TERESITA
The Voice from the Grave

TERESITA
The Voice from the Grave

The incredible but true story of how an occult vision solved the murder of Teresita Basa

John O'Brien
and
Edward Baumann

Bonus Books, Inc., Chicago

96 95 94 93 92   5 4 3 2 1

Library of Congress Catalog Card Number: 91-77023

International Standard Book Number: 0-929387-67-8

Bonus Books, Inc.
160 East Illinois Street
Chicago, Illinois 60611

Printed in the United States of America

To Teresita — Mabuhay!

CONTENTS

CONTENTS

PREFACE

In January of 1979 an accused murderer was brought to trial in Chicago based on evidence provided by a "voice from beyond the grave." To this day police and prosecutors are skeptical but agree, to a man, that it actually did occur. They also agree that it was, without a doubt, one of the strangest criminal cases ever recorded in a city where violent death has never been a stranger. Whether you believe in reincarnation, extrasensory perception or the great beyond, it is an undisputed fact that a voice, identifying itself as that of Teresita Basa, a murder victim buried half way around the world, possessed the body of a woman she barely knew. The voice spoke the name of the killer, described the homicide, and supplied hitherto unknown evidence to aid police in their investigation. The story of Teresita Basa is true.

John O'Brien and
Edward Baumann
January 1992

ACKNOWLEDGMENTS

The authors are grateful to Teresita Basa's cousins, Ron Somera and Kenneth Basa, for providing intimate details of her life; and to homicide investigators Lee Epplen and Joseph Stachula, for making available their notes on the investigation of her death. All of the people in this story are real. Several were identified by assumed names—Felipe Dayoc, the former Manila policeman, because of personal circumstances; Edward O'Meara, who broke Teresita's heart, at the request of Teresita's family; and Ronnie Sparrow, murder suspect, because he was a juvenile. Mrs. Rader, one of the jurors, also asked that her name be changed for story purposes.

THE PLAYERS

In Teresita's Life:
    Dr. John Abella, fellow band member
    Justino R. Alfafara, foreign affairs officer
    Corbillita Astroquillo, college friend
    Jean R. Auguste, fellow employee
    Gary Bailey, fellow employee
    Stephan Barath, her ghost writer
    Kenneth Basa, her cousin
    Pablo Basa, her uncle
    Pedro Cruz Basa, her father
    Socorro Basa, her mother
    Joseph Battista, music professor
    Rev. Wilfred Brimley, C.S.P., her priest
    John D. Bulkeley, commander, U.S. Navy
    Bruce Campbell, neighbor
    Remebios Chua, fellow employee
    James Clomey, neighbor
    Dr. Alfredo R. Corpuz, family physician
    Ron Correa, her friend
    Virginia Dudley, rental agent
    Elizabeth II, Queen of England
    Ted Ellis, her supervisor
    Etta Enriquez, Philippine consul
    Ramona Espada, friend
    Sidney Foster, music professor
    Nonoy Gangoso, band member
    John Gleason, neighbor
    Joyce Kaltman, building manager
    Ray King, close friend
    Vernon Kliewer, university professor
    Katherine Knazze, neighbor
    Mario Knazze, neighbor
    Robert Knudson, friend
    Robert Krauth, pen pal

Connie Kuehn, hospital supervisor
Joe Laguda, band member
Dr. Edward R. Levine, medical director
Ruth Loeb, close friend
Petro Lulusa, janitor
Ralph Magner, friend
David Martinez, cousin
Fermin Martinez, grandfather
Dr. Maurice Mazel, hospital operator
Pete Molina, band member
Amada Santos-Ocampa, university friend
Dr. Mario Oliveros, hospital official
Edward O'Meara, suitor
Jun Pascal, band member
Richard Pessotti, close friend
Manaham Pressler, concert pianist
Manuel Quezon, Philippine President
Zeneida Quezon, the President's daughter
Elisa Romero, ambassador's wife
José Romero, ambassador to England
Tessie Romero, their daughter
Emile Salnave, fellow employee
Arthur Shields, janitor
Allan Showery, fellow employee
Ron Somera, cousin
Ronnie Sparrow, murder suspect
Alexander Tcherepnin, pianist and composor
Ming Lee Tcherepnin, his wife
Lorenzo Teves, uncle
Cornelia P. Villa, cousin
Myron J. Walters, lawyer

In Teresita's Death:
Dr. Tae An, pathologist
Joseph Andruzzi, policeman
Al Ballard, criminal court bailiff
Frank W. Barbaro, criminal court judge

Aldonna Barrows, waitress
George Behnle, medical examiner
Walter Bosco, homicide commander
Joseph Chambers, police sergeant
Willie Chester, jail inmate
Dr. José Chua, Filipino physician
Joe Cummings, radio newsman
James Cunningham, jury foreman
Theodore Czerwionka, fire chief
C.J. Dockery, police sergeant
Egon Donsbach, policeman
James Dunbar, evidence technician
John Durkin, homicide investigator
Lee Epplen, homicide investigator
Richard J. Fitzgerald, criminal court judge
Edward Flynn, homicide sergeant
James Frankenbach, crime lab technician
Julien Gallet, homicide lieutenant
Bernard Gavin, medical examiner
Emil Giese, police captain
Leonardo Gonzales, hospital worker
Christian Grogman, homicide investigator
Walter Hayes, police lieutenant
Michael Herigot, task force patrolman
Gilbert James, karate expert
Yanka Kalmuk, suspect's paramour
William Kinahan, bomb and arson lieutenant
Walter Klein, homicide investigator
Blanca Lara, court reporter
Jerry Lawrence, homicide investigator
Paul Linton, assistant state's attorney
August Locallo, police lieutenant
Kip MacMillan, Evanston police lieutenant
Floyd McKinney, Evanston detective
Richard Meyers, crime lab technician
Steven Miller, police officer
Joseph Mohan, task force patrolman

Edward O'Connell, police sergeant
Ted O'Connor, police sergeant
John Olejniczak, police evidence technician
Joanne O'Hara, bookkeeper
W.M. O'Malley, youth officer
Dennis O'Neill, police evidence technician
Thomas Organ, assistant state's attorney
Mark Palenik, hair expert
Samuel Palenik, hair expert
John W. Philbin, homicide investigator
Daniel Radakovich, assistant public defender
Marie Rader, juror
John Redmond, police evidence technician
Robert E. Reese, crime lab technician
Robert M. Reilley, crime lab technician
Manuel Rios, bomb and arson investigator
A.B. Russele, police officer
Richard Sandberg, homicide sergeant
Mildred Schafer, juror
Lee J. Schoen, assistant state's attorney
Sue Serkowski, waitress
Edward J. Shilney, bomb and arson investigator
Joseph Stachula, homicide investigator
John Stout, polygraph examiner
James Emmet Strunck, criminal court judge
William Swano, assistant public defender
John Teening, homicide investigator
Bruce Thompson, polygraph sergeant
Karen Thompson, the governor's sister
R.G. Wagner, homicide supervisor
Thomas Walsh, polygraph examiner
Richard Webber, juror
Robert Webster, hospital security chief
John Whalen, homicide investigator
Warren Whelan, fire lieutenant
Kathleen White, suspect's neighbor
Revele White, neighbor's husband

"In police work I take the attitude that, while some things may be strange—even incredible—there is a solution, somewhere..."

—Chicago Homicide Investigator Joseph L. Stachula

CHAPTER 1

A GRIM DISCOVERY

The day after Chicago's firecracker-popping Chinese held their festive New Year parade down Wentworth Avenue in Chinatown—ushering in the Year of the Serpent, 4675—had been cheerful and sunny. It provided a welcome respite from what would go down on the record books as the bitterest winter in the city's history. The outside temperature hovered right around 32 degrees Fahrenheit, not quite warm enough to melt the mounds of snow piled high along the curb fronting the reddish brick apartment building at 2740 N. Pine Grove Avenue.

The Pine Grove apartment stood in the city's New Town area, the latest "in" spot for young marrieds, mixed marrieds, singles, swingles, gays—you name them.

As the day moved into its final hours, warm lights glowed randomly from windows of the residential hotels and high-rises clustered around the intersection of Pine Grove and Diversey Parkway, a block west of Lincoln Park on the city's picture-postcard lakefront. In Lincoln Park Zoo the stillness was interrupted by the muffled roar of a lion as he bade the zebras, elephants, and other citified creatures of the jungle good night.

In their fifteenth floor apartment, a little over two-thirds of the way up in the 2740 building, Mario and Katherine

Knazze had just finished dinner. Katherine, a 25-year-old accountant, was stacking dishes in the stainless steel sink in the tiny kitchenette. "I'll wash 'em before we go to bed, Mario. Why don't we just relax for awhile?"

Her 27-year-old husband pushed himself slowly away from the table and walked into the adjoining living room. He stood in front of the window, his hands jammed into his blue jeans pockets, looking at his reflection in the glass. Beyond the image of the handsome, brown-skinned face, with Afro hairdo and bushy sideburns, Knazze could see nothing but darkness. Apartment 15G, on the front south end of the twenty-one story building, faced eastward out over the still icy Lake Michigan. Glancing down at the little concrete balcony outside the sliding glass doors he pondered the snow heaped atop his portable barbecue grill and wondered if summer would ever come.

Katherine switched on the television, and made herself comfortable on the couch. Knazze dropped into a chair opposite the TV and picked up the latest edition of the *Chicago Tribune*. The front page picture portrayed an angry looking dragon, winding its way through Chinatown amid dancing children. He smiled at the caption, which quoted the Chinaman inside the papier-mache dragon head as complaining about how cold it had been.

Above the picture, with the *Trib*'s familiar American flag logo, and Old English type, was the date, Monday, February 21, 1977.

"What time is it, honey?" he asked.

"Just about 8:30."

"Anything good on tonight?"

"I don't really know. Maybe there's an early movie. Busy day at the store?"

"Nah. Lotsa people had Monday off for Washington's birthday. I let most of the help duck early. What the hell."

Katherine clicked the channel changer experimentally from 2 to 5 to 7. She was on her way to 9 when she wrinkled her nose and asked, "Do you smell anything, Mario?"

"Something's burning," he said, sniffing the air. "You take everything off the stove?"

"Everything's all right in here," she said, making a quick check of the kitchen.

Mario laid down the paper, walked quickly across the room, and pulled open the door leading to the long corridor alongside the twin self-service elevators. The hall was filled with an acrid, gray haze. He coughed, rubbed his burning eyes, and yelled, "Grab your coat, Kate. We're getting the hell out of here!"

They slammed the door to 15G behind them, leaving the lights on and the TV going. Mario punched the down button on the elevator as he ran past, and the two began banging on neighbors' doors yelling, "Fire! Fire! Everybody get out!"

The elevator door rolled open and Mario took his wife's arm and pushed her into the cozy three-by-six foot car. At the far end of the hall he spotted Bruce Campbell from 15A scurrying toward the stairwell, along with other tenants. The 1 and 7 squares lit up as Mario poked the buttons on the elevator panel. "You go all the way down and stay outside, Kate. I'm gonna jump out on seven and get the janitor."

He bolted from the car before the door was all the way open, yelling over his shoulder, "See you out on the street." He took a quick right and was banging on the black painted wooden door marked 7H two giant steps later. Petro Lulusa, the same age as Knazze, had been on the job only a few weeks. It was a good, modern building, in a good North Side neighborhood, and he liked it. There were few things to go wrong and the residents rarely complained.

The frantic pounding on his door and all that yelling in the hall made him uneasy. He peeked cautiously through the eye-level peep-hole and recognized the features of the man from upstairs. Opening the door apprehensively he asked, "Is there something . . . ?"

"The joint's on fire, I think. There's something burning on fifteen. C'mon!" Knazze urged. He turned back toward the elevator and hit the "up" button in time to catch the car he had just left on the way back up. Lulusa pulled the door to his apartment shut and was right on his heels. The smoke was filtering through the rest of the building, and they could smell it well before the elevator door rolled open and they stepped back into the fifteenth floor corridor.

Several apartment doors were open, indicating the haste in which their occupants had gotten the hell out of there. The two men worked their way down the burnt-orange carpeted hall, from south to north. As Mario pounded on each locked door, the janitor slipped his passkey into the opening in the doorknob and swung each door inward to make sure everybody was out. As they yelled into each apartment they also noted that the air inside was clear. Whatever was burning was farther down the hall.

At approximately the same time the Knazzes detected the smell of smoke, James Clomey in apartment 16B, one floor up on the opposite end of the building, heard what sounded to him like a muffled explosion.

Curious, he slid the glass patio door open and edged out onto his small balcony to take a look. Two blocks away he could see the lights of cars crawling north and south along Clark Street between the flashing neon shop signs. He glanced down toward the parking lot. All quiet.

Then Clomey looked directly below, and in the darkened 15B he could see the orange reflection of flames dancing across the frosted window panes. Ducking back into his apartment, he grabbed a jacket and headed for the door. Once down in the lobby he called the fire department. Within minutes after Clomey had joined other tenants clustering in the chill night air in the narrow street outside he could hear the wail of sirens.

Then the flashing red and white lights swung south off Diversey into Pine Grove, and rigs from the 13th Battalion thundered up in front of the building. Helpful hands held the inch-thick glass doors open as excited voices directed the firefighters in their heavy boots and rubberized coats toward the elevators.

Knazze and Lulusa, coughing and gagging, were still on fifteen when firemen began pouring out of the two elevators, carrying gas masks, pike poles, portable lanterns and hand extinguishers. The smoke was most dense at the north end of the corridor, and they could see it curling from beneath the door of 15B.

Lulusa was trying to open the door with his master key, but for some reason it was stuck. Just as the firefighters began to hunch up behind him the lock clicked and the door swung inward. Thick black and grayish smoke billowed into their faces like an erupting volcano.

The janitor reeled back as the firemen pulled on their face masks and dropped to their knees. They crawled into the darkened room, the powerful beams of their electric torches cutting through the smoke as they made their way to the west wall and smashed out the windows and balcony doors with their pike poles for ventilation. Crawling in behind them was another fireman, who had unlimbered the hose line in the hallway and was dragging it at his side.

The fire was in the bedroom, just off the combination living-dining area of the three-room apartment.

Two firefighters with portable extinguishers and the man with the hose, still on hands and knees, worked their way into the room, spraying in the direction of the heat, smoke and now visible flames. Whatever it was that was burning was in the middle of the room, on the floor beside the bed. The sharp hiss of steam and the stench of burned cloth leaped at them as the water met its target.

The air was beginning to clear somewhat, with the draft created by the open door and broken windows sucking the smoke out into the night. Battalion Chief Theodore Czerwionka could see what appeared to be the remains of a burning mattress, pulled partly off the bed. Tossing it aside, his men played their water on what looked like a large pile of burning rags that had been partly covered by the mattress.

"It's a bunch of clothes or something, Chief," Lieutenant Warren Whelan of Engine No. 55 advised Czerwionka, as the men soaked it down. The flames seemed out, but the pile of material continued to smolder from underneath, where the water couldn't penetrate.

Whelan put the toe of his boot against the edge of the burning pile and kicked it out of the way. He could tell now, it was a pile of clothing and bedding, with flashes of flame still flickering around the bottom edges.

"Wait a minute, guys," he said, stooping over and digging into the pile with his gloved hands, tossing the smoldering rags aside so the men with the hand pumps could get at the base of the trouble. Then, in the beams of their lanterns, they all saw it. First a knee. Then a naked breast.

"Good god!" coughed Whelan, tearing away at the charred remnants of fabric and bedclothes. "Get some water down here, and . . ." The man nearest the door spun around and headed for the street to alert the ambulance team, which routinely stands by at any fire call to an apartment or hotel building.

By the time the men with the pumps had sprayed down the area and the last wisp of smoke had curled away, the paramedics were coming down the hall. As the firefighters focused their lantern beams on the soaked object in the puddle of soggy rags on the bedroom floor, nobody had to tell them it was no use.

Whelan expelled his breath. "Holy Mother . . ."

"Jesus!" said Czerwionka, almost to himself. "Look!"

She was lying on her back, stark naked. A rather small body, but a well-formed adult. Her head was nearest the west wall. Her knees were drawn up and her legs were wide apart at the thighs, coming together at the ankles. Her bare arms were flat on the floor, bent upward at the elbows, with her slender, delicate hands at the side of her head.

"Well, I'll be dipped," somebody remarked, breaking the silence.

She had been dreadfully burned on both sides of her body. The right side was the worst, with the flesh seared away. Her head was also badly burned, with little left of her jet-black hair.

The destructive flames had not had a chance to work their way down through all of the clothing that had covered her, so her face, chest, abdomen, pubic area and her upper legs had been mercifully spared.

Whelan pointed a beefy arm at her breasts. "Do you see that?"

In the exact center of her chest, casting a wavering shadow in the unsteady light, protruded the wooden handle of a large kitchen knife. It was umbedded to the hilt.

Blood seeped slowly from the wound, red turning to pink as it joined the little rivulets of water that trickled casually down the sides of her rib cage. For a long moment they stood staring down at her.

"Don't anybody touch a goddam thing," barked Whelan. "Let's get everyone back out into the hall. One of you guys, get your ass downstairs and tell the cops directing traffic out there to radio the dicks. Tell 'em we got a dead one here, and it ain't from takin' too much smoke."

Chief Czerwionka stood in the apartment doorway and surveyed the cluster of firefighters and curious tenants gathered in the still smoke-smelly hall near the stairwell. "You the building engineer?" he beckoned to Lulusa, who was still clutching his ring of keys.

"Yes, sir?" the janitor responded, as though asking a question himself.

"Who lives in here? Do you know her name?"

"Number 15B? That would be the Basa lady. She's a nurse, I think. Over at Edgewater Hospital. I seen her in a white uniform."

"Basa, you say? B-A-S-A?"

"Yes, I think so. They call her Teresita."

CHAPTER 2

TERESITA

The macabre discovery of Teresita Basa's grotesquely violated body set in motion one of the most unusual criminal investigations in homicide history. The conclusion fired the imagination of every true believer in spiritualism, reincarnation, and extra-sensory perception, and taxed the skeptics' minds to headache proportions.

The victim's picture appeared in syndicated newspaper articles and magazine stories and Chicago police, who were not overly anxious to discuss the case, found themselves fielding worldwide inquiries they hoped and prayed would soon go away.

Teresita Basa had been a member of the Philippine aristocracy. To hard-bitten street cops at the moment, however, she was Case No. 059 292—lying naked with her secret parts shamefully exposed and a bloody knife sticking out of her sternum. She would, in due time, be cleaned up, embalmed, boxed and crated, and shipped away for burial ten thousand miles across the sea.

She rests there now, beneath the cool soil of Negros Island, which glitters like an emerald in the tropical sun in the romantic Sulu Sea. It was there, in a place called Dumaguete, that Teresita cried her first cry. . . .

Negros Island—1929

The lethargic gray carabao wallowed in the water-filled ditch by the side of the road. Only his massive leathery head, with wide, brownish horns and broad, black nose protruded above the muddy surface. The ever present flies buzzed in angry circles, competing for space on the flat landing field between his dark, bovine eyes. Lush green foliage climbed the sides of the ditch and clustered around the roots of the coconut palms lining the dirt thoroughfare on the outskirts of Dumaguete City, on the lee side of the island. The sun was comfortably warm and the old water buffalo offered only a bored glance at the slender young Filipino who walked briskly along the road, which soon became little more than a passageway between the bright rows of sugar cane.

Pedro Cruz Basa, the 28-year-old lawyer who had given up the urban bustle of Manila for the slower pace of "Sugar Island" was wearing woven sandals and a white *barong tagalog*, a loose-fitting embroidered shirt that hung comfortably out of his black trousers. He had just come from Silliman Mission Hospital and was hurrying to the office of his father-in-law, Fermin Martinez, at the sugar plantation.

A scruffy brown cur scampered out and yapped a warning as Basa passed a small clearing with a one-room farmhouse. The simple dwelling, with woven bamboo walls and thatched roof of palm leaves, stood six feet off the ground on sturdy bamboo stilts.

Its four windows, one to a side, were guarded by red-painted shutters that could be closed for protection during the rainy season. Today they gaped openly in anticipation of any breeze that might drift through. Glancing through the shanty as he passed some 15 meters away Basa could see the silhouette of a kerosene lantern hanging from a roof beam.

A two-wheeled ox cart stood tilted forward in the yard, and tethered in the shade of a nearby coconut palm lazed the family carabao. Several small pigs rooted in the sheltered area beneath the house, and a dozen or so chickens scattered in a flurry of white feathers and clucking as the mongrel circled back to his dozing place beneath the wooden-wheeled cart.

The young lawyer thought of the old man as his feet kicked up dust along the road. Martinez, like himself, was a son of Luzon, the big island to the north. A one-time insurrectionist, Martinez had fought with General Emilio Aguinaldo against the Spanish in 1898. And then he battled briefly against the United States. After Aguinaldo settled his differences with the new American government Martinez sailed the 650 kilometers down from Cavite to Negros, to begin life anew. He used his flair for organization to help bring people together, becoming the island's first representative to the First Philippine Congress. Now, a little more than a quarter of a century later, he owned one of the largest plantations in the islands.

Martinez was waiting on the veranda of the main building as his son-in-law, who handled legal work for the local sugar industry, approached excitedly.

"*Mabuhay*, Pedro. Long life to you."

"*Mabuhay*, Grandfather," the young man beamed, somewhat out of breath.

"Grandfather?" the old man smiled, baring his gold-capped teeth.

"A beautiful little girl, with eyes like her mother's and a voice already as loud."

"Oh-ho!" laughed Martinez, clapping his weathered hands together. "And my little girl—is she . . . ?"

"Socorro is all right now, sir. But she had the doctor worried. Me to, I might add. She didn't have an easy time of it, and he said there can be no more children. We are blessed with this one."

"What happened, my son? Are you sure she's all right?"

"Complications. That's what the doctor said. But, yes, thank God she is fine. When I left the hospital they had just brought the little one to her and Socorro was singing softly in her ear."

"And my grandchild! Forgive me, Pedro. How will you call her?"

"We have named her Teresita."

"Teresita," the older man repeated. "Little Terese."

Martinez put his left arm around his son-in-law's shoulders and guided him into the small office. He pulled a bamboo tube, more than two feet in length and three inches in diameter, from a corner of the airy room, and removed the homemade stopper, fashioned from sun-baked carabao dung pressed between palm leaves.

"This calls for something special," he said, fetching two drinking glasses from a woven bamboo tray atop a rattan stand by the open window. "Best *basi* around! The field workers make it in the barrio. I provide the sugar, of course." He tilted the bamboo sideways and poured some of the clear fermented beverage into the glass. "They don't know what they're missing in the States, do they?"

"What do you mean, father?"

"You can't get this—or anything else—over there. Not legally, anyhow. Prohibition! The Americanos have their rum wars. We have fine *basi*. To my granddaughter."

"To Teresita."

"And to Socorro."

"Socorro."

"To the new father!"

"Ha-ha. To me, and to you."

The warm wine went down well.

"Now I must see that granddaughter of mine," Martinez said, putting his glass down on the desk. "We'll go back together, but first . . ."

Taking a pen from the top of his desk, he dipped its metal point into a small inkwell. Then he went over to the wall calendar, advertising a 1929 Oakland motorcar for $1,145, and scratched a blue circle around Wednesday, the thirteenth of March.

"Teresita Basa's natal day!" he proclaimed. "Come on, papa. Let's take a ride."

The *tartanilla*, the decorative two-wheeled pony cart that was the island's major means of transportation, waited in the flower-filled yard in the shade of the tall coconut palms. The reins of the tiny Filipino horse, Admiral Dewey, were looped loosely around the branch of a small tree. Martinez had long ago made his peace with the Americans, but he could not resist naming his horse after their hero of the battle of Manila Bay. After all, hadn't the Americans named the road running along the waterfront Dewey Boulevard?

"Sktttt! Sktttt! Sktttt!" hissed the old man, stomping his foot at the macaque monkey that was mischievously tugging at the horse's rein. "Damned monk! The other day he ran off with some papers I left out for the messenger. Just ripped the envelopes open and scattered the papers around when he couldn't find any food inside." The monkey retreated, turned to utter a piercing, high-pitched scolding, and skittered squirrel-like up the side of a palm tree.

The fragile-looking pony seemed as though he would be lifted clear off the ground as the two men settled into the wooden seat between the high spoked wheels of the *tartanilla* and leaned back under the sunroof.

Basa had called the cart a *calesa* when he first came down from Manila—the Tagalog word. The old man marveled at how quickly he had picked up Cebuano, the language of the Visayan Islands.

There are 7,100 islands in the Philippines, where 73 distinct dialects and seven major languages are spoken. Of course, the young lawyer had no trouble courting the alluring Socorro Pinili Martinez, the belle of Dumaguete, since both spoke fluent Spanish, the old language, and English, which was now a required subject in the schools.

"Do you think you'll ever get a motorcar?" Basa absent-mindedly asked Martinez, as the Admiral's hooves plip-plopped along the dusty road into town.

The old revolutionist smiled. "Where would I go with it? There are no roads when you get out of town. Hell, you have to take a boat to visit another barrio. Where would I get the damned thing repaired? Where would the petroleum come from to make it go? And how could I ever explain to the Admiral that I gave him up for a machine, eh?"

Basa nodded. "Makes sense."

The rhythm played by Admiral Dewey's hooves changed its tune from plip-plop to a steady clip-clop as they fell upon the macadam pavement that announced their entry into Dumaguete, pronounced Doo-ma-ghetty. Since coming down from the north at the turn of the century, the old man had seen it grow from a seaside barrio to a city of 17,000. It was now a major port from which half of all the sugar in the Philippines was exported, along with vast amounts of copra from dried coconut meat.

"You know, Socorro was the town queen until you came and stole her from me. She really was," Martinez jested. "I sent her to the finest schools to become a pharmacist, and to develop her beautiful singing voice. Do you know how many female pharmacists there are—not just here, but anywhere? And how did she thank me? She married a lawyer. A word-twisting foreigner from Luzon who couldn't even speak our language."

"Just like yourself," laughed Basa. "You didn't grow here like your sugar cane. I heard they had to chase you out of Cavite for raising so much hell among the Spaniards."

As the *tartanilla*, now sharing the busy street with dozens of similar brightly-painted pony carts and two-wheeled carabao drays, neared the center of town, Pedro said, "I'd like to get off at the plaza. I'll meet you at the hospital in a little while."

Basa jumped nimbly to the ground as Martinez brought the Admiral to an easy halt in the shade of one of the flowering acacias surrounding the plaza. He remained in the wooden seat and watched rather proudly as his daughter's young husband strode quickly across the wide lawn, waved happily to the statue of José Rizal, the Philippines' national hero, and disappeared into the coolness of the old Spanish limestone church.

"That young man, he'll be somebody some day," Martinez smiled to himself. "He and his lawyer friend, José Romero—the two of them. My daughter chose her man well."

Looking across the plaza at Santa Catalina's Roman Catholic Church he immodestly acknowledged that he was of no small importance on Negros, himself: Congressman, plantation owner, and generous contributor to the church which had become the seat of the Bishop.

It was the Bishop himself who concelebrated the nuptial mass in that very church when he gave Socorro to Pedro. He remembered well the colorful procession from the Martinez home to the church, Socorro in her flowing white gown, escorted by her parents, the attendants, the relatives who came all the way from Luzon—four days by boat—for the elaborate ceremony. He smiled as he recalled Pedro, uncomfortable in a formal suit, as the Bishop placed the ring, first on the groom's finger, then on the bride's, and blessed them both "in the name of the Father, and of the Son, and of the Holy Spirit."

Then, as the young couple stood before him, with the palms of their outstretched hands cupped, the Bishop dropped 13 silver coins into Pedro's hands. And he, in turn, let them trickle into the waiting hands of Socorro, saying, "My wife, I give you this ring and these coins as a sign of our marriage." "I accept them," she said softly. Then a cord was looped around the couple, tying them together, and they were covered with a single veil.

After the ceremony the many guests, including priests, repaired to the Martinez home for a wedding feast of *lechon*, pig roasted over an open fire on a giant spit.

Tears welled in the old man's eyes, and he made the sign of the cross, as he somberly recalled that Pedro's best friend, José Romero, had lost his wife, Pilar, in childbirth less than two short years before, leaving Romero with an infant son. The reason for the stop became clear. Fermin Martinez knew, now, that Pedro Basa was on his knees inside the old Spanish church, giving praise and thanks that Socorro had come through the ordeal, and for the healthy child God had permitted their happy union to produce.

Martinez would wait for his son-in-law, and the two of them would go to Silliman Hospital together to see the new baby.

CHAPTER 3

D.O.A.

Pine Grove Avenue had assumed the carnival appearance of a giant outdoor discotheque. The street outside the apartment building was ablaze with lights. Firemen from the 13th Battalion were still on the scene and the red and white flashing lights from the snorkel unit, Engine No. 55, Ladder Truck 44, the chief's car, rescue squad unit and attending vehicles cast a kaleidoscopic pattern as their reflections danced off the sides of the high-rises and nearby hotel buildings. The firefighting apparatus was soon joined by siren-screaming police cars with flashing blue Mars lights on their roofs, vying for parking space among the emergency rigs on the narrow street.

Barricades had been erected at both ends of the block and uniformed patrolmen stood at the corner of Diversey on the north and Wrightwood on the south, to wave curious motorists on their way with long, red flashlights.

When the bored looking plainclothes dicks arrived in their "soft" cars with telltale wire antennae protruding innocuously from the trunk lids, they bounced over the curb and pulled onto the sidewalk in front of 2740.

Through the double-door glassed entry they went, past the mail lock-boxes with buzzers for each apartment. Through the inner lobby, beneath the three hanging plants, past the building office on the left and into the self-service elevators, oblivious of the onlookers and newsmen clamoring for information. Moments later they were plodding methodically down the 40-foot long smoke-smelly corridor.

Inside apartment 15B the lifeless body of 47-year-old Teresita Basa lay on its back, still wedged between the burned bed and the wall, legs still wide apart before a dozen sets of curious and sympathetic eyes. The ugly knife handle still protruded from between her small breasts. Several detectives tried the light switch, as though expecting it to work after it had refused for everyone else. The blaze had knocked out the electric power in the apartment, and the only illumination came from the firemen's battery-torches and the cops' flashlights. The firefighters methodically gathered up their equipment. Their work was over, except for filing a written report.

"Watch your goddam feet where you step," somebody barked. "Remember that jerkoff who used to leave a big pile of crap in the middle of the floor like a trademark every time he killed someone? Looks like we got a real sex nut on the loose here—no telling what the fuck you might find."

"Wasn't that Heirens?"

"Yeah, somebody like that."

William G. Heirens, teen-aged "lipstick murderer" of the 1940s, confessed killing a six-year-old girl and two grown women and committing an undetermined number of break-ins in what psychiatrists called "pursuance of an abnormal sexual urge." After he was caught police found a cardboard box containing more than 40 pairs of women's panties stashed in his home. One of the victims, a 33-year-old former WAVE named Frances Brown, was slain in her apartment at 3941 N. Pine Grove—this very same street. Afterward the killer dragged her, the murder knife still protruding from her neck, to the bathtub where he rinsed the blood from her body with a douche hose. Then he lifted a bright red lipstick from the victim's purse and scrawled in bold letters across her bedroom wall:

For heavens
Sake catch Me
BeFore I kill More
I cannot control myselF

Now, more than 30 years later, Heirens was still in prison, but the mention of his name caused several flashlight beams to instinctively sweep across the bedroom wall over Teresita Basa's defiled corpse. There was no message.

Homicide Investigator John W. Philbin, a Viet Nam veteran now assigned to Area 6, knew he would have to make the initial police report and was busy keeping score. Notebook in hand, his eyes darted from chest to chest, copying names and badge numbers of fellow cops.

Moving in and out of Teresita's private bedroom where she still lay naked and exposed on the water-soaked carpet, her sightless eyes focused unmoving on the soot-blackened ceiling, were Chief Czerwionka, Lt. Whelan and "numerous firefighters." Philbin did not record their names. He could get them from the battalion commander if needed.

He jotted down the presence of Capt. Emil Giese, 23rd District watch commander; Lt. Walter T. Hayes; Sgt. Joseph Chambers; district officers Joseph Andruzzi, A.B. Russele, Steven Miller and Egon Donsbach; crime lab technicians Robert E. Reese and Richard Meyers; Fire Lt. William Kinahan and investigators Edward J. Shilney and Manuel Rios of the bomb and arson squad. From his own unit he noted Homicide Sgt. Edward Flynn and fellow investigator Theodore O'Connor. George Behnle was there from the Cook County Medical Examiner's office.

Philbin moved into a position over the body while O'Connor held the flashlight, and made laborious hand-printed notes he knew must be legible because they would have to be followed up by detectives on other shifts.

From papers found in the apartment, and the tentative identification by the janitor, Philbin listed the victim in his report as Basa, Teresita; female; Oriental; DOB 13 March, 1929; respiratory therapist; 2740 N. Pine Grove.

Location of victim on premises, bedroom. Nature of injuries and location of body, knife wound, chest. Possible point of entry, front door. Unusual characteristics of crime (trademarks), unknown.

"Homicide R/Os [reporting officers] spoke to Fire Chief Czerwionka, 13th BN, and learned that the Fire Department received a call of a fire at 2045 hours. While putting out the fire in the bedroom Lt. Whelan, Fire Dept. truck #44, was picking up burned clothing off the floor and found victim naked with a knife embedded in victim's chest. Victim's body was partially burned. Laying on the floor. Numerous firemen were on the scene by the time of R/Os arrival. Fire Dept. Chief Czerwionka stated upon the arrival of the fire dept they found apt. rifled. Apt. door was locked and had to be opened by Mr. Lulusa, Petro, Apt. 7H . . . bldg. janitor."

The apartment windows had been smashed out to clear the smoke, and the February wind whipped through the bedroom and into the open hallway. Policeman Manuel Rios, 57-year-old youth officer assigned to bomb and arson, huddled next to Philbin as the homicide dick took notes. Rios, the first Mexican-American to join the force, had quit a $654-a-month railway switchman's job in 1951 to become a cop at an annual salary of $3,432. He shuddered now. A chill ran over him as he wiggled his cold, wet toes. The water had seeped into his shoes as he gazed at the violated corpse. He jammed his hands deeply into the pockets of his trenchcoat and turned his head slightly to whisper to Shilney, his partner.

"A doll. Doesn't she look like a doll? That look on her face. Placid. Almost angelic."

Shilney grunted.

"There's no trace of horror at all. What a terrible way to go. The knife— it's buried to the hilt. How could anyone be so cruel?"

"It had to be somebody she knew," Shilney offered. "Did you get a look at the frickin' door? Three locks on it—two dead bolts and a chain. Nothing forced, either. Whoever did it, she let 'im in."

"An angel," Rios repeated. "Her face looks like an angel. I really feel sorry for her. I know, I know . . . don't get personally involved, but jeez . . ."

"Hey, nobody touch the knife," Behnle, the medical examiner, cautioned, squatting beside the body. "Leave it in her, just the way it is. It stays with the body."

"How long you figure she's been dead, George?" asked Sgt. Flynn.

"From the condition of the body, I'd guess she bought the farm about an hour ago," Behnle surmised. "Give or take a little."

Reese, the crime lab tech, waved everyone back so he could photograph the scene. First he crouched at Teresita's feet, making an almost floor-level shot of her widespread thighs, the upturned arms, showing the body's position in relation to the west wall. Then, standing at her right knee, he stepped back several paces through the debris for a full angle view of the corpse, showing the extent of the burns to her right side and arm. Finally he stood over Teresita and pointed his camera straight down, snapping her sightless eyes as they peered into the lens.

Next Reese knelt beside the body and gently placed plastic bags over the victim's delicate hands. "This'll preserve them for fingerprints," he explained. "Can't get anything in here at this time. Too damn wet." Turning to Behnle he said, "I'm through with this part of it for now."

The medical examiner's concern was for the body and what had killed her. Reese was more interested in picking up anything that might help tell who killed her. He moved about the rest of the small apartment.

Against the south wall of the bedroom was a partly charred dresser. Several jewelry boxes atop the dresser had been opened, and necklaces and bracelets had been strewn about. Also on top of the dresser was a woven straw wastebasket. It appeared to have been thrown there. Beside the dresser was an upholstered vanity bench, turned on its end. On the floor near the body was a badly charred suitcase that had been opened and apparently ransacked. Its top was completely burned away. The floor around the dresser and under the broken bedroom window was littered with debris and remnants of charred wearing apparel. Reese painstakingly photographed it all.

He also snapped the inside of the bedroom closet, where every item of clothing had been pulled from hangers onto a heap on the floor. It definitely appeared as if someone had been frantically searching for something, and then set the fire to cover up his trail.

Reese moved into the living room, where Teresita had kept her many books and classical phonograph records. Music was obviously one of her loves. There were several overturned plants in vases near the shattered patio doors, and a potted palm, still upright, at the end of the plaid upholstered sofa. An upended cocktail table appeared to have been tossed against the couch by firemen making their way through the dense smoke to get to the window. Soot marks on its surface showed the outline of a book, and a circular object—a beer can or glass—indicating the table had been upright on the floor during the fire.

Teresita had two television sets, Reese noted. They were arranged side by side, a console and a large portable. Two large upholstered pillows had been propped against the larger TV. She probably sat on the floor, on the giant pillows, when she watched TV, he figured. Ashtrays, napkins, and items of clothing were strewn about the room. A Budweiser can lay on its side under the edge of the couch. Against the opposite wall was a well used piano.

Reese caught it all with the crime lab camera. He moved quickly and efficiently. Nothing could be touched until he completed his job, recording for future reference the exact position of everything when police arrived. He also photographed the inside of the apartment door, showing the eye-level burglar chain and two dead-bolts.

After the photos were taken Flynn and O'Connor removed a small brown box containing what appeared to be the victim's personal papers—notes, bills, receipts, checkbook stubs. They also picked up a memo pad on which someone had noted, "Get tickets for A.S."

Preliminary work at the scene completed, the meat wagon men were called in from the corridor—two burly representatives of Chicago's finest, carrying a well-worn brown stretcher. The litter was placed on the floor beside the body, and a plastic sheet, with a zipper running around its edges, was unfolded and placed atop the canvas. Teresita's legs were pulled down so that her thighs came together and her upturned arms, with her hands encased in the plastic sacks, were placed at her sides. The body was gently hefted onto the stretcher and the plastic sheet was wrapped around her, knife and all, and zipped shut. The two men lifted the stretcher, and Teresita Basa left her apartment for the last time.

After the body was removed, apartment 15B was temporarily closed, with seal number 35696 placed on the door in order to preserve any evidence that might still be inside.

Teresita's cold body was taken unceremoniously in Police Squadrol No. 2373 to nearby Columbus Hospital. The physician on duty, Dr. Thomas Topper, was called outside and into the back of the squadrol where the plastic liner had been unzipped to expose the upper portion of the body. At 11:05 p.m. Teresita was officially pronounced "dead on arrival" as required by law.

CHAPTER 4

CHILD OF DUMAGUETE

On the twenty-fifth day of November, the feast day of Santa Catalina, the patron saint of Dumaguete, 8-month-old Teresita Martinez Basa was solemnly baptized along with all the other Roman Catholic children born in the parish during the past year. The event signalled the beginning of the annual fiesta. It also occasioned a gala feast in the new home Pedro Basa had acquired, with the help of his wealthy father-in-law, who would be paid back. From the new house on Colon Street, on the south side of the plaza, the Basas could walk across the street to mass at Santa Catalina's, next to the imposing home of the bishop.

Since Dumaguete was the provincial capital of Negros Oriental, the eastern half of the island, he had made Santa Catalina's parish his seat.

Next to the bishop's, the Basa home was one of the more impressive dwellings in town. The two-story white stucco structure with ornate mahogany trim, towering cathedral windows, and a tiled roof, was surrounded by a red-tiled veranda with an ornamental wooden railing, where the Basas would sit for hours on warm nights.

The lush yard, bursting with tropical foliage, became Teresita's private Garden of Eden. Besides her music, Socorro loved flowers. She grew her own orchids in the shade of the latticework on the patio along the east side of the house.

Bauno trees, with their delicate pink blossoms, and coconut palms towered over the ferns, poinsettias, hibiscus, plumed banana plants and lush bougainvillea surrounding the home, where busy red dragon flies hovered over the flowers like hummingbirds.

During the rainy season little Teresita would sit in the airy livingroom and plunk out what to her were pleasing tunes on the massive grand piano. The varnished mahogany Steinway had been brought by boat all the way from Manila in a crate as big as an automobile, and hauled from the docks on an ox cart. Teresita would also sit for hours, absorbing classical music from 78-rpm records on the wind-up Victrola with the long metal horn.

Although she was an only child, Chita, as her doting father called her, was never a lonely one. Among her earliest friends was little José Romero, Jr., son of her father's closest friend. Romero, who like Basa drew much of his legal business from the sugar and copra interests, was emerging as one of the town's most prominent citizens—just as old Martinez had predicted. He served on the Provincial Board, a position comparable to the State Senate in America, and in 1930 the 32-year-old widower took a new wife, Elisa Villanueva.

"Come on, Chita. Let's go for a walk," Basa called one warm afternoon in Teresita's third year.

"Where are you two off to now?" Socorro teased.

"Just over to listen to the news."

"Just over to listen to the news," his wife mocked. "Wasn't that the main reason we had to have that radio you bought in Manila?"

"Si! But it's more fun across the street," Basa laughed. "C'mon, Chita. Hold Daddy's hand so the horses don't run over you crossing the street."

Socorro sat down to pleasure herself at the piano as Pedro and Teresita left the house, like two children, hand in hand.

The plaza was the social gathering place. Nearly the size of a football field, it was surrounded by flowering acacias, coconut palms and bougainvillea. The air was filled with the music of tropical birds. In the center of the green was a circular kiosk, with a galvanized sheet metal roof, where bands played regular concerts that the Basas could enjoy from their veranda. The kiosk also sheltered a cabinet-model radio, from which the people of Dumaguete—few of whom had radios in their homes—could learn the latest news, or listen to music, as they relaxed on wooden benches.

Farther back were the lovers' lanes, cozy brick pathways covered with lattice-work to provide shade, and containing swinging seats where young people could sit and giggle self-consciously at strollers. Teresita soon discovered the lovers' lanes were wonderful places to run through and giggle back at the older boys and girls, while the men of the town sat around the kiosk talking politics in the shadow of the ever-present statue of Rizal, the Filipino martyr executed by the Spaniards in 1896.

". . . and in the United States, President Hoover has vetoed the Hare-Hawes-Cutting Act granting independence to the Philippine Islands after a ten-year period of tutelage, because of the 'Japanese threat' . . ." the radio in the kiosk chattered, as the men moved from their benches and clustered around the set so they could hear better. "However the U.S. Congress overruled the veto. But, in a still later action, our own Senate leader, Manuel Quezon, has announced that the Philippines will not accept the proposition because of the clause permitting American retention of military bases. . . ."

Basa and the other men in the plaza would wait two more years before the radio would announce an agreement had been reached in which the United States would give the Filipinos their independence in one decade—1944.

Meanwhile Teresita would be confirmed, by the Bishop himself, at the age of six, the same year she was enrolled as a first-grader in St. Paul's College. Despite its small size, Dumaguete already had one college and two universities, the

main one being Silliman, which was supported by the Pres-
byterian Church. Nearby St. Paul's, operated by the Sisters of
Charity, contained an elementary school where Teresita
would receive her first 12 years of formal education.

Teresita's seventh year was a solemn one for the growing
child. It was the year of her first Holy Communion, a coming
of age with God. It was also the year Teresita began her formal
piano training. The giant Steinway became an obsession with
the child, an object of love and expression that would guide
her actions for the final 40 years of her life.

It was about this time, also, that Teresita acquired a "big
sister." Cornelia P. Villa, who was really an aunt, although
only a few years older, had come to live in the Basa home
because of the exceptional educational opportunities offered
in Dumaguete.

"It's good that you came when you did, Cornelia," Pedro
Basa joked. "Chita has been very lonesome since her boyfriend, José, moved away. His papa is in the House of Representatives now, and they must spend a good deal of their time
in Manila."

The Romero family had been increasing in size, and the
Basas and Romeros continued to spend occasional weekends
together whenever possible. They recently returned from an
outing in the hill country near Mount Canlaun, where the
children had seen Negritos for the first time. The black-
skinned pigmies, with kinky hair and broad heads, had come
to the Philippines some 30,000 years before when land
bridges connected the islands of the China Sea. Oblivious to
the jet age, they continue to live a stone-age existence, coming
into the villages only when it becomes necessary to trade.

Back at home, Pedro recalled the trip to the uplands, the
last time the Basas and Romeros were together. If the truth
were known, he and Socorro missed Elisa and José far more
than their children missed one another. A Filipino's life
centers around his family, his church, and his work—and it
was the work that took Romero to Manila, where he had been
made floor leader of the National Assembly.

And it was work that kept Pedro away from his wife and daughter longer than he cared to be apart from them. One of the most successful men in Dumaguete, he was now legal representative for several sugar plantations, the copra company, and the new paper mill, where *bagasse*, the residue from sugar cane, was turned into bond paper and cardboard.

Not that hard work did not bring its just rewards. The Basa home, with its newly-installed electric wiring and indoor plumbing, was one of the finest in town. Pedro also had his own *tartanilla* now, and a spirited pony that Teresita had christened Jacinto. Furthermore, he was giving serious thought to investing in a motorcar.

Could anyone deny that little Teresita faced the brightest of futures?

CHAPTER 5

THE HUNT BEGINS

From Columbus Hospital Teresita's body, the ugly knife handle still protruding from her chest, was taken in the police squadrol to the grim, gray Cook County Morgue on West Polk Street. The disinterested officers shoved the stretcher onto an elevator, where their burden was taken to a basement storage area. The plastic wrapping was unzipped, and the naked corpse was placed into a large refrigerated drawer to await the post mortem examination that is required in cases of death not due to natural causes.

From the Basa apartment on Pine Grove, arson investigator Manuel Rios headed for his home. It was a homicide case now, and he was out of it. Arriving shortly before midnight, he told his wife, Irene, of the dreadful scene he had witnessed. "I can't get that angel face out of my mind," he said, sitting on the edge of the bed. "Her body. Her bedroom. A totally desolate scene. Christ, how could anyone do such a thing as that?"

While Rios tossed in his bed, where sleep came slowly that night, homicide investigators still on the scene outside the sealed apartment were picking up momentum. Starting on the fifteenth floor, they fanned out through the building, knocking on doors, recording names, and asking tenants:

"Did you know the occupant of apartment 15B?"

"When was the last time you saw her?"

"Did you, or anybody in your family, see, or hear anything unusual tonight?"

Lulusa, the janitor, said Miss Basa had been paying $275 a month for her three-room apartment. "She was a very private person, you know? I never did know her well enough to talk. She never complained about anything."

"You see a lot of people coming and going, in your work. Had you noticed anything unusual about her lately?"

"No, nothing that I can think of. Well, maybe this is unusual. About three weeks ago, I think it was, I was in the lobby by the manager's office, and I seen her there with this man."

"What kind of man, Petro?"

"What kind of man?"

"Yeah, you know—white? Black guy? Filipino? Can you tell us what he looked like?"

"Oh. Well, he was a white guy, yes, about 50 years old, I'd guess. He had gray hair. He seemed like he'd been drinking, and they were arguing about something."

"Now we're getting somewhere. Did you by chance hear what the argument was about?"

"No. Just when I got there they went out of the building."

Bruce Campbell, the dead woman's 29-year-old neighbor in apartment 15A, overlooking Lake Michigan, said he heard nothing through the common wall that separated the apartments. "I smelled smoke and got myself downstairs. Her apartment was unusually quiet. She was a good neighbor. Never any disturbance. Once she had me in to meet some of her friends. There were maybe five, seven people present."

"Can you tell us who any of them were?"

"No, I'm sorry. I can't remember any of their names. They were all Filipinos who worked with her except this one guy. He was about 50, gray hair, kinda balding. I think he said he was a sheet metal worker. But I can't remember his name. I never was too good at names."

James Clomey, who lived directly above Teresita in 16B, told detectives, "I was in my apartment when I heard the explosive sound. I ran and looked out of the window. I saw flames coming out of the apartment below me. I ran out of the building and called the fire department."

Mario and Katherine Knazze, who had lived in 15G for about four years, said they had only a nodding acquaintance with the woman at the opposite end of the hall. "We'd say 'hello' and 'so long' to one another when we met in the hall, or on the street out front, but that's about all. We figured she was a nurse, because most of the time she wore a white dress and white shoes," Knazze related.

"Oh, there is one thing," his wife recalled. "About two weeks ago some lady in the building told me that the Basa woman was attacked, or raped, or something like that. She said she just got home from work at the hospital and forgot the key to her apartment. While she was standing in the hall, trying to get into her room, a man wearing a ski mask grabbed her and attacked her—in the hall or in the elevator, I don't know. I just heard that somewhere, but no police came around or anything like that."

It was, in fact, the first time police heard of the alleged attack.

The building manager, Joyce Kaltman, was interviewed in her own apartment, 2B, one floor up from the lobby office. She produced the lease for 15B, showing that Teresita Basa had moved in on September 15, 1974, almost two and a half years earlier. "There was never any trouble with her of any kind," she said. "Well, there was one incident in which her apartment was broken into, and we had to have the lock changed."

An undated memo in the file with the lease indicated the tenant had once reported several articles taken from the apartment. The memo listed the items as a Parker pen, a paper cup filled with coins and some Scotch whisky. The manager had no knowledge of the rumored attack.

The Basa slaying was the second homicide that night in Area 6, a section of Chicago having a population approximating that of Omaha, Nebraska. There are five different police districts within the Area, which includes the Rush Street honky-tonks, Old Town, New Town, North Michigan Avenue's "Magnificent Mile," the ultra swank Gold Coast, the Cabrini-Green public housing projects, and the homeowner neighborhood of Rogers Park. In a given year Area 6 records 110 to 120 homicides, a startling number of them having homosexual overtones—but most are solved.

Area 6 Homicide Headquarters, on the northwest corner of Belmont and Western Avenues, is on the site of the old Riverview Amusement Park, forerunner of today's theme parks. It's a neighborhood of antique galleries, locksmiths, small industry, and the Slammer Inn, a cop saloon featuring Old Style Lager.

The police building, directly across from the Slammer, looks more like a college administration building than a cop house. The two-story brown brick structure occupies the plot of ground where Aladdin's Castle once amused and terrified the adventurous. The tall red radio antenna out back, the view from homicide Commander Walter Bosco's office window, is precisely on the site of the old Pair-O-Chutes tower. The building houses the headquarters unit for the northeast section of Chicago. Within its walls are also the district headquarters with its complement of patrol officers, a detective headquarters, and a branch of Cook County Circuit Court. The building, which fronts on Belmont, anchors the south end of a sprawling parking lot—acres of blue and white Dodge police squads with the motto "We Serve and Protect" on every door.

Interspersed among the police vehicles are dozens of Volkswagen beetles, Chevies, campers, pick-up trucks, nondescript autos, and fancy sports cars of working cops.

Those entering from the parking lot walk under a large canopy providing protection from the weather, through the swinging glass doors, and into the vast lobby.

It could be Holiday Inn, minus the potted plants—brown brick walls, clay tile floors and fluorescent lighting. The waiting room walls are lined with blue plastic seats, the kind that stack for mopping. The tile floor leads up a stairway to the second floor, and down a yellow cement block corridor into the large, antiseptic squad room. Plastic liners in the waste baskets reflect the total absence of spittoons—long-time fixtures in all the older station houses.

General assignment, homicide, robbery, burglary and auto theft dicks share this room around the clock. There is an Olivetti typewriter and push-button phone on each of the eighteen formica topped desks where the cops make out their reports. There are 24-hour clocks on the east and west walls, and a conventional one on the north wall, above the head of Lt. August Locallo, on duty behind the brick reception counter. Around the perimeter are five "interview" rooms. Each is a 9-by-15 foot, windowless cell with cement block walls, a two-inch thick door, and a pair of handcuffs bolted securely to the wall.

On the far wall of each interview room are two glass framed "Rights of Prisoners Under Arrest." One is in English, the other in Spanish, a concession to the city's mushrooming Hispanic population.

The earlier homicide that evening involved a so-called "Ma and Pa" squabble over a liquor bottle. It ended with a woman stabbing a neighbor man to death. It was cleaned up on the spot by Investigator Joseph Stachula and his partner, Lee Epplen.

The two of them were seated now in the big squadroom, at one of the far desks alongside the stainless steel water cooler. Stachula was pecking haltingly at the typewriter as his partner lit a cigarette and flipped the match into the Danish Camembert cheese can serving as an ash tray. The pair were winding up their paper work on the whisky bottle killing when investigators Philbin and O'Connor came in with their notes on the Basa homicide.

The 40-year-old Stachula (pronounced Sta-HOO-la), senior member of the team, was considered a copper's cop. His personnel file bulged with an incredible 85 honorable mentions.

A native Chicagoan, the oldest of five children, he joined the Marine Corps in 1958, and stayed on as a reserve Leatherneck, serving as first sergeant of Echo Company of Chicago's 2nd Battalion, 24th Marine Regiment. He joined the police force in 1967 at the age of 30, was promoted to investigator in 1972, and had been working homicide out of Area 6 ever since. Still tough as rawhide, Stachula stood a muscular 5 feet 8 inches tall, weighed 165 pounds, and carried a perpetual look of sincere consternation under a mop of brown hair that frequently flopped down over his dark eyes.

Burly Lee Epplen, the junior member of the partnership, was nine years younger. His father, Robert, used to manage a grocery until his legs gave out. Now he worked as a city sewer inspector. Lee was a football standout at Lane Technical High School. After graduation he worked as a factory hand until a relative persuaded him to try out for the police force. Before taking the patrolman's exam in 1968 he went on a crash diet of meat, salad, and strenuous exercise, dropping from 284 to 185 pounds in four months. Now he was carrying 225 on his 6 foot 2 inch frame.

If it is true that opposites attract, Joe Stachula and Lee Epplen had to be the perfect combination.

Both men preferred the middle watch, because four to midnight was when most of the action was. Stachula also liked to keep his days free to pursue college courses. A year earlier he had attended a special course for homicide detectives at the FBI Academy in Quantico, Virginia. The course dealt mostly with bizarre and multiple murders, with emphasis on the psychological makeup of killers. He was about to put what he learned to good use.

Epplen ground out a Marlboro in the cheese can as Philbin and O'Connor described the scene they had walked in on at the Pine Grove apartment building. Stachula, who did not smoke, gave his partner a weak grin of approval.

"You guys have got a hot one," he commented. "Rape, murder, arson, robbery—all in one. Sounds like a weirdo out there. If we don't nail him fast he could do it again."

"What do you mean, we?" Philbin chided. "You guys are off duty. You busted your big case for the night."

"As Joe always says, a policeman is working when his eyes are open," Epplen laughed. "Actually, I think someone said that about newspaper reporters, but it goes for us, too. And me? I'm wide-ass awake. I'm in the middle of a divorce and nobody's waiting for me to come home. Come on. What can we do? What have you got so far?"

"Well, we've got some next of kin listed in her personal papers," Philbin said. "There's a David Martinez out in L.A., and a Kenneth Basa up in Evanston. Both cousins, the way it looks. Ted and I were gonna try to track them down before the newspapers did, then go back to the joint on Pine Grove and see what else we can stir up."

"Why don't you and Joe take the kinfolks and I'll go back with O'Connor," Epplen said, anxious to get a look at the scene before it was cleaned up. "That'll give you time to make out your report."

As it turned out, Stachula's immediate assistance was not needed. Philbin was able to reach both Martinez and Basa by phone. He told them briefly what had happened, offered his condolences, and asked Kenneth Basa to come by in the morning to tell police what he could about Teresita. Stachula finished pecking out the report on the whisky bottle killing and filed it for future court action. O'Connor and Epplen returned to the murder scene at 2:00 a.m. "What we're looking for," O'Connor told him along the way, "is an address book, or Christmas card list, or something with the names of friends we can start with."

"You know what day this is, Ted?" Epplen asked casually.

"Tuesday, soon as it gets light out."

"Washington's birthday," huffed Epplen. "Think we'll find somebody who will tell the truth?"

The street in front of 2740 Pine Grove was clear of emergency vehicles when they pulled up, except for one district blue and white, posted to make sure the murder scene remained undisturbed. A representative of the medical examiner was waiting for them, as requested, to remove the coroner's seal from the door so they could enter. Epplen was instantly struck by the disarray, the odor, and the cool blast of air whipping in from the broken windows after the warm elevator ride up to the fifteenth floor.

"Jeezuz Christ!" he whispered.

Teresita's bedroom was drenched with water, and the smoke had blackened the walls. In the beams of their flashlights the two detectives painstakingly sifted through the charred, wet remnants of clothing that had been piled atop the body. There were several pairs of pantyhose, a piece of wool knit material, beige in color, and what was left of a colored bedsheet and a burnt mattress pad.

There was a pot on the stove in the kitchenette, containing a slab of spare ribs. The ribs were cold to O'Connor's touch, and he noted that the grease was caked.

A small quantity of meat, wrapped in white butcher's paper, rested on the counter top next to the stove. Some chopped lettuce and half a tomato were on a wooden cutting board on the counter on the other side of the stove.

"Do you see what I don't?" O'Connor asked.

"Yeah," Epplen replied, eyeballing the area around the cutting board and scanning both counter tops. "No knife!"

"But she had obviously been using one," O'Connor noted. "That's gotta be the one that's in her."

A thorough shakedown of the apartment, easily accomplished now that the firemen and district coppers had cleared out, netted more personal papers, $30 in currency, which O'Connor inventoried by serial numbers, and—under some clothing strewn about the room—a small address book. "Abella, John; Correa, Ron; King, Ray; Knudson, Robert; Loeb, Ruth; Pessotti, Richard . . ." O'Connor read, flipping randomly through the pages. "This is what we came for, Lee. Let's head back to the station. Then you can go grab a couple hours of sack while Philbin and I go a-calling."

"You get your jollies waking people up in the middle of the night, don't you," Epplen remarked wryly.

"If it'll help nail a killer, you're damn right."

When O'Connor and Epplen got back to Area 6 Stachula was still there, having coffee and doughnuts with Philbin and Joe Cummings, lone-wolf police reporter for radio station WBBM. Cummings, who always wanted to be a cop but couldn't because of a "bum ticker," carried a radio scanner in his car to monitor police calls. He was often the first newsman on the scene, and he was there on Pine Grove earlier that night, along with other reporters, getting what little info was available at the time. He took what he had back to the radio station and put it on the air.

Now, softening the homicide dicks with coffee and rolls he had purchased himself, Cummings was talking out of the side of his mouth—the confidential way he had seen cops do—and meticulously putting together the story. Cummings was not the college dandy type of reporter who was slowly filling the jobs of the old rough-and-tumble beat men of Chicago journalism. He was a throwback to the glory days of flash powder, and the cops could relate to him. How many other newshawks come by the station house with coffee and doughnuts in the middle of the night, just to talk? Epplen and O'Connor filled in their partners, and Cummings, on the slim pickings at the Basa apartment. Cummings, who had long ago earned the policemen's trust, knew from experience how much of the information he could use, and what he would have to sit on while they checked it out. He never betrayed a trust.

"So, what did you put out on this one, Joe?" Epplen asked. Cummings mocked a look of astonishment. "I know," the detective added quickly. "I should have turned on News-Radio 78, but I was working on this case, ya know?"

"Same as the other guys," the news man said evenly into his styrofoam coffee cup. "A woman tentatively identified as Teresita Basa was found dead after fire broke out in her apartment at 2740 North Pine Grove. City Press carried a bulletin, so it was probably on all the ten o'clock news."

"It was," Philbin confirmed. "Couple of guys who knew her from the hospital called while you two aces were out.

They heard it on the news. I asked 'em to come in and talk to us. They should be down any time now."

"Do we know them?" O'Connor asked.

"Ahhh, let's see," Philbin said, consulting his notebook. "King, Ray, and Pessotti, Richard. They share an apartment over on Marine Drive."

"They're in the victim's address book," O'Connor said. "This whole thing is starting to look too easy."

"Well, fellers. As long as it's gonna be that easy, I think I'll take a duck," Stachula said, draining the coffee cup. "I told Pat not to wait up for me but I got a feeling she will anyhow. With five kids, this is the only time she has to herself."

"Wanna grab a quick belt at the Slammer?" Epplen asked, rising to his feet and giving Cummings a good-night pat on the back. "Thanks for the coffee, buddy. Some day you're busy at the station I'll run get some for you."

"If the Slammer's still open at this hour we'll have to find a cop and close him down," Stachula smiled. "It's past closing time."

"G'night," Cummings said, not turning around. "Remember what I told you, Lee. If you want me to help you line up a nice apartment." After Epplen and Stachula got up, Cummings gathered up the coffee cups, put them into a bag, tossed them into the wastebasket, and took off. He would go out to his car, turn on the police scanner, and probably repeat the scene in another stationhouse before sun-up. Epplen, meanwhile, changed his mind about needing any shut-eye and decided to stick around.

A few minutes later 27-year-old Ray King and 21-year-old Richard Pessotti were ushered in to talk with Philbin and O'Connor. At first it appeared they had little to offer. King had been a friend of the victim, having worked with her at Edgewater Hospital. Pessotti knew Teresita through King.

"How about other friends at the hospital? Did she have any other close friends?"

"Mrs. Loeb. She's an administrative aide to Dr. Mazel, the medical director. She and Teresita were very close," King explained. "We called her about one o'clock this morning and gave her the news. She said she just talked to Teresita on the phone last night."

O'Connor and Epplen caught each other's eyes. O'Connor opened Teresita's address book to the "L" page, and Epplen copied down the home address of Mrs. Ruth Loeb. She lived near the hospital.

"How about you two guys?" O'Connor asked. "You ever been to her place?"

"Mrs. Loeb's or Miss Basa's?"

"Basa."

"We've been there a number of times. She'd just have us over for an evening, or maybe the three of us would go out for something to eat. Stuff like that. She was a fantastic musician, and she liked to play the piano for us. Or sometimes she'd put on a classical record and we'd just sit and soak up the music."

"Did she have a boyfriend that you know of?"

"No, not a boyfriend," said King. "She liked men for their company, I'd say, but we never knew about any romances, did we, Rich?"

Pessotti shook his head.

"How about steady visitors? Anybody like that?"

"Well, there was this Robert Knudson."

"What about Robert Knudson?"

"He's a construction worker. Likes beer a lot. He used to stop by Teresita's apartment and have a couple of beers."

"How did Teresita get along with him?"

"Well, sometimes they argued."

"Could you tell us what this guy looks like?"

"Gray haired. Fiftyish."

Philbin and O'Connor exchanged glances. The janitor had seen the victim quarreling with a gray haired man about 50!

Epplen, standing behind the two men so they could not see his motions, held up his note pad with Mrs. Loeb's name on it, tapped the page with his finger to indicate he was going to check her out, and made a bye-bye gesture with his hand as the other two detectives chatted with Teresita's friends.

At 3:30 a.m. he was at Mrs. Loeb's door. The 60-year-old widow cautiously checked his identification and let him in. She needed little prompting as the detective hung his coat over the back of a chair. "You don't have to tell me why you're here," she said. "You know, I had to be the last one to speak with Teresita before she was murdered."

"Can you tell me about it, Mrs. Loeb?"

"Well, as you probably know by now, I work closely with Dr. Maurice Mazel, who is the medical director at Edgewater Hospital. Miss Basa worked with us as a respiratory therapist for the last three years, and she and I became rather close friends. I had been on vacation in California, and just got back. Teresita gave me this beautiful scarf, made in the Philippines, as a going-away present. The first thing I did when I got home and got settled was to call and let her know I was back. I phoned her about eight o'clock to see if the two of us could get together for lunch today. . . ."

The woman's voice faltered. Epplen looked up from his note-taking and gently pressed her to go on. "I know this is hard for you, but the time factor could be important," he added.

"We chatted awhile, just small talk, you know. And she agreed to meet me tomorrow noon. Oh, that would be this noon, wouldn't it. Oh, dear. I just can't believe any of this."

"What kind of mood would you say she was in, Mrs. Loeb?"

"Oh, she was in good spirits, if that's what you mean. She mentioned something about writing a book of some kind."

"What about the men in her life? Do you know whether Miss Basa had a, uh, lover? Or a boyfriend? Was she seeing any particular guy?"

"She did have one close male friend at one time, but they discontinued seeing one another last summer. I couldn't even tell you his name, or anything about him."

"How about last night, when you talked to her? Was she alone?"

"No, now that you mention it. She wasn't. While we were talking I could hear a male voice in the background. I had forgotten all about that until now."

"Did you recognize the voice, Mrs. Loeb?" Epplen asked, seriously leaning forward on the edge of his chair.

"Oh, no. It was rather indistinct. I couldn't hear what he was saying, but he was speaking calmly—not loud or excited like. And Teresita was giggling. I asked her, 'Am I interrupting anything?' in a kidding sort of way, and she said, 'No.' We talked just a little longer, and then I said, 'Since you have company, I'll call you back later.' She didn't sound upset or anything like that. It didn't seem like anything was wrong."

Mrs. Loeb's recollection of the telephone chat told Epplen two things: One, Teresita Basa was alive and apparently well as late as 8:15 or 8:20 p.m., just 10 to 15 minutes before residents of her building got the first whiff of smoke. And two, the person—almost certainly a man—who was in the apartment was someone she knew quite well. It would appear that Teresita's killer was no stranger.

The presence of the mysterious visitor in the Basa apartment was discovered by Philbin and O'Connor at almost the same time, while they were dialing numbers in her address book. Dr. John Abella, of suburban Northbrook, offered no protest at being awakened by the jangling telephone in the middle of the night. "Doctors are accustomed to being called at all hours," he said. "It goes with the job."

Abella told the detectives that he had telephoned the victim at around 7:10 p.m. Monday. "I might explain here that Teresita and I both played in a small Filipino band which I direct, The Mahogany Five. The purpose of my call was to discuss ticket sales for a concert we're planning at a local dance hall.

"During the course of our conversation, Teresita excused herself for a moment to answer the door. When she returned to the phone, she advised me that she had company. She indicated this was good, because it was someone who she thought might buy a ticket. We were speaking in a Philippine tongue, and she used the term that does not denote gender, however, so I cannot apprise you as to whether the visitor was a male or a female."

The doctor promised to make himself available should the officers desire any additional information, and to provide them with the names and addresses of the other three members of The Mahogany Five.

Upon returning to the station from Mrs. Loeb's, Epplen compared notes with Philbin and O'Connor. The visitor— most certainly the killer—arrived at the Basa apartment at 10 minutes past seven. He had been in the place for about an hour before Mrs. Loeb called to discuss lunch. During the phone conversation Teresita indicated no sign of distress. The visitor had to have been a trusted friend.

The investigators called Connie Kuehn, a supervisor at Edgewater Hospital. She said she would try to speak with fellow employees of the slain woman Tuesday afternoon in an effort to determine whether Teresita had discussed any plans she might have had for Monday evening, or if she expected any callers.

The last person Philbin and O'Connor contacted, from the list of Teresita's immediately known friends, was 37-year-old Ron Correa, who lived in west suburban Oak Park. The telephone chat with Correa was brief. He had been a friend of Teresita's for some time. He mentioned Dr. Abella as another long-time friend of the victim.

Correa also said he understood Teresita had been having some difficulty with someone named Sandor Barath over possibly publishing a book. "If I'm not mistaken, the problem was one involving finances," he said.

"Do you know of any frequent visitors to the Basa apartment?"

"Ah, only one I can think of at the moment—Robert Knudson."

After a long night of it Philbin and O'Connor typed up a detailed report of their activities and discoveries for their supervising officer, R.J. Wagner, who would assign dayside detectives to follow it up. The last notation at the bottom of page five said: "Attempts were made to contact Robert Knudson at his home by telephone and in person. No response from 0100 hours to 0800 hours, 22 Feb. 77."

CHAPTER 6

COMING OF AGE

Teresita had spent an hour at the Steinway and was ready for some fresh air as Socorro slipped quietly into the room and asked, "Who wants to go to the market?"

"Me! Me!" chimed Chita and Cornelia, who had come in from the veranda with a bouquet of orchids to decorate the dinner table. Pedro Basa had offered to leave the *tartanilla* behind for their use, paying the yard boy to act as a driver, but Socorro had told him, "The walk will do us good. I sing in the concert in the plaza tonight, and I will have to be relaxed. Trying to sit passively as Jacinto lurches down the street between carabao carts and sputtering cars will be more than my nerves could stand."

Leaving the house open, they headed down Colon Street. Socorro carried a large wicker basket over one arm and her purse, made from woven pineapple fibers, on the other. The girls toted another basket between them, bumping it against their knees as they walked. Along the way they passed the "house of mystery," a sheet metal structure where only men were allowed. Every town in the Philippines had one—a cockfight pit. Magellan found them when he arrived in the 1500s.

The Dumaguete market was a place of wonderment. At one end were the coconuts, split in half and drying in the sun, white meat surrounded by brown shells resembling a thousand eyes staring skyward.

There were stalls, covered with palm leaves to keep off the sun where Moros sold brightly colored carpets, straw hats and wind chimes made from bamboo. Concrete tables with built-in drains displayed wild deer, carabao, pig and monkey meat drying in the sun. There were squawking chickens, alive in bamboo reed cages, and headless, silent ones hanging by their talons from bamboo racks. The fruit stands were piled high with mangos, papayas, jackfruit, avocados, eggplants, taro, squash and *camotes*—Philippine sweet potatoes. There were baskets of all sizes filled with rice, beans and pineapples. Bananas hung in bunches across the stands.

In another section could be found the produce of the Sulu Sea—anchovy, tuna, mackerel, perch, scad, slipmouth, sardines and herring, snapper, shark, shrimp, lobster and oysters with their shells tilting open as they dried in the tropical sun. Around the market were the shops of the Chinese merchants who offered shoes—both leather and wood-carved—embroidered shirts, trousers, house dresses and *balintawaks,* the elaborate "butterfly" gowns with long sleeves puffed at the shoulders; watches, jewelry and tinware.

"Mama, can we have a centavo for a sugar cane?" Teresita begged, her brown eyes sparkling. Socorro dug into her purse and gave each girl a copper coin, worth one-half of a U.S. penny.

Chirping excitedly, the girls ran over to a small booth where each bought a six-inch length of sugar cane. As they chewed into the fiber the delicious sugar-taste ran down into their throats. Chewing on their cane, they stopped at an open stall where a Moro with a soiled red turban on his head had several frightened macaque monkeys for sale—as pets or for dinner, take your choice. A rope tied tightly around the waists of the monks kept them from wandering off, or chasing any of the scrawny mongrels that wandered sniffing aimlessly around the market.

The giggling youngsters watched the monkeys until Socorro came up with both baskets filled and called, "Come on, girls. Time to be getting back." The monkey man lifted one hand and offered a slight wave as they departed. One of the monks strained at the end of the tight, yard-long line, trying to reach a lizard that was sunbathing on a post supporting the thatched roof of the neighboring stand.

The evening's musical program in the plaza was a special one, and it seemed that almost everyone in Dumaguntn had come to hear the lawyer's wife sing. While waiting for the entertainment to begin, Pedro Basa bought each of the girls an orange-flavored frozen sherbet cone. Then, seeing theirs, he called the vendor back and said, "Make that one more, for myself."

The band played several classics and a few novelty numbers, "Pop! Goes the Weasel," being one of them, as the sun slowly set over the plaza. Then the lights in the kiosk glowed as Socorro appeared before the hushed audience. A coloratura soprano, she sang a Visayan serenade, called a *balitaw,* a love song of the islands. First there was silence as she finished the song, which had begun in a plaintive manner and ended lilting and gay. Then came the applause, with the men in the audience rising to their feet. Teresita and Cornelia tried to clap louder than anyone else as Pedro looked proudly from side to side, accepting admiring glances from his friends and neighbors. The final musical number on the program was a *tenis-tenis,* a comic song from the Sulus. Accompanied only by a bamboo xylophone, a trio of young men improvised the song, in four-line verses consisting of humorous anecdotes aimed at various members of the audience.

Then the lights were dimmed and men came forward with blazing torches. It was time for the *tinikling,* a folk dance in which the participant acts the part of the Philippine rail bird.

Two barefoot men in short pants squatted on the stage facing one another, holding sturdy bamboo poles nearly two inches thick and a dozen feet in length in each hand. Holding the poles parallel and about four to six inches off the floor, they clapped them together to the music while a young couple in costume danced between and beside them. The audience cheered as the dancing feet darted in and out from between the poles as they cracked together, faster and faster, barely missing their ankles. Then, the wild dance over, the lights went back on in the plaza. Socorro joined Pedro and the children and they walked arm in arm across the lawn to their home.

The next morning at the breakfast table Teresita asked, "Daddy, do we have any bamboo poles?"

"Bamboo poles? Why in the world would anybody want anything like that?" he responded, winking across the table at Socorro.

"Oh, I just wondered," Teresita mused, innocently.

"Well, I think if you looked out under the trellis by the orchids you might find one or two," Pedro said wryly. "Although I can't imagine why you would want them."

As Basa left for work the girls skipped out into the yard, where he could hear them calling to the neighbors' children, "Rosalinda, Josephine, come over quick! We're going to do the *tinikling*." The game lasted through the morning, with delighted cries of false pain echoing through the garden whenever one of the youngsters failed to get her ankle out of the way before two of the others cracked the poles together. When Pedro came home for dinner Teresita found it necessary to limp, just a bit.

"Oh, it really doesn't hurt, Daddy," she offered. "I just got my ankle caught dancing the *tinikling*."

Negros enjoys a mild Mediterranean type climate, protected from the storms that often rage across the Pacific to the east, attacking the neighboring islands of Leyte and Samar. Socorro liked the rainy season because her garden sprouted so rapidly you could almost see the buds pop open. The end of the season meant it would soon be time for the fiesta of Santa Catalina. The parishioners began preparing for the festival at just about the same time people over in the States were getting ready for Thanksgiving.

The blaring of trumpets, the rattle of snares, and the muffled boom-boom-boom of the bass drum awakened the Basa household, along with just about everyone else in town that late November morning. A uniformed band strutting by in Colon Street to the tune of a rousing Sousa march proclaimed that the fiesta had begun. "Get out your best *balintawak*, Socorro," Pedro said, motioning toward the closet where her puff-sleeved butterfly dresses hung. "I'll wear my new *barong tagalog*. And look," he smiled, displaying a colorful scarf embroidered from pineapple leaf fiber. "I stopped at Mr. Chong's across from the market and picked up a *panuelo* for Chita so she'll have one like Cornelia's."

"Daddy, how late can we stay up tonight?" asked Teresita, over her breakfast mango.

"As long as you can keep your brown eyes open," he laughed. "Nobody should miss a moment of the festival."

That afternoon they joined in the religious procession through the town. The festive parade was alive with bands and floats from neighboring barrios, and even from nearby islands, joining the people of Dumaguete in the march to the plaza.

A brass band contest, the highlight of any festival, began late that afternoon. Two bands, invited from neighboring barrios so neither could be accused of being a local favorite, faced one another between the kiosk and the José Rizal statue.

When each was in position the band facing east opened up loudly with "Happy Days are Here Again," quickly followed by "Sweet Georgia Brown," then a series of Latin numbers, Filipino folk tunes and, finally, the "Hungarian Rhapsody." Not one bandsman was dry of perspiration by the time the nonstop concert ended, and several sat down on the grass to catch their breath. No sooner had they lowered their drumsticks and horns, however, than the band facing them broke into an ear-splitting rendition of "La Traviata." Playing each number from memory, like the opposing band, the musicians blared, oompahed, tweedled, tooted and drummed until they, too, seemed exhausted. As soon as they stopped for breath the first band, somewhat rested, picked up the tempo with a Dixieland march.

For the remaining three days of the festival the bands blared away, each trying to out-dazzle the other. While one played, members of the opposition band dozed, munched on fried chicken provided by townspeople, or made necessary trips into the bushes. By tradition, the band still playing when the festival ended would be the winner.

"I'll bet you each a sherbet that the one from LaLibertad wins," Basa challenged the enthralled Teresita and her young aunt as they walked over to the plaza for the dizzying finale. He knew he'd buy a sherbet anyway because, in true Filipino fashion, neither band ever gives up. Eventually the mayor, as always, walked between the contestants with his arms raised and proclaimed—to the delight of everyone—a tie!

"You were half right, Daddy," Teresita chirped. "You owe us each half a sherbet."

"I'll let you in on a secret, girls," he laughed. "It's always a tie. Nobody wants to be second, especially at fiesta time." A roving band of guitar minstrels strolled through the departing crowd as the Basas returned to their home. "I have good news," Pedro announced as they approached the house. "The Romeros are coming home for the holidays."

The Christmas season in the Philippines begins December 16, with the first of a series of daybreak masses that will continue for nine days. Each mass is paid for by one of the nine most well-to-do families in the parish, selected for the honor by the priest and a committee of parishioners. Among the nine who achieved the social distinction this year were the Martinez family, the Romeros, and the Basas.

Early on the sixteenth Socorro got the Chinese lanterns out of the store room. These were elaborate star lanterns made from bamboo, paper and tinfoil. They also got out the creche, a Martinez family heirloom, to set up in the living-room. In past years Pedro laboriously hung the lanterns across the veranda, facing the street. This year he settled back in his rattan chair and supervised as Teresita and Cornelia carried out the happy chore.

"I can't believe where the time has gone," he said. "In less than three months you'll be 12 years old, Chita. A young lady. Will you be going carolling with the others tonight?"

"Yes, Daddy. All the girls from our class."

A group of friends stopped off at the Basa home at sundown and Teresita, wearing a brightly colored dress, joined them. Each evening, for the next eight days, they went through the neighborhoods, singing the same carols that children have sung at Christmastime through the ages. On the ninth night, Christmas Eve, Teresita put on her white dress and joined the other carolers at the church. There her group was met by other carolers, who formed one giant chorus comprised of most of the children from the parish. They bought hot rice cakes from vendors in the churchyard while waiting for the procession to begin.

As the group formed for the march through town, two of the older boys, chosen to lead the procession, were given alabaster statues of Joseph and Mary to carry.

Following the boys with the statues, the singers wound their way through the streets, stopping at designated houses to ask for shelter, and to reenact the story of Bethlehem. The occupant of each home they stopped at would come to the door and sing out that there was no room, and the procession would continue.

Socorro was waiting on the veranda when the retinue moved down Colon Street and arrived at the Basa home, the last stop before returning across the plaza to the church. The two boys held the alabaster statues aloft as the children announced that Joseph and Mary had traveled far, and asked Mrs. Basa if she could shelter them for the night. Her ringing soprano voice sang out, like the others, that there was no room. The procession slowly turned away and returned to Santa Catalina's, arriving at midnight to discover that the infant Jesus was now present in the nativity scene.

This would be Teresita's last Christmas festival as a child. The following year, 1941, just nine days before the festival was scheduled to begin, the Japanese attacked Pearl Harbor. Ten days later the emperor's forces invaded the Philippines, and the tranquil Pacific was embroiled in war.

CHAPTER 7

TAE AN DROPS A BOMBSHELL

Tuesday, the twenty-second, was a rarity for February in Chicago—sunny and warm. The temperature soared to a balmy 55 degrees before slipping back to 34 at nightfall when it started to rain. The morning *Tribune* carried an item about the murder at the bottom of page five:

WOMAN FOUND SLAIN IN BURNING FLAT

A hospital therapist was found stabbed to death Monday night when firemen were summoned to fight a blaze in her North Side high-rise apartment.

The body of Teresita Basa, 47, a respiratory therapist at Edgewater Hospital, was discovered under a bed in her 15th-floor apartment at 2740 N. Pine Grove Av. Police said a knife was imbedded in her chest.

The apartment appeared to have been ransacked, according to 13th Battalion Chief Theodore Czerwionka. He said a mattress and some clothing had been set afire, but the damage to the apartment was minor.

Police said firemen found the front door to the apartment locked when they arrived. They said the fire apparently had been set to cover up the murder.

Teresita Basa, after nearly 48 years of life, rated a total of four paragraphs on an inside page. Her body lay on a dissecting table in the basement of the county morgue, where Dr. Tae An, the medical examiner's pathologist, was performing a routine autopsy. Dr. An's interest in the naked subject before him was strictly professional. The slightly built Korean had performed more than 2,000 post mortems as county pathologist, and this was just one more assignment before lunch.

He had already posted the North Side man who'd been stabbed in the dispute over a whisky bottle. This one, he told himself, would be a bit messier. Furthermore, he was not particularly enthused over the presence of the burly, lumbering police officers in the room, trespassing on his territory. They told him that whoever did this to the cadaver on the table was still at large, and "no woman will be safe until the offender is apprehended." Whatever Dr. An found they wanted to know as soon as he did, without waiting for his written report to filter down through channels.

The pathologist, speaking aloud while an assistant took notes, observed the ugly burns about the face and head, and particularly along the right side of the body. He noted that the skin on the victim's throat was "bruised and peeling off . . . the larynx is fractured . . ."

"What do you mean, the larynx is fractured?" interrupted James Frankenbach, a police crime lab technician who was standing by.

"Her windpipe is broken," the doctor explained impatiently. "She was choked as well as stabbed."

Dr. An then moved efficiently down to the knife, which still protruded like a signpost from the victim's chest. Cutting carefully, he determined that the five-inch blade had penetrated the heart, and had also pierced the left lung. "Cause of death is stab wound lacerating the heart and strangulation," he announced.

Dr. An removed the knife with difficulty. It had been plunged into Teresita's chest with such force that it had become wedged in place. He finally worked it free and handed it to Frankenbach. It was a wood-handled kitchen knife with a curved blade, and a sharp, serrated edge. It was, undoubtedly, the knife Teresita had used to slice the tomato shortly before she was attacked. Dr. An made several more routine observations about the body, and concluded by calmly noting in his Korean-American monotone that the hymen had not been penetrated.

"Say that one more time, doc," Frankenbach stammered.

"The hymen has not been penetrated."

"Are you saying she wasn't raped, doctor?"

"Not this lady."

"Are you sure?" the detective asked incredulously.

"A lack of, or rupture, of the hymen, or maidenhead, as some call it, cannot be considered proof of loss of virginity," the doctor impatiently pointed out. "But an unimpaired hymen—which is what we have here—is certainly evidence of the opposite."

"Do you mean to say, doc . . ."

"Your lady is as pure and chaste as the day she was born. She died a virgin!"

The implication was obvious. Teresita had not been murdered by a sexual psychopath, as police suspected, but by someone clever enough to have arranged the scene to throw them off the track. It would have worked, except for Dr. An's thoroughness.

The autopsy completed, the body was released to the next of kin, Ron Somera, Teresita's 41-year-old cousin from Gurnee, about 40 miles north of Chicago. Somera had been named executor of the estate. Like Teresita, he was a native of Dumaguete. He had come to the United States because of greater opportunities, and was married to a Filipina nurse employed at a Waukegan hospital. He also worked in Waukegan, for Sears, Roebuck & Co.

Somera had arranged to have the body removed to the nearest funeral home, Mrazek & Russ, for preparation to be returned to the Philippines.

Mrazek's hearse had already picked up the body by the time Robert M. Reilley, another crime lab technician, arrived at the morgue to take the victim's fingerprints for the record.

Her prints were needed to compare with those found on various objects in the murder apartment, so they could be separated from those of the possible killer. After talking briefly to morgue attendants, and checking the record book on the first floor, Reilley drove over to Mrazek & Russ on West Jackson Boulevard.

He found Teresita lying on her back on a basement embalming table. He grimaced at the horrible chest wound and severe burns on the woman's right side. "I can't do anything with that right hand," he remarked to a funeral home employee who stood by to assist if necessary. "Too damned charred. The ends of those fingers are just meat." Working slowly and painstakingly, he was able to get a satisfactory set of prints from Teresita's left hand.

While Reilley carried out his grim task in the brightly lit basement of the undertaking parlor, homicide investigators from Area 6 were preparing to pay a return visit to the scene of the slaying. Philbin and O'Connor, after only a few hours sleep, were joined at Belmont Area headquarters by investigators John Teenings and Walter Klein. They briefed them on the case while driving back to 2740 N. Pine Grove.

Bernard "Turk" Gavin, an investigator for the medical examiner's office, was standing by as requested, and removed the coroner's seal from the door. Joining the detectives at the scene was officer John Redmond, an evidence technician. The eeriness of the night before and the swaying flashlight beams were gone now. In the morning light the apartment seemed one of utter desolation. "Just think," O'Connor remarked, scanning the blackened mess. "Yesterday this was her home."

With daylight on their side, the detectives scoured the apartment for anything that might point to the identity of Teresita's killer. An opened pack of Salem cigarettes was found on the floor in front of the television. About three feet away lay a half a pack of Mores, a new brand on the market. Just under the west end of the couch was an empty Budweiser can, tipped on its side. Redmond gingerly placed a pencil in the opening in the can, picked it up, and examined it. The side was dented in the middle, possibly by the thumb or palm of someone who squeezed the can after emptying it—a habit some people have. One that could put a murderer in jail.

Taking out his fingerprint kit, Redmond dusted the red, white and blue can with powder from a soft brush. Then, applying clear plastic tape, he lifted a latent print from its side. "This can could have belonged to the lady," he said. "Or, maybe we're looking for a guy who likes to squeeze beer cans, and then does the same thing to someone's neck."

"We got two more in here, John," Philbin called from the kitchen, where he and his partner were sorting out the contents of a brown paper garbage bag. Among the egg shells, crumpled pieces of paper, celery leaves and coffee grounds were two more Bud cans, both crushed in the middle. Redmond dusted them, and lifted prints from each. The two cigarette packs, which might have contained the killer's prints, were soggy with water. He couldn't do a thing with them.

He put the cans into plastic bags for further study at the crime lab. The investigators left the apartment, and Gavin reaffixed the coroner's seal to the black wooden door.

On their way out of the building the detectives ran into Arthur Shields, the tall, lean, and balding day janitor. The 54-year-old Shields, who did not live in the building, said he was at home on North Clarendon Avenue the previous evening. "I didn't know anything about what happened here until I came to work this morning," he said. "Boy, talk about a shocker!"

"Well, how about yesterday, before you went off duty? Did you notice anything unusual around the building, or anything like that?"

"Not that I can recall. Well, wait a minute. I did see this guy knocking on Miss Basa's door. I'd say it was about a quarter to four. I was on the floor picking up trash, you know, and he was by her door at the end of the hall."

"Did this man see you, Mr. Shields?"

"Oh, hell yes. I talked to him."

"You talked with him? What did you talk about?"

"Yeah. I told him it was a building policy to challenge anyone walking around on the floors. Security, you know. And he says he just wanted to see if she was home. Then he leaves, and I go down and report it to the office."

"What did this guy look like, Mr. Shields? Can you remember anything about him? His dress? His appearance?"

"Oh, I'd seen him maybe three times before. Miss Basa was the kind, she wouldn't let anybody in if she didn't know them."

"Alright, now. Can you describe this gentleman for us?" Philbin asked, pulling out his notebook.

"Oh, middle 30s, I'd say. Tall. White guy. Six feet, maybe six two. About 190. He had brown hair, combed back. And he kind of walked with his shoulders hunched over, ya know?"

The janitor hunched his shoulders and lowered his head, to illustrate his point. "He reminded me of an immigrant."

"How about his clothes? What was he wearing?"

"When I seen him yesterday he had on one of those brown Ivy league hats, and he was wearing a brown plaid jacket. What he had on the other times, I don't remember."

"Mr. Shields, you've been a big help," Philbin said. "I'm going to give you my card, and if you think of anything else, call me at Area 6. If I'm not there, they'll know where to find me, day or night."

O'Connor asked the janitor if he would be available to come down to headquarters and look at pictures of possible suspects. "Any time. You know where I am. If I ain't here, you can get me at home."

On the way back to Belmont Avenue, Philbin and O'Connor made another sweep by Robert Knudson's home on North Sayre Avenue. This time he was there. After the detectives stated their business, the 47-year-old unemployed sheet metal worker agreed to accompany them to the station. There Knudson was questioned at length, but they were unable to shake his story. He insisted he had gone out for groceries between 9:30 and 10:45 a.m. the previous day but, other than that, had never left the house.

"If you never left the house, how come we couldn't get hold of you? We tried half the damn night."

"I can't explain that," Knudson shrugged.

"Well, there is a way we can settle this," Philbin suggested. "Mr. Knudson, would you be willing to submit to a polygraph examination—a lie detector test?"

Knudson rubbed his stubbly chin. "Why not?" he said slowly. "Yeah. You guys set it up and I'll take it. I know I didn't do anything to Teresita."

While Philbin and O'Connor were questioning Knudson in one of the small interrogation rooms, Detectives Teenings and Klein scooted back to the murder building and picked up Shields. They drove the janitor back to homicide headquarters, where he eyeballed the suspect through the one-way glass.

"Nope, that isn't him," Shields asserted. "He ain't the guy I seen knocking on the lady's door yesterday. Doesn't look anything like him, in fact. The guy I saw had brown hair, not gray."

A lie detector test was scheduled for Knudson for seven o'clock that night. In the meantime he was requestioned by homicide investigators John Whalen and Jerry Lawrence. Lawrence, a serious Christian active in prayer groups and Bible study, used the gentle approach. He was friendly, sympathetic, and wanted to do what he could to help. The results were the same as Knudson's bout with the other detectives, however. "Like I told the other officers, I was home all evening yesterday," he insisted. Visibly upset over being questioned about the death of a friend—a woman with whom he had been seen regularly—Knudson gulped down a Valium to settle his nerves. One of the detectives brought him a paper cup from the water cooler to wash it down.

Whalen and Lawrence then escorted Knudson to the crime lab at Central District Headquarters, 1121 South State Street, where Thomas Walsh, a polygraph technician, administered the test. At the conclusion of the exam Walsh approached the two detectives, shaking his head.

"Well, what gives?" asked Whalen.

"He told me you guys let him take a Valium to calm his nerves."

"Yeah, what's wrong with that?"

"Oh, it calmed the hell out of his nerves," Walsh said. "He's so frickin' calm now I might as well have put the lie box on an empty chair."

"You didn't get anything?"

"The test was inconclusive. You're gonna have to bring him back another time."

For Knudson it was a frustrating experience as well. He would have to go through it all over again. The detectives drove him back through the rain to his North Side home. "We'll be in touch," Whalen told him. "I ain't goin' anywhere," Knudson replied.

So the night wouldn't be a complete waste, Lawrence and Whalen headed for Marine Drive to take another crack at Richard Pessotti and Ray King. Anyone knowing anything about the victim had to be questioned thoroughly while things were still fresh in their minds. Any cop will tell you that once a murder trail cools, it seldom heats up again.

At this point, no one had been ruled out as a suspect. The detectives had achieved good luck in the past by questioning someone who had been interrogated by other investigators earlier. A fresh approach occasionally uncovers something that might have slipped by the original questioners.

The two men were relaxing in their high-rise apartment overlooking the lake when the detectives called. King was lounging in blue jeans, while Pessotti was wearing an expensive looking leisure suit with his shirt open at the neck to display a gold chain and cross. "Both of us knew Teresita from working at the hospital," he related. "I'd say I've known her—had known her—for about a year. The three of us liked to go out to dinner, or maybe a movie. Sometimes we'd go and hear her band play. I guess you could say the three of us were close personal friends. Strictly platonic, you understand."

The detectives understood. During the discussion Lawrence casually injected Knudson's name into the conversation. King and Pessotti said they'd been trying to contact the man all afternoon, but got no answer at his home. "We wanted to discuss Teresita with him, as one of her friends, to see his reaction," King said.

The detectives did not mention that Knudson had been with them.

"I might point out that Rich and I heard that Teresita's publisher was at her apartment last night," King continued.

Several of the dead woman's friends had told police she had been involved in a writing project, but none seemed to know what it involved. "Where did you hear that?" Whalen asked.

"From some girl who works at the hospital, named Maria."

"This Maria. How did she know this publisher was at the apartment?"

"Well, I don't think she really did know," Pessotti interjected, with the emphasis on "really." "She kind of just gave it to us as a rumor. Everybody there was talking about what happened last night."

He and King offered to talk to Maria in the morning and relay any information they might come up with to the investigating officers. On the way back to the station Whalen and Lawrence stopped off at Edgewater Hospital to chat with personnel on duty in the respiratory therapy department. They had all known Teresita, but none could offer anything of what detectives like to refer to as "evidentiary value."

Back at Belmont, reviewing reports of other investigators from the previous night, they came across the notation that Ron Correa had mentioned someone he believed named Barath, with whom Teresita had been having difficulties. Whalen and Lawrence tried several people by that name, and when they came up with Stephan Barath they hit the gong. The 47-year-old musician and teacher admitted that he was, indeed, the mysterious "publisher" that the victim had mentioned to friends. Only he wasn't really a publisher at all. They drove over to talk to him.

"This could be a little embarrassing," he told the detectives. "Not for me, you understand—it was a matter of business—but for Teresita Basa. And, after all, she's gone now."

"What, just exactly, was the nature of your business with the Basa woman?" Lawrence pressed.

"Ghost writing, I guess you'd call it. I was writing a master's thesis for her, for a price. I answered an ad she had placed in the paper, let me see . . . in 1974. That was how I first met the lady."

"What was this thesis about, Mr. Barath?" Whalen asked.

"Tcherepnin, and I'll bet you never heard of him. Most people haven't, unless they're deep into heavy music. Teresita was fascinated by him. He's a Russian born composer— Alexander Tcherepnin. She said she had met him in Paris. She was working on her master's at Indiana University, doing her thesis on the composer's life . . ."

"But you were doing the actual writing."

"Exactly. In fact, it was nearly complete. A hundred and fifty pages. It was very difficult, because biographical material on the subject is quite limited. I asked her how she happened to choose him, of all people, and she told me, 'Because I like him. He's a nice man.' I found that she really liked Tcherepnin's music, but she was unable to analyze it properly. It was too deep for her."

"What kind of a person would you say Miss Basa was, Mr. Barath?"

"Well, as I told you, I saw her perhaps only half a dozen times, or less. I had never been to her actual apartment. I went to the building last week and rang the bell, and she came down. We had words about how much she was going to pay, but you couldn't call it an argument. It was a lively discussion."

"And?"

"As I recall, an employee of the building came by while we were talking, so we left. Neither of us wanted it known that I was doing this writing for her. That's why she referred to me as her 'publisher,' if anyone asked questions.

"Teresita was a good Christian person, I do know that," he added. "She believed very strongly in her faith. I would also say she was a somewhat stern person. I always had the feeling she was in a hurry. When she talked, her words were quick, like 'da-dum da-dum.' Then she'd say, 'Well, I must go now.' And away she'd go."

In thanking Barath, Whalen casually asked if he'd object to being fingerprinted.

"For what reason?"

"Well, so we can compare your prints with any that might be in the apartment. This is how we rule out possible suspects, as well as identifying anyone who may have been there. Not that you're a suspect, of course. This is something we're asking everyone who was associated with her to do."

"I have no objection, if you put it that way," Barath said.

Whalen and Lawrence left Barath's home on West Winnemac Avenue and drove back to Knudson's neighborhood. Parking their unmarked car a block away, they went from door to door, briefly questioning neighbors. Nobody had seen Knudson either coming or going the previous day.

One more piece had been fit into the puzzle, however. It was undoubtedly Barath, and not Knudson, whom the janitor Lulusa had seen arguing with Teresita in the lobby of her apartment building a week before the murder.

And the unexpected discovery that Teresita had guarded her virginity—a secret that hadn't occurred to the killer—ruled out sex as a motive for her murder. The position in which her body was found, stripped naked and with her legs spread wide apart, had been a carefully arranged stage setting, designed to point homicide investigators in the wrong direction.

CHAPTER 8

A MEMORY THAT
WON'T GO AWAY

It happened ever so swiftly. The Japanese penetrated the Philippines with remarkable ease. The islands, under American domination since before the turn of the century, had been every bit as unprepared as Hawaii. And, lying just below the Tropic of Cancer from Japan itself, they were directly in the line of attack. On Christmas Eve the Japanese hit Manila.

Teresita's second cousin, Lt. José Basa, a fighter pilot, had been on patrol with a fellow Filipino airman in their American-built P-40s. They were returning to base when they spotted the Mitsubishis with their Zero support planes coming in over the city. Like a pair of troublesome gnats the Filipino fighters, along with a pitiful handful of American planes that were able to get off the ground, flew into the face of the enemy with guns blazing. Basa went down in flames, the first Filipino to be shot out of the sky in warfare. After the bloody conflict was over his grateful country would honor him with a postage stamp bearing his likeness.

Gen. Douglas MacArthur did what he could to defend the islands with 24,000 ill-equipped American troops, 120,000 inadequately trained Filipinos, and 250 obsolete airplanes. He declared Manila an open city to protect its inhabitants and historic buildings from destruction, and set up headquarters on Corregidor in Manila Bay. The ailing President Manuel Quezon and his vice president Sergio Osmeña reluctantly joined MacArthur on the island fortress.

Dumaguete, on the southern tip of Negros Island, was a beehive of activity during the closing days of 1941. Ships of every kind were being loaded with food from the Visayan Islands for the defenders of Corregidor and Bataan, a Florida-shaped peninsula jutting into Manila Bay. Only a few of the ships ever got through.

By February President Quezon himself was on his way to Negros, dodging between islands, one step ahead of Gen. Masaharu Homma's Imperial Japanese Army. At MacArthur's urging Quezon and his party, including his wife and three children, left Corregidor aboard the U.S. submarine *Swordfish* to avoid capture. From the *Swordfish* the Presidential party transferred to the steamer S. S. *Princess of Negros*, which plied a nervous path toward Negros Oriental, arriving February 27.

Quezon's last days as President in residency of the Philippines were spent in Dumaguete, preparing his people for the inevitable. Teresita squeezed her father's hand the first time she saw him, slouched in a wheelchair, where he spent much of his working day. "He's such a tiny man, Daddy," she observed. "I always thought the President would be a huge person. He's not even as big as you."

"He is a very sick man," Basa explained. "The President has tuberculosis, and every day when one of our islands dies, he dies a little bit with it."

In the days that Quezon spent meeting with community leaders, Teresita became friends with his youngest daughter, Zeneida, her own age. She filled Teresita's ears with endless stories of the great city of Manila, and how she and a group of girlfriends had spent their final days there wrapping Christmas gifts for the soldiers. "On the day that Manila was bombed my father became very angry," she related. "His face turned red and he said, 'How dare those Japs!'"

On the sixteenth of March, while the Quezon party was still in Dumaguete, their escape ship, the *Princess*, was captured by Japanese destroyers off Negros in Tanon Strait. Then came the electrifying word that MacArthur had run the enemy blockade in a PT boat and had flown to Australia.

Enemy bombers were pasting the neighboring island of Cebu almost daily as their troops swept across the Sulu Archipelago and captured Davao and Zamboanga on the great island of Mindanao. Word reached Quezon by radio that he could remain behind no longer. Three U.S. PT boats, the same craft that had hustled the general away from Corregidor, were out on Macajalar Bay, ducking the Japanese in hopes of repeating their derring-do mission with the Philippine president.

On March 18 Quezon conferred for the last time with the town leaders in a home near Zamboanguita Beach, where he hoped to be picked up. Because of his position of dominance in the community, Pedro Basa was among those present. Over Socorro's muted objections, he had brought Teresita along—partly so she could see Zeneida for one last time, and also because he wanted her to be a witness to history.

One of the three rescue boats racing toward Dumaguete under cover of darkness failed to make it through the blockade. The other two, led by U.S. Navy Comdr. John D. Bulkeley, who had evacuated MacArthur two days earlier, throttled in and tied up at the Dumaguete wharf shortly after midnight.

"There is simply no time to delay, Mr. President," the bearded PT commander announced. "We've got to get the hell out before sun-up, or we don't get out at all."

Teresita hugged Zeneida, and both girls were sobbing as they promised to write one another—how, they didn't know. Then the president's group was hustled aboard the two boats, which thundered out into the bay at 3:00 a.m.

With the end in sight Dumaguete, like Manila, was declared an open city to protect the historic baroque cathedral, the college and university buildings, and other structures of importance. Pedro and Socorro Basa agonized for days over whether to join Teresita's uncle, Lorenzo Teves, and many of their friends who were disappearing into the mountains. A number of townspeople prevailed on Basa to remain behind, however, saying his counsel would be needed more than ever.

The cocky little men in brown uniforms met no resistance as they marched warily into town and set up headquarters in the municipal building on the plaza. Teresita and Cornelia were told to take no notice of them. The girls were also admonished to take no notice of Pedro Basa's occasional absences from the home on Colon Street. Only a trusted few knew he was working with the guerrillas, providing them with information on Japanese operations and the strength and location of the occupation forces.

A number of young women and girls from the working class families in Dumaguete, as elsewhere under Japanese domination, were forced into prostitution in local "pompom" houses in order to help provide for their families with the men gone. Members of the elite, such as the Basas, were treated with begrudging respect. For the teen-aged Teresita, the greatest personal change in her life came at school, where the invaders dropped English language classes and replaced them with compulsory lessons in Japanese.

As guerrilla harassment continued, the small airfield on the outskirts of Dumaguete, where light propeller aircraft once landed and took off on island-hopping missions, was turned into a military airdrome for fighter planes and medium bombers. The first step toward liberation of the Philippines came on October 20, 1944, when American GIs swarmed ashore on the neighboring island of Leyte.

General MacArthur, who had promised the Filipinos, "I shall return," had himself photographed wading ashore from a landing barge. President Quezon did not return. He died in the United States, and was succeeded by Osmeña, who was at MacArthur's side in the Leyte landing. With the landings the Japanese airfield at Dumaguete assumed major importance, both as a fighter base to attack the American invaders and as a target itself.

Teresita's most indelible memory of the war came late that year, at about the time the townspeople would normally have been celebrating the feast day of Santa Catalina. "The Americans are coming over again, Mama," she said early that morning while preparing for school. "Listen, you can hear them."

The Basas went cautiously out onto the veranda as the P-38s soared high over the city, amid the rapid coughs of the ack-ack guns and puffs of black smoke. Then the graceful silver planes with their twin fuselages swooped beneath the range of the anti-aircraft fire, coming in from the sea at tree-top level to another attack on the airfield with gunfire and 50-pound bombs.

After dropping their loads, the planes could be seen gaining altitude over the trees as they made a wide circle over the town to head back out to sea. "Look at that one! Look at that one!" Teresita shouted, pointing skyward over the plaza. One of the P-38s was trailing black smoke and fire.

As the Basas watched, the pilot flipped open his hatch, aimed his damaged plane out to sea, and tumbled head first out of the cockpit. His parachute billowed open almost immediately, and he swayed from side to side as he drifted slowly toward the plaza directly across the street from their home.

The roar of a fast-moving truck coming up Colon Street signaled the arrival of trouble. It was a Japanese-made Ford, full of helmeted soldiers. The vehicle's brake linings squealed as the driver brought the lorry up fast at the edge of the plaza.

A platoon of soldiers poured from the back end, gripping their rifles and pointing toward the sky as they chattered in Japanese. Then they waited as the American airman drifted slowly to the ground, not 200 meters away.

"Oh, what's going to happen, Daddy?" Teresita asked, holding her hand to her face.

"The flier is caught, and there is nothing to do about it," Basa consoled her. "I suspect they will take him away and ask him a lot of questions. Then he will be put in a prison camp until the war is over."

As the pilot hit the ground his legs buckled and he rolled over onto his side. His chute settled to the plaza and collapsed like a giant handkerchief. Before he could struggle to his feet he was surrounded by shouting Japanese, some of them poking at him with their bayonets. The American was jerked to his feet and his parachute harness was disengaged and fell to the ground. The pilot looked warily at his captors as he raised his hands to surrender. As he lifted his right hand, he unsnapped his flight helmet and let it fall to his feet. Teresita could see that he had blond, curly hair and a suntanned face. He was, perhaps, 10 years older than she.

"It's best that we go inside now. It's all over," Basa suggested, taking Teresita by the shoulder to guide her back into the house.

"I can see his face, Daddy. He isn't hurt," Teresita said, still watching the drama across the street.

She had barely uttered the words when a rifle cracked and the American reeled backward, a look of dismay on his face, and dropped to his knees. As the pilot looked up in disbelief, one of the Japanese soldiers lunged forward with his bayonet.

"Oh, my God," the shocked Basa uttered, crossing himself. "Go into the house, everyone!"

The flier was still on his knees, hunched over with his head almost on the ground. One after another the soldiers drew Yankee blood with their bayonets, then stepped back to give the next man a turn. Then there was a shot, and another, as the life blood spurted from his wounds and the American rolled onto his side and flopped over on his back. The torn body continued to jerk as the soldiers gleefully emptied their rifles into it.

Teresita could only cry, "Daddy," as she fell sobbing into her father's arms. The Japanese had the dead American by his feet, making a bloody path as they dragged him across the plaza to the truck in front of the Basa home.

It was a memory that Teresita would carry with her to her grave.

CHAPTER 9

SUSPECTS GALORE

Lee Epplen and Joe Stachula rolled in to work early Wednesday afternoon, February 23. The Basa murder case was nearly two days old, and the cops had yet to come up with a solid suspect. Epplen lit up a Marlboro, and the two of them sipped coffee from styrofoam cups while waiting in the conference room for the 4:30 p.m. roll call.

Stachula paged through a well-read copy of the morning *Tribune*, left behind by the day shift. On an inside page he discovered that the death of Teresita Basa, the biggest thing in his life at the moment, had been relegated to one paragraph status:

> INVESTIGATORS Tuesday were seeking several male acquaintances for questioning in the fatal stabbing of Teresita Basa, 48, a respiratory therapist at Edgewater Hospital, whose body—with a knife embedded in her chest—was found in her 15th floor apartment at 2740 N. Pine Grove Av., where firemen put out a small fire.

He read it aloud to Epplen. "They didn't even get her age right," he said. Stachula leafed back to the comic section, where he read Dick Tracy. Finally, as his eyes dropped to the bottom of the page, he exclaimed, "Son of a bitch!"

"Now what?" Epplen asked.

"Some bugger worked the crossword puzzle."

"What the hell do you expect, Joe? Somebody's gonna pay 15 cents for the paper and leave the best part for the moochers? Here, lemme have the sports section."

"Hey, listen to this one," Stachula said, rattling the paper. "Story out of New York about a dedicated copper who put three punks behind bars, and listen how he did it. These gang members beat up a Puerto Rican girl who resisted their advances. She gets scared and takes the hell off for home. The cop goes down to Puerto Rico at his own expense and talks her into coming back to testify against the punks who jumped her."

"Guy must be nuts," Epplen grunted, scanning the basketball scores. "I mean, at his own expense? Gimme a break."

The second floor room was rapidly filling up as 4:30 approached and Sgt. E.R. O'Connell strode briskly onto center stage. He called the roll and then briefed the assembly on what had happened on the day shift. Then there followed a case-by-case discussion of unfinished business. He held the Basa homicide for last.

"On this one, I've got news for you! We seem to be looking for an offender who is either nuttier than nuts or sly as a fox, one or the other. How do we know that? Because the autopsy showed—now get this, fellas—that Teresita Basa was a virgin. She was not, repeat NOT, raped, as we were led to believe. Now, this info has not been given out to the media, and we don't want it to get out. So, if some nut wanders in and confesses that he raped and killed the victim, just to get his name in the paper, we know he's whippy as an antenna. This little tidbit is also going to help us in questioning the real killer when we find him, because nobody but him and us knows that he didn't rape her.

"It now looks like the offender tried to make it look like a sexual attack to throw us off the track. So you guys who have been checking known sex offenders have been pulling your puds. Maybe that's what this *ganef* wanted, enough time for his trail to get cold. He could be in California by now."

"I could go out there and look for him," volunteered Epplen, eyeing the mounds of snow out the window.

"Nobody needs a smart-ass," O'Connell droned.

"Hey, Sarge. How about if the broad was a lesbo, and some dame killed her?" a voice questioned from the back of the room.

O'Connell looked down at the front row. "Philbin?"

"Not a chance, sergeant," Philbin answered. "We've checked the Basa woman out every way from Sunday. She definitely wasn't a lesbian. This lady was as pure as the driven snow."

"Thanks, John. You and Lawrence, Epplen, and Stachula —you four keep after this one. We've got another name for you to check out, and we're going to need prints of everyone you've talked to so far, to compare with evidence found in the home. It now looks—and I think we're right this time—like the killer had to have been someone who she knew well enough to have in her apartment, but who didn't know her well enough to realize she still had her cherry."

Epplen and Stachula were assigned a car, given the ignition keys, and advised of their radio call letters for the night—a four digit code that can be read by police throughout the city. The number 8 signifies homicide, and the second digit denotes the police area, 6 in their case. The last two numbers identify a specific team car. Epplen and Stachula were 8612.

It was raining as they pulled out of the lot and Epplen switched on the wipers and defroster. It was 40 degrees and dropping. Puddles of dirty slush splattered noisily against the bottom of the gray Plymouth as Epplen pointed the unmarked car toward Marine Drive.

The detectives had been instructed to ask Ray King and Richard Pessotti if they would come in voluntarily to be fingerprinted. They readily agreed, saying they wanted to help out in any way they could. On the way back to the station

Stachula sat sideways and chatted with the occupants of the rear seat about the victim.

"You know, Chita wasn't just an ordinary person. She was SOMEbody," King remarked.

"You called her Chita?" Stachula questioned.

"Her old man gave her that nickname back in the Philippines. He was a judge, did you know that? He's dead now. She let only her closest friends call her Chita."

"And you guys were her closest friends?"

"We went around a lot together," Pessotti interjected. "Chita, well, she kind of needed someone to watch out for her. She was worldly wise, but gullible as hell. She'd give you everything in her purse if she thought you needed it more than she did."

"What do you mean by worldly wise?" Stachula asked.

"She'd been all over," Pessotti said. "She was even received by the Queen of England. And in France she knew Tcherepnin. You guys know who that is?"

"Tcherepnin, Tcherepnin," Stachula mulled, tongue in cheek. "He's that Russian composer, isn't he?" King and Pessotti gawked at one another, amazed at how much a simple cop might know, as Stachula poked Epplen triumphantly on the leg.

After being fingerprinted at Area 6 the two men were driven back home. The prints were turned over to fingerprint technician Dennis O'Neill, who checked them against those found at the murder scene, including those on the Budweiser cans. There was no comparison.

O'Neill also checked Robert Knudson's prints against those found at the scene. Again, there was nothing to show any of them had been there on the fatal night.

Lawrence and Philbin brought him one more set of prints, those of a male white, Ralph M. Magner. Once more, the results were negative. While Epplen and Stachula were working with King and Pessotti, the other two detectives had located Magner, whom they had learned was another close friend of the victim. They telephoned him at his North Side home and he agreed to come in voluntarily for questioning. Arriving a short time later, he parked his 1970 Chrysler New Yorker behind the station house and sprinted through the rain to the shelter of the canopy over the back door.

An engineering draftsman for a large electric company, Magner was a handsome man of 48 with thick, sandy hair. After being printed and photographed for the record he was taken into one of the interview rooms. He told the detectives he had learned of Teresita's death two nights earlier from the ten o'clock news.

"How did you happen to know the victim?" Philbin asked.

"I met her through a guy I knew from one of the jobs I was on," he replied.

"This guy who introduced you to her. What was his name?"

"Knudson. Bob Knudson."

The two detectives exchanged glances. Then they talked some more about Teresita. Magner said he had "socialized" with her on three or four occasions—"cocktail parties, and a picnic."

While Philbin and Lawrence were questioning Magner, Stachula and Epplen, back from returning King and Pessotti to their home, were given a mug shot that had been made earlier. They telephoned Shields, the janitor, to make sure he was home, then drove over to his place with the snapshot. Shields studied the picture, and handed it back to Stachula.

"It looks like the guy I seen at Miss Basa's door that day—the one she was killed. Like I say, it looks like the guy, but I can't be sure."

"Would you mind coming down to the station with us and take a look at someone for us?" Epplen asked. "It would be very helpful to us."

"Sure. Like I told you before, anything I can do to help."

Back at Area 6, Shields was stationed behind a one-way glass so he could look into the interrogation room where Magner was casually sipping coffee and chatting with the other two detectives. "Do you recognize any of those men in there?" Stachula asked.

"Sure do," Shields replied after a short pause. "That one in the middle," he said, pointing to Magner. "He's the one that was knocking at the lady's door the afternoon of the murder."

Confronted with the janitor's identification, Magner calmly returned the detectives' stares and insisted, "It wasn't me. I don't care what anybody says."

"Look, Ralph. The guy made you. What's the percentage of denying you were at Teresita's apartment on the day of the murder? The witness is willing to testify that he saw you there, that he talked to you, and that you talked to him," Philbin persisted.

"No way. You've got a witness. O.K. I don't dispute that. And he says he can identify me. O.K. But I'm still not the guy he saw, or thinks he saw. I wasn't there."

"How about later in the evening, Ralph? Where were you around eight o'clock Monday night?"

"I can't recall right now. I'd have to think about it."

"Would you be willing to submit to a polygraph examination?"

"No, I'm not nuts about the idea, but—yeah—I would take a lie test if I had to. Just to get you jokers off my back."

Magner was free to leave, after being advised that the dicks would probably want to talk to him again. On the way out he encountered Stachula and Epplen, who asked if he needed a lift home in the rain. "No thanks, my wheels are out back," he said.

Before calling it a night the two detectives decided to get a noon start the next day. In going through Teresita's personal papers they had come across the name of a lawyer who had done work for her. They wanted to catch him while he was still in his office.

* * *

By Thursday morning the bitter rain had turned to wet, heavy snow. Stachula and Epplen met at noon at the Slammer for a quick bite before hitting the streets. The gray shingled building, that looked as if it might have pre-dated the Great Chicago Fire of 1871, was decorated across the front with vertical one-inch wood strips, painted black to resemble the bars of a lockup. Over the front door was a sign proclaiming "Old Style—Cold Beer," and beneath that, "Food." If the Slammer's food wasn't good enough, there was a sign on the roof directing motorists crossing the Western-Belmont overpass to McDonald's.

Stachula was already parked at the far end of the garish red formica bar when Epplen wandered in, blinked his eyes to focus in the dim light, and made his way across the soiled red Ozite carpet to join him. As he breezed past a group of vice dicks huddled near the door he picked up snatches of conversation.

". . . Jesuz Christ. They brought the fuckin' broad in and were going to have her pose in the nude!"

"No shit! In the station?"

"Fuckin'-A. Right in the station! I got the hell outa there . . ."

Frank was behind the bar, stacking glasses under the giant portrait of Mayor Richard J. Daley.

Augmenting the back-bar decor was a blue Mars light salvaged from a wrecked squad car, a large color TV, and a two-way radio mike—not hooked up to anything. On the opposite wall was a publicity photo of Joseph Wambaugh, the L.A. cop turned author, and a string of arrest photos from various newspapers. The bartop was cluttered from end to end with ash trays.

"How's Pat?" Epplen asked his partner, as Frank banged a glass of beer down in front of him, splashing part of it on the bar top.

"She's fine," Stachula smiled. "Bitching a little because I don't spend enough time at home, but she understands. Talk to Rose Mary lately?"

"Yeah. I called her at work this morning," Epplen said. "There's still a lot of stuff we've got to get straightened out before the divorce goes through. The kids, the house, who gets what . . ."

"She still at the Anti-Cruelty Society?"

"Yeah. It takes two incomes these days, even to get unhitched."

Frank, waiting patiently behind the amber glass he had plopped indelicately in front of Epplen, queried, "You guys gonna eat?"

"May we see a menu please?" asked Stachula, innocently raising his eyebrows.

"Fuck you! See all them people at the bar? I ain't got time for jokers," Frank answered, feigning anger. "Exactly what would youse like on your hot dogs?"

"Whatever you can spare without bleeding," Stachula said.

"Put the stuff up here, Frank, so we can put it on ourselves. We don't know where your hands have been," Epplen added.

After finishing their sandwiches they ducked across the street through the snow to their building, waved to the sergeant behind the reception desk, and took the stairs two at a time up to the squad room.

While Epplen examined the bulletin board on the east wall, Stachula checked the mail box, with its 200 pigeon holes, to see whether he or his partner had any messages. At 1:30 p.m. they checked out the same Plymouth they had the night before and headed west to see Myron J. Walters, attorney at law.

"What a terrible, terrible thing," the lawyer said, shaking hands with the two detectives and ushering them into his office. "She was a wonderful person. It's hard to fathom how, or why, anyone would do something like that, especially to someone like her."

"Happens every day in Chicago," Stachula mused. "In going through her personal effects, we noticed that you seemed to have had some legal dealings with her."

"Yes, she asked me to represent her, relative to obtaining a permanent resident visa," Walters explained. "Miss Basa had been to this country twice, on student visas, and it was her desire to remain here and to continue in her chosen field at Edgewater Hospital." The lawyer said he knew little about Teresita's personal life, but he did recall a recent incident.

"It may, or may not, be helpful in the police investigation," he speculated. "Miss Basa was quite concerned that I had not received a check she had sent me for my services. I had been having problems with a 16-year-old black kid I had working for me, Ronnie Sparrow. He did odd jobs around the office. I finally had to let him go."

"Why did this concern Miss Basa?"

"Well, I'd been missing things even before she said she mailed me this check, which I never received. I suspected for some time that the kid was stealing checks mailed to me by clients, but I could never prove it. And I can't tell you for a fact that he took the check Miss Basa said she mailed.

"But—and you may or may not consider this to be important—this boy had been present during one of Miss Basa's visits to me, and he knew who she was. Also, as an office employee, he could have had access to my personal files regarding her. He could have gone into things while cleaning up. Frankly, I wouldn't put anything past the little shit."

The lawyer gave Stachula and Epplen the boy's address on Felton Court, a half block from Cooley High School. It was not one of Chicago's better neighborhoods. "Could I tell you officers one more thing?" he asked, as he handed them the slip of paper containing the house number.

"Anything at all," Stachula said.

"This has nothing to do with my relationship with the client, but I was aware of the fact that she had been having some problems with various personnel on her job. I can suggest the name of a person, Gary Bailey, who might give you some information if you were to talk to him at the hospital."

"Who is this Bailey, Mr. Walters?"

"He worked with Miss Basa, and can possibly provide you with some insights as to her relationship with certain other individuals on the job. I don't know any of this for a fact, you understand. I'm just tossing out this name because I realize, in the position you gentlemen are in right now, you must want to touch base with anyone who knew anything at all about the victim."

The detectives thanked Walters and went to a nearby drug store, where they dropped a dime to call the Edgewater Hospital personnel office. They learned that Gary Bailey had worked with Teresita as a therapist, but was no longer employed there. The hospital listed his last known address, a transient hotel on West Ontario Street.

The 29-year-old Bailey was not at all hesitant about talking to police. He said he'd been a close friend and co-worker of Teresita for some time.

"We have received information, Mr. Bailey, that your friend might have been going through some problems with someone at work," Stachula explained. "Maybe more than one person. You were close to her, we've been told. What can you tell us about this?"

"Well, Teresita was having what I would call a serious problem with these two guys there, Gene August and Emil Salnava."

"What do you mean by 'serious problem?' Were they bothering her, you know, like making advances or anything like that?"

"No, no. Nothing like that. I can't really say what it was all about, except that she felt these two guys were on her back all the time. She always acted cheerful, like nothing was going on, but these two were over her, you know, and she felt they were purposely assigning less desirable jobs to her. Giving her all the shit details."

"Were they?"

"I suppose it depends on how you look at it. Teresita thought they were, and she was very disturbed about it. She complained about it being unfair labor practice, and this Emil and Gene, they just belittled her and called her names. They even threatened to write unfavorable letters to the immigration people so she couldn't get a permanent visa. That was when she started asking people to write letters for her. Around Christmas, I think it was."

"Did Miss Basa do anything about this, ah, persecution, if you could call it that?"

"She told her lawyer about it, I know that," Bailey continued. "And she began keeping a record. She would document, as she put it, each unfair practice, and she kept the records in her apartment. This Emil is an alien, too, and she was threatening to go to immigration about him if he didn't let her alone."

"Do you have any idea why these guys were doing this to Miss Basa?" Epplen asked.

"You'd have to ask them about that. I have my own ideas, but I really couldn't be sure. All I know is, Teresita was real up-tight about the whole thing."

One more thing happened that night before Stachula and Epplen sat down in the squad room and typed out their supplementary report for Sergeant O'Connell. Not long after they talked with Bailey, an anonymous telephone call was received through the Centrex System in the police communications center. The unidentified caller said, "I think the police should know that Teresita Basa fought bitterly with Emil Salnava."

* * *

Stachula and Epplen pored over hospital employment records to see what they might come up with. While there was no Emil Salnava or Gene August, Edgewater did have in its employ an Emile Salnave, 24, listed as an Asian, and a Jean R. Auguste, 28, a male Haitian. They turned this information over to their supervising sergeant, who on Saturday assigned homicide investigator Christian Grogman to check out the two men. Grogman had come over to Homicide from the department's C-5 Internal Corruption Unit.

"This is right up your alley, Chris," O'Connell told him. "Internal corruption in the therapy department."

Before Grogman could follow up on the anonymous call, however, Area 6 Communications received a phone call from another individual who said, "I would like to talk to someone who is working on the Basa murder." Communications switched the call to Grogman. It was Petro Lulusa, the maintenance man, who suggested he had some new information that might be relevant to the investigation. Grogman checked out a car and drove over to the Pine Grove apartment building to talk to Lulusa as he worked.

Lulusa related that he and the janitor, Arthur Shields, had been talking about the murder in their building. Later that day he mentioned the slaying to Virginia Dudley, weekend rental agent on duty in the building office. Mrs. Dudley, in turn, mentioned a conversation she had with Shields about Teresita several weeks earlier. Lulusa said it concerned an incident Shields had neglected to mention to police. Grogman found Mrs. Dudley in her second floor office, and asked her what it was all about.

"The thing I mentioned to Peter involved a complaint Miss Basa had made to this office about a month ago," she explained. "She said someone had entered her apartment and taken some loose change and a bottle of liquor. She seemed to think somebody had a key to the apartment, since it hadn't been broken into, so we arranged to provide her with a new lock. I took the matter up with Mr. Shields at the time."

This was the same incident the building manager, Joyce Kaltman, had pointed out to police shortly after the slaying. She had produced the undated memo from her file reporting that the lock had been changed.

"Now, about a week after this, I happened to be talking to Mr. Shields again, about something else," Mrs. Dudley continued. "And he volunteered that he had run into the Basa woman in the hallway, and she told him she'd solved the theft herself. She told him she discovered that one of her 'boyfriends' had a key to the apartment and had taken the articles.

"Both Peter—Mr. Lulusa—and I felt that this information might be significant in your investigation."

Grogman tried without success to locate Shields. Saturday was his day off and he was not at home. The detective was curious as to why Shields had neglected to tell the other detectives about his encounter with the victim. It may have been an oversight.

More important, Grogman wanted to ask Shields whether Teresita, in telling him about the incident, had mentioned the name of the person who had committed the theft, or if she just described the thief as one of her "boyfriends." Any little piece of a puzzle, when fitted into another small piece, can become a big piece.

After several unsuccessful attempts to nail Shields, Grogman went back to his original assignment—Salnave and Auguste. Salnave lived on North Halsted Street, about two miles from the hospital. Grogman found him at home, and explained the nature of his call. Rather than talk in the apartment, Salnave agreed to accompany the detective back to Belmont and Western.

Upon arrival at Area 6 headquarters Salnave was photographed and fingerprinted. Grogman pointed out that all of Teresita's friends were undergoing the process to help rule out their presence in the apartment prior to the slaying. Afterward, as the two talked in one of the bleak interview rooms, Salnave acknowledged that he and the victim had not been the best of friends of late.

"We were friends at the beginning. Good friends," he emphasized. "We met about two years ago at the hospital, when we worked together, and found that we shared a common interest in the piano. Teresita was an excellent pianist. She could play anything—classical, popular, anything you wanted. I told her I envied her because I couldn't play a note, but I always wished I could. You know, like those guys in the movies, who sit down and play tunes at parties? Well, she said she could teach me. She gave piano lessons on the side."

"And so you took lessons from her?"

"Yeah, at her place. In her apartment. I went up there three times, at least, and took lessons. Then we had a falling out, and I didn't go back any more. I still don't know how to play the piano."

"What do you mean by a falling out? Tell me about it."

"Oh, Teresita was very straight, if you know what I mean. In fact, I never met anyone like her before. She didn't drink, or anything like that—just kept beer and liquor if any of her company wanted it."

"Did she have a lot of company, as far as you know?"

"From what I heard around work, I'd say she entertained quite a bit. Yes."

"How about boyfriends? I understand she had a few."

"Not the way you might think," Salnave interjected. "You must understand that in the Philippines, when a woman says she has a 'boyfriend' she literally means a male person who is her friend. You see, Teresita had a number of male acquaintances that she called boyfriends—but they were not 'boyfriends' as you think of them here in the States. Teresita did not have any lovers or anything like that, as far as I know. She was too up-and-up, so to speak. That's why she stopped giving me piano lessons."

"You try to make a pass at her?"

"Oh, no. Hell no. I'm half her age. I was dating this other girl at the hospital, see? And Teresita didn't approve because I was still married at the time. She told me straight out, 'I don't approve.' Then one day at work she told this girl bad things about me, in order to try to break us up. So, after that, we just weren't friends any more. I was no longer her boyfriend."

There was no phone listed for Jean Auguste, so the next day—Sunday—Grogman drove over to his apartment on West Lakeside Place on the outside chance of finding him home. He knocked at the door of apartment 703 and the 28-year-old Haitian invited him in. Grogman explained his business and, like Salnave, Auguste agreed to accompany him to the station to be fingerprinted for the record.

"Oh, mon, I was never one of Teresita Basa's friends," Auguste insisted when Grogman put the "boyfriend" question to him. "We worked together, that's all. I have never been to her home. I have never been anywhere with her."

"But she seemed to enjoy the company of younger men, did she not?" Grogman asked. "Don't you fit the pattern?"

"She preferred men with feminine tendencies. I don't know, unless she was sure these people wouldn't bother her."

"Well, who, at the hospital, would you say had been closest to Teresita Basa during the time you worked with her?"

"I would say her nearest friend at work was Richard Pessotti. He isn't there any more. I don't know what he does now—fashion designing or something. I know he'd been to her apartment for parties and things."

"Can you recall anyone else?"

"Mr. Ted Ellis. He's a supervisor in the Inhalation Therapy Department. And Allan Showery. I think they had both been there to a party not too long ago."

"O.K. Mr. Auguste. Now tell me about your disagreements with Miss Basa," Grogman pressed. "From talking to other people at the hospital, we get the picture that you and she didn't exactly hit it off."

"You couldn't call them disagreements. We just didn't get along. She seemed to have ill feelings toward me because, at times, I was in a supervisory position over her. In that capacity I occasionally assigned jobs to other employees. She seemed to resent taking orders from me, and we argued over work she was assigned to do. It was just a personality thing between us, that's all."

"You don't think Miss Basa had a thing against blacks?"

"No. That didn't matter to her. If she liked you, she liked you."

After the interview Grogman drove Auguste back to his apartment. On the way back he swung by Pessotti's apartment on Marine Drive. Both he and King were enjoying a Sunday afternoon at home. "I really apologize for bothering you," he said after introducing himself. "But, now that you've had several days to think about it, we're wondering whether you might have recalled the names of any other friends Teresita Basa entertained in her apartment.

"Well, I remember that Chita had been quite friendly with a music professor from Loyola University," Pessotti mused. "I can't recall the gentleman's name, but she mentioned once that he had been to her apartment. She said he was helping her with her thesis."

Grogman wrote on his note pad: (Stephan Barath).

CHAPTER 10

MANILA

Late in 1947, as the Islands gradually returned to normal, Pedro, Socorro and Teresita Basa gathered at the Dumaguete airport on the edge of town for an occasion that officially marked Teresita's coming of age.

"You can still change your mind, you know," Socorro said, putting her arm around her only child. "You can continue at St. Paul's College, or even go to Silliman University, if you like."

"I know, Mama. We've been through that. I really want to get away from this island for awhile," Teresita replied, almost pleading. "Whenever I look at the plaza I still see that American flyer. I dream about him, and the Japanese soldiers standing over him with their bloody bayonets. I want to get away from everything, and study my music. The opportunities are so much greater in Manila. You told me that yourself. Now that grandfather Martinez is gone, you and father are all I have, and I know you'll come to visit me often in Manila."

"Well, of course. That will give me a chance to look in on José Romero," Basa smiled. "Now that he's in the Senate, who knows? Maybe some day he'll become our President."

"At least we won't have to worry about Chita being alone in the big city," Socorro added. "With the Romeros she'll have more company than she did here at home."

"How many children do they have now, Mama?"

"What is it, Pedro—four boys and three girls?"

"Five boys, I think. And three girls. Tessie is nearest your age, Chita."

Justice Basa was paged over the loud speaker. He and his wife and daughter crossed the field and clambered up the metal staircase into the Douglas DC-3, a converted U.S. Army Air Corps C-47. He and Socorro were going to take the flight to Manila with Teresita. Teresita, who had never flown before, took the window seat, with her mother beside her holding her hand. Basa shared the seat across the aisle with a business-man who was returning to Luzon.

For most Filipinos the vast inter-island fleet of more than 6,000 vessels, from small boats to modern ships, was still the only way to travel—inexpensive but time consuming. The trip to Manila, at best, took two to three days. Justice Pedro Basa, however, could easily afford the four-hour flight. He had been elevated to the judicial bench at about the same time Romero was elected to the Philippine Senate.

Teresita grabbed the arm rest with her left hand and squeezed her mother's hand with the other, as the C-47's engines began to cough. The two-engined aircraft vibrated mightily as the Filipino pilot locked the brakes and revved the motors for all they were worth. Then he released the brakes and the craft rumbled forward—slowly at first, but soon the ground beneath Teresita's window became a blur. As quickly as it had started the rumbling stopped, and the bulky craft was airborne. The tops of palm trees were now flying past beneath the window, and then they were out over the sea.

After brief stops at Cebu City, Iloilo, and Mindoro the DC-3 passed over Batangas and Basa Airfield, named for the World War II hero, and made a wide circle over Manila bay, still dotted with the ugly rusting hulks of both American and Japanese ships.

As the craft flew over Corregidor its passengers stared silently at the gaunt, broken concrete walls of the garrison barracks of the island fortress. Then, as the plane came in low over South Harbor and cast its darting shadow across Dewey Boulevard, there were gasps of "My God," and "Look at that," from startled passengers. Two years after the end of World War II Manila—the Pearl of the Orient—was still in ruins.

"The Japs didn't give up without a fight," Basa's seatmate commented, pointing out the window. "General Yamashita declared it an open city, as MacArthur did when he left, but his men disobeyed him. Our beautiful city was four-fifths demolished. Four-fifths blown to pieces or burned, block by block . . . I cry when I think about it."

"It gives me a bad feeling in my stomach," Basa nodded.

Teresita tightened her seatbelt as the plane made its final approach, landing smoothly at Nichols Field, alongside the Paranaque River south of town. After retrieving their luggage the Basas were met by Pedro's brother, Pablo, the mayor of Caloocan, a well-to-do suburb north of Manila. Teresita found the ride in her uncle's 1932 Chrysler Imperial almost as fascinating as the plane ride, as they followed the Manila South Road into the wide Taft Avenue and headed north through Pasay, Malate and Ermita.

As they moved closer to the center of the city the avenue became clogged with colorfully-painted Jeepneys—World War II army jeeps abandoned, sold, or stolen and converted into jitney cabs capable of carrying up to a dozen passengers; two-wheeled pony carts, pedicabs, ox carts and bicycles; army six-by-sixes from nearby Fort McKinley; buses and cars of every description. The city's vast streetcar system had been blown to bits, and it was everyone for himself.

Here and there new buildings were slowly rising amid the stark skeletons of the old, and busy workers were painstakingly transforming piles of debris into neat stacks of reusable bricks.

"You can thank your friend, Romero, for much of this," Mayor Basa told his brother. "For the past two years he headed the Joint Committee on Rehabilitation and Reconstruction. It was he who really got things moving again after the fighting."

"We're looking forward to seeing him before we return to Dumaguete," Pedro commented as they passed the old walled city—Intromuros—a relic of the original Spanish settlement. As the Chrysler approached the Santa Cruz bridge over the dog-legged Pasig River they could see the muddy water choked with boats of every description, bobbing among the lush green hyacinths.

On the north side of town the Avenida Rizal emptied into Manuguit Extension, which took them past the giant Chinese Cemetery with its ornate mausoleums, and directly into Caloocan. The mayor's home, as in most Filipino communities, was on the plaza, opposite the church.

The Basas spent the next several days with Pedro's brother taking care of business in Manila, sightseeing, and getting Teresita settled at St. Scholastica College, where she would spend the next four years.

Separated from her family for the first time, she plunged deeply into the study of music, which had become the center of her life. The famed Manila Symphony Orchestra was re-formed after the war by director Herbert Zipper, and Teresita and her classmates took in every performance. On weekends she joined the Romero family for outings to Baguio, the resort city to the north, or Lake Taal and Tagaytay Ridge, in Southern Luzon. She also became proficient in Tagalog, the national language, while at the same time honing her English by reading English-language daily newspapers printed in Manila.

An event that would have a lasting effect on Teresita's life came during her second year in college. In 1949 the Honorable José E. Romero—one-time Provincial Board member from Negros Oriental, member of the Philippine House of Representatives, floor leader of the National Assembly, and Senator—was appointed Minister Pleniponiary to the Court of St. James in London.

The lawyer's appointment as his government's representative in England gave Teresita an extra chance to see her parents, who flew in for the gala going-away party for the Romero family. After dinner guests gathered around the grand piano, and Teresita played while Socorro sang in her rich soprano voice.

The departure of the Romeros, on whom Teresita had leaned so heavily, left an unexpected void in her life. She had considered them second parents, and they had accepted her as one of the family—"Tessie's sister." She plunged deeper into her music and also became a voracious reader, building a vast collection of hard-cover books.

When she was graduated from St Scholastica with honors in 1952, Justice and Mrs. Basa flew to Manila for the ceremony. Afterward, the three of them returned to Dumaguete together.

"Well, Chita, what do you think you'll do with your life, now that you've put college behind you?" her father asked, as the trio sat relaxing in rattan chairs on the veranda across from the plaza. "We have a judge in the family, and a pharmacist who teaches Spanish, and an accomplished pianist. Do you think you'd like to teach at one of the local universities like your mother?"

"I've been thinking about it, Daddy," she said quietly. "I know exactly what I want to do. I've just been waiting for the proper time to discuss it with you and Mama."

"The proper time might be now," Socorro added softly. "They need a music teacher at the college, you know."

"Tessie and I have been writing back and forth," Teresita continued. "She sent me some information about the Royal College of Music in London. I would dearly like to go there to continue my studies, father. They say it's one of the finest music schools there is, and it offers a degree in pianoforte."

"And costs a small fortune, I presume," Basa added.

"I could stay with the Romeros."

Pedro and Socorro exchanged glances as Teresita tried to read their faces. Socorro nodded to her husband, as he rose and walked over to the veranda railing. He turned and sat gently on the edge.

"I've been in contact with the ambassador myself," he smiled. "I know about your letters from Tessie, and by a strange coincidence José mentioned how nice it would be if you could visit his family in London. As a matter of fact, he says the Philippine Embassy, where you would stay, is within walking distance of the Royal College."

Teresita looked incredulously, first at one parent, then the other. Suddenly there were broad smiles all around. She put her arms around the judge and said, "Oh, Daddy. Would you and Mama really let me go to London?"

"It will be our graduation present," he said.

CHAPTER 11

NUTS AND BOLTS POLICE WORK

It was a truly miserable March Tuesday in Chicago. A freezing rain pelted Carl Sandburg's "City of the Big Shoulders," coating them with up to half an inch of ice. Police were forced to cordon off Franklin and Adams Streets, bordering Sears Tower, as sheets of ice weighing 20 to 30 pounds disengaged themselves from the smooth black facade of the world's tallest building and plummeted to the asphalt street below.

"It's like shrapnel when they hit and the chips start to fly," yelled Traffic Patrolman Charles Bennett, warning an occasional drenched passerby to keep a respectable distance. "Knocked the windshield right out of a '75 Buick! Lucky as hell nobody got hurt. Look at Sears Tower there—twenty-six windows out! If we don't have ice bombs, it's falling glass. A guy oughta get combat pay for this beat, I tell ya. I saw one . . ."

A sudden gust of wind whipped away the end of his sentence.

Over at 2740 N. Pine Grove, Ron Somera, Teresita's cousin, was going through what was left of her personal belongings. The police were done with everything in the apartment and it was turned over to him as executor of the estate. He had just come from the funeral, and made arrangements to have her remains flown back to the Philippines for burial in Santa Catalina Cemetery, next to her father.

Somera was attempting to determine whether there was anything else of value that should be sent home. Teresita's clothing would all be discarded. What hadn't burned had been ruined by smoke and water. The two television sets and the piano would be sold to help pay expenses. Somera looked over her extensive collection of books and phonograph records. These reflected her personality, he thought. They might give enjoyment to others as they had done to her. He would send them to Teresita's grieving mother, Socorro.

Downstairs, in the same building, Philbin and O'Connor were talking once again with Lulusa, the janitor. He was still their best bet as far as identifying anyone who might have been hanging around on the day of the killing. They showed him police photos of several men, and asked whether he recognized any of them.

"Yeah, I know this guy," he said, pointing to the photo of Ralph Magner, whom Shields, the other janitor, had already fingered as having been at Teresita's door on the afternoon of the murder. "I don't know his name, but I saw him with the Basa lady down in the lobby one day, maybe three weeks before it happened."

The detectives turned this information over to their supervisor, Sergeant Edward Flynn. "O.K.," he said. "Now you guys get out there in the real world and find out for us just exactly where the hell Ralph was on 21 February."

Epplen and Stachula, meanwhile, were having another go at Robert Knudson, the man who seemed so anxious to cooperate but could never come up with anything. They stopped at his home on Sayre Avenue just to ask whether there was anything new since their last talk. This is the nuts-and-bolts of police work—the kind people don't see on television. Minute detail work. Retracing steps. Talking to people who might know nothing. And then talking to them again, just in case they might know something.

"Yeah, well, there is this one thing, but I don't know if it means anything," Knudson said, rubbing his chin. "While I was at the wake, in the funeral home, I saw this one friend of hers that I hadn't seen in a long time, and we talked a little."

"This friend—what was his name, Mr. Knudson?"

"Not a him, a her. Ramona. Ramona Espada. She used to work at the hospital, but doesn't now. She was telling me that somebody from the hospital told her that Teresita was supposed to be entertaining some composer shortly before her demise."

"Did she mention the name of this composer?"

"No, she didn't seem to know any more than that. We were just talking about Teresita, and she mentioned it, you see."

"Well, you knew Teresita pretty well, didn't you?"

"I guess I knew her as well as anybody. We went out together, but it wasn't like a romance. We just valued each other's company, if you know what I mean."

"Did she ever mention any composer to you?"

"Nope. Nobody except this old Russian guy she met once, living in France, I think."

"Would that be Alexander Tcherepnin?"

"Yeah, something like that. Oh, say. There was this music professor from Loyola. I think it's ah, Barrett. No, Barath. Yeah, that's it. Barath. Professor Barath was doing some work for her. Maybe he's a composer."

Stachula and Epplen thanked Knudson for his help, shook hands, and urged him to call them if he should think of anything else. From the personnel department at Edgewater the detectives learned that a Mrs. Ramona Espada had worked there at one time, in the same department as Teresita, but had left in October 1975.

She was now working as a respiratory therapist at St. Joseph's Hospital on North Lake Shore Drive, not far from Teresita's Pine Grove apartment. The records office at St. Joseph's provided Mrs. Espada's home address on West Palmer Street. They headed back, Epplen, as always, behind the wheel. Because of his size he preferred to do the driving.

"If you drove, I'd have my legs on the dashboard," he told Stachula.

Unlike the old time dicks in their wide-brimmed fedoras, Epplen and Stachula seldom wore headgear. Stachula generally wore a business suit, while Epplen's "work clothes" consisted of sports coats and slacks. Both wore topcoats this time of year.

"You know, Joe, there are very few homicides I've seen where the victim didn't deserve what he got," Epplen commented as they slowed for traffic in Fullerton Avenue. "This is a rare one, where she really seems to be, as they say, pure as the driven snow."

"Yeah. And that's what's going to make this one all the harder to nail down," Stachula added. "There doesn't seem to be a motive. Not a damned thing. Hey, did I ever tell you I was born in Edgewater Hospital?"

"No shit! Funny coincidence, isn't it?"

"Yeah, I just thought of it myself. Palmer's 2200 West. Take a right up here."

"You got shot once, too, didn't you, Joe?"

"You thinking of plugging me for being a back seat driver?"

"No. But when you mentioned the hospital, it came to me that one of the guys said something about you getting shot one time."

"Yeah, I still take a ribbing about it. I didn't get shot, though. Somebody threw something at me."

"Yeah?"

"There was a rock concert in Lincoln Park, five-six years ago, and we were questioning a suspect about an armed robbery. Some of the kids from the concert started calling us names, and we could tell trouble was brewing so we called for back-up. When the other squads pulled up a barrage of rocks and bottles started flying. It was like a battlefield. I took one on the leg. Had to go to Henrotin to get patched up. Jim MacMillan got his arm broken. Couple of other guys got hurt, too. We arrested a couple of punks and it was all over."

"Those can be bad scenes—rock concerts."

"Nah. There were maybe 3,000 people, and only a handful —maybe 50 or 60 wise-ass punks—gave us any trouble. It was over so fast a lot of people didn't even know it happened."

Epplen pulled the Plymouth up in front of the house on Palmer. Mrs. Espada was unable to disguise her surprise to find two detectives knocking on her door.

"How in the world did you get my name?"

"From the people who attended the wake," Epplen said. "I guess you signed the book, huh?"

"Oh, my. I don't even remember, I was so upset. I hadn't seen Teresita since I quit Edgewater. Then Mrs. Kuehn called and said she had been stabbed to death. I couldn't believe it." Mrs. Espada made the sign of the cross.

"Would that be Connie Kuehn from the hospital?" Stachula inquired.

"Yes. She was our boss. Mine and Teresita's."

"Had you heard anything about Miss Basa supposed to have been entertaining a composer, or anything to that effect?"

"Yes. Mrs. Kuehn mentioned it when she called me."

"Did she happen to mention the person's name, by any chance?"

"No, she didn't know the name. Teresita hardly ever mentioned anybody by name. She liked to be a bit mysterious."

"Do you know whether Miss Basa had any particular boyfriend?"

"No. She was with a fellow named Bob Knudson quite a lot. But I don't know if you could call him her boyfriend."

The detectives gave the Espada woman their card, with the usual suggestion that she call if she thought of anything.

"Well, where to now, Joe?" Epplen asked, as they got back into the unmarked car. Stachula flipped open his notebook. "How about Ruth Loeb? The woman over on Edgewater, that you talked to the night the body was found? She's supposed to be the last person who talked to the victim. Maybe if we bring up this composer jazz to her it might ring a bell."

"It's worth a try," said Epplen, turning the ignition key. "I know the way."

At the Loeb home the two investigators carefully went over her final conversation with Teresita, the night of the murder. Her recollection of the telephone chat was the same as the story she had given Epplen earlier.

"And this voice you heard in the background, when Miss Basa said she had company—it was definitely a man's voice?" Stachula pressed.

"Yes, I'm certain it was a male."

"Did Miss Basa say anything about a composer? You know, like, could this male guest have been a music composer?"

"She didn't say," Mrs. Loeb responded. "She was very mysterious, and giggly."

"Have you heard any gossip around the hospital about her supposedly entertaining some composer, or someone connected with music in any way?"

"No, I have not, gentlemen. I'm sorry. But I can ask around at work. Maybe somebody else heard something. I still have Officer Epplen's card, and if I learn anything, I promise I will call you."

"That's the second person in less than an hour who mentioned that the victim was 'mysterious' about her house guests," Stachula noted as they got back into the car. "She could have made our job a lot easier by being a little more open."

When he and Epplen got back to headquarters there was a written laboratory report from Thomas Walsh the polygraph examiner, on the lie test administered the week before to Knudson. The letter told them what they already knew, but made it official:

Re: Teresita Basa
   Homicide
   On 22 February 1977, Robert Knudson was brought into the laboratory by Officer Whalen of Area 6 - Homicide. This subject was to be given a polygraph examination in connection with the above captioned crime which occurred 21 February 1977, at 2740 N. Pine Grove.

Robert Knudson was given four polygraph tests. There were no significant emotional disturbances in this subject's polygraph records on questions pertaining to this crime being investigated. It is, therefore, the opinion of the examiners that this subject is telling the truth when he denies committing this crime.

However, this subject did take medication prior to this examination to calm his nerves. Therefore, this report must be qualified and a re-examination should be rendered if the investigator deems it necessary.

"Well," mused Stachula. "That's what the lie box is for—to help clear the innocent. I don't see any percentage in giving him another go at it, do you?"

"It's not up to us to decide," Epplen pointed out. "But I agree with you. I don't think he'd have taken it in the first place if he had anything to hide. We can keep in contact with him, though. Sooner or later he might think of something that might help."

"This is going to be a long one, do you know that, Lee?"

"What do you mean, Joe?"

"If you don't nail your killer within 36 hours, it generally means you might not catch him at all. Or, if you do, it's only after one hell of a lot of digging."

"Which is what we're good at," Epplen observed. "We're gonna get this bastard, Joe. I don't know how, or why, but we're gonna win. I don't give up on this one. She didn't deserve what she got, and somewhere, somebody is going to have to answer for it. To us!"

Chicago averaged four homicides a day in 1977—one murder every three days, roughly, in Area 6 alone—and each demands immediate attention. All of the area's investigative resources are thrown into each one while the clues are still hot. If they aren't solved on the spot, or very soon thereafter —as most of them are—detective teams must, by necessity, move on to new cases.

The unsolved case is never dropped. It is kept open, and investigators are reassigned to it as time and manpower allow. Any loose ends in the Basa case—and there were plenty—

would be tied up in due time. But the urgency of catching the perpetrator before he got away was gone. He had gotten away. Now they would have to track him down.

Ron Somera had Teresita's book-of-the-month selections and her classical records crated. He was amazed at how many books and records she had accumulated in such a short time. It cost $500 to ship them back to the Philippines.

*   *   *

On Wednesday, March 9, Lee Epplen selected his wardrobe with the usual care. After shaving and showering, and dabbing on a liberal amount of lotion, he laid out a checked blue and white sports coat, selected a pair of blue slacks, and a white, open-collar shirt. Then he looked out of the window at the still frozen ground and grumbled, "Crap."

Epplen had a personal interest in the ground. The burly, ham-fisted ex-football star was a home gardener, and he was anxious to get at it. "Nothing beats growing things for relaxation," an uncle once told him. Epplen tried it, and discovered that it worked. Whenever he had a tough case, one that kept eating at the lining of his belly like the Basa homicide, he found solace in the soil. Until he could get his seeds into the ground, though, he could only think about it.

Vegetable seeds; no flowers.

"If you can't eat 'em, I won't grow 'em," he told Stachula. "Got my list already for spring—beets, asparagus, tomatoes, cucumbers, lettuce, green peppers and hot peppers. When I get home I go to bed, and the next morning get up and go into the garden, and there are all my plants. And, just like that, I get my sanity back."

Last year his sanity got a boost by an invasion of potato beetles. "They really took my mind off things," he laughed. "I sprayed 'em. I stomped 'em. I did everything but shoot the sons-a-bitches."

His garden would, as in other years, be in the back yard of the house on Mulligan Street. Rose Mary and the two kids were still living there, even though he had moved out. He visited the place regularly to see if anything needed fixing. Epplen thought of how things used to be, and would never be again, as he drove in to work that afternoon.

After roll call, as O'Connell gave out the assignments, Epplen drew Ralph Magner. There were a lot of things that still didn't add up, and the sergeant wanted Lee to try his hand at Teresita's friend. Despite the fact that the janitor had identified him as the man seen knocking on the apartment door several hours before the murder, Magner insisted he hadn't been near the victim's building in more than a year.

Epplen drained his cup of coffee, checked the basketball scores in the paper, and then put in a call to Magner at the electric company. Magner agreed to come in to Area 6 for another talk. "I'll be in as soon as I get off work," he said. "I'd just as soon not jeopardize my job by ducking out early." It was a little before six o'clock when his battered Chrysler rolled into the parking lot behind the police building.

"You're a little older than Teresita, aren't you, Ralph?" Epplen said, trying to think of a way to kick off the conversation.

"Yeah, by a year. She was 47, going on 48. I'll be 49 a month from today."

"Now, I know we've been through all this before, Ralph, but I want you to start at the beginning once more and tell me everything, exactly what you did on Monday, February 21st. The whole bag, from the time you got up in the morning on the day of the murder, and try not to leave anything out."

"Well, I went to work," Magner said, matter of factly. "You can check the records at Cherry Electric. They'll show I was there all day."

"We already did that. You were there. So, what did you do after work?"

"I knocked off at five o'clock, and decided to do some shopping. So I drove up to Lakehurst Shopping Center at Waukegan."

"O.K. That would take you maybe an hour, depending on traffic. So, now you're in Waukegan, and it's six o'clock."

"Yeah. Well, I wandered around a little. And then I got hungry, and decided to grab some dinner."

"At the shopping mall, or did you head back home?"

"Right there. At Lakehurst. I found this Hickory Farms restaurant in the mall and went inside."

"How long would you say you were in the restaurant?"

"Until maybe 7:00 or so."

"Which would have given you time to get back to Chicago by 8:00. Am I right?"

"Yeah, if I would have left then, but I didn't. Frankie Yankovic's polka band was doing a show in the mall, and I stuck around. I stayed until the show was over, and then I headed home."

"And you didn't go anywhere near 2740 North Pine Grove?"

"No way. Like I told you guys before, I haven't been in that building in over a year. The last time I was there was for a Christmas party a year ago, 1975. That was the last time."

"But there is a witness who says he positively saw you there, knocking on Teresita Basa's door, around four o'clock."

"Around four o'clock? Hell, I was at work. You can check."

"Maybe this witness was a little off in his time," Epplen suggested. "We have this problem, Ralph: Who saw you up at Lakehurst? Frankie Yankovic? How the hell do we know you were up there at all?"

"The waitresses in the restaurant saw me," Magner insisted.

"Oh, great!" Epplen said, rolling his eyeballs toward the ceiling. "We just go up there and get all the waitresses together and say, 'Anyone who saw Ralph Magner here on the night of the twenty-first, raise your hand.' Right?"

"Their names are Sue Serkowski and Aldonna Barrows," Magner said, condescendingly.

"These two waitresses *know* you?"

"No. They just waited on me."

"Aw, cut the shit, Ralph. What do you take us for? You go up to a strange restaurant, two women who never saw you before wait on your table, and two weeks later you're giving me their names? Come on. Why don't you start leveling?"

"I am leveling with you. No bullshit! Those are the broads who waited on me. Why don't you check them out?"

"Oh, we will. Do you always take down the names of waitresses when you go to strange restaurants?"

"Hell, no. But I did this time. I knew I was going to need an alibi."

"Pardon me while I roll up my pants, Ralph. It's getting pretty deep and these are my good clothes. You knew you were going to need an alibi? How come? No crime had been committed yet, even if what you say is true."

"Not that same night. I went back there," Magner explained. "After you guys talked to me the last time, I thought back and remembered where I was that night, because that's the night Frankie Yankovic was in Waukegan. So, I went back up there and asked this waitress if she remembered me, and got her name. The other one wasn't there, but this one gave me both their names."

Magner would have made a good detective. Epplen shook his head and mumbled, "Jezus Christ, Ralph. You've got to be some operator. Tell me. Would you be willing to go on the lie box with all this shit?"

"Yeah. I said so before."

"O.K. How about right now, while everything's fresh in your mind?"

"Now? This very minute?"

"Why not? As soon as I can set the test up. Is it O.K. with you?"

"Let's get the damned thing over with. The sooner the better. You guys are beginning to wear me down, like in the movies."

"That's the game we're playing, Ralph. Only it's no game. If you did this, I'm gonna find out. If you didn't, maybe you can help us find out who did. That's what we all want, isn't it?"

"You bet," Magner agreed. "Let's go."

Epplen called Sergeant Bruce Thompson at Eleventh and State, and scheduled a polygraph exam for 9:00 p.m. Thompson and his assistant, John Stout, were all set up when Epplen and Magner breezed in. In all, they administered a total of six tests. When the ordeal was over, Thompson greeted Epplen with a weak smile.

"Well?" Epplen shrugged. "I thought you were gonna keep him all night. What gives?"

"We ran him through more than once. In fact, we went the whole route six times. Six. And we came up with the same answer every time. A big, fat zero."

"What does that mean, zero?"

"He wasn't responsive to anything we put to him, even the control questions. The box registered no emotion whatsoever. It didn't say he was lying and it didn't say he was telling the truth. It didn't say anything."

"Are you sure the damned thing was working, sergeant?"

"Oh, yeah . . ."

"So, you're telling me he found a way to beat it?"

"I don't think the gaffer was trying to fool us," Thompson continued. "That's why we retested him so many times. He appears fatigued. Maybe he had a rough day at the office, or maybe you wore him down before you brought him here. Anyway, the tests didn't register. I suggest he be re-examined at a later date."

Epplen and Magner talked it over. A new appointment was scheduled. Epplen would bring him in at 7:00 p.m. March 16—one week hence. As Epplen drove Magner back to pick up his car, the detective decided his next best bet would be to look up the two waitresses in Waukegan.

* * *

Epplen never got the chance. Sergeant O'Connell sent him back to the Pine Grove apartment to talk to Virginia Dudley, the assistant manager, to see whether she had picked up any rumbles from any of Teresita's neighbors.

Epplen found her in the second floor office. "I was in the neighborhood, and thought I'd touch base," he said. "Hear anything?"

"Not really," she said. "The other day there was a man in to see about renting an apartment, and he asked me if this was the building where the girl was murdered. When I said it was, he began asking me all kinds of questions about it. I was extremely busy at the time and had to tell him I couldn't discuss it at the moment, so he left. I couldn't even tell you what he looked like.

"Oh, yes. At the same time this was going on, a couple of women were chattering something about the Basa woman drinking with a tenant named Charles up on six."

"Who would that be?"

"Well, let's look at the book here. Ah, here we are. The only Charles on the sixth floor is Mr. Epstein in 6D. Now, as I say, I don't know anything about this. I just overheard these two mention it, and I had never seen either one of them."

"Right now we're grabbing at straws, Mrs. Dudley," Epplen confessed. "Anything at all will be helpful at this point. Thank you very much, and if you think of anything else, you know where to find me."

Epplen found Charles to be of little help. He said he had just moved in after Christmas and knew hardly any of his neighbors. "I never heard of the Basa woman until I came home that night and police were all over the place," he said. Epplen suddenly wished gossipy old women would mind their own business.

Sergeant Whalen, meanwhile, drew the waitress assignment from O'Connell. He drove up to Lakehurst, sniffed out the Hickory Farms restaurant, and asked the hostess if there was an Aldonna Barrows or a Sue Serkowski working there. "I'm Aldonna," she said quizzically.

The detective stated his business, and asked Mrs. Barrows whether she could possibly recall a customer who had been in the restaurant three weeks earlier, name of Ralph Magner. It turned out she did.

"Normally I wouldn't remember that far back, but that was the night Frankie Yankovic's band played in the mall here," she explained. "This gentleman came in, alone, some time between 6:00 and 7:00. I seated him at that table over there. Then I sent Sue over to wait on him."

"And you remember this particular customer, out of all the people who eat here?" Whalen asked incredulously.

"Well, he sticks in my mind because of something else that happened. You see, Sue served him, and after a period of time—maybe a half hour or so—he got up and walked away. I assumed he'd left the restaurant and we cleared the table. After Sue removed his dishes and wiped everything up, he came back and says, 'What happened to my food?'"

"He made a point of calling attention to himself, then?"

"Well, he just wanted to know where his food went. We both explained that we thought he was finished, and we apologized. I made an adjustment on his bill, of course, and he left."

"Did he seem angry?"

"No. He just wanted to know what happened."

"Do you remember what time he left?"

"Well, he was in here no more than half an hour, I'd say. He came in some time after 6:00 and left before 7:00."

"And did he then come back and talk to you on a different occasion?"

"No, not me. I was off the night he came back, but Sue told me about it. She said he wanted to know our names. Sue was a little suspicious, but he told her he was the subject of a police investigation and might need our names to prove where he was that night."

"And this was definitely the same person who was in on the night of Frankie Yankovic?"

"Yes. Sue remembered him, because of clearing his table off prematurely."

"I know this might be difficult after all this time, Mrs. Barrows, but do you think you could describe the gentleman?"

"Well, I'd say he was about 45 years old, medium build, and light hair, or maybe gray. Combed straight back." She ran her hand over the top and back of her head, as though she were combing her own hair.

Whalen thanked her and headed back to Chicago. Magner checked out. Few people realize how much time cops spend spinning their wheels on wild goose chases like this—all necessary to narrow down the field of suspects. Arriving at Area 6 in less than an hour, he had time to spare, so he checked over the Basa file for any other loose ends.

He came across the name of Bruce Campbell, Teresita's neighbor. He noted from the reports that Campbell had told detectives he'd been a guest at parties in the murder victim's apartment. He called Campbell and asked if he'd mind coming in for a follow-up talk. No problem.

Whalen also spotted the name of Robert Krauth, Teresita's friend in the Boston area. On a hunch, while waiting for Campbell, he telephoned Boston police, who connected him with a Sergeant Walters in the identification section. At Whalen's request, Walters ran a check on Krauth, and determined that he had no police record. He was clean.

Knowing that, Whalen then put in a call to Krauth. The Bostonian said he learned of the murder early the next morning when King and Pessotti called him. They were the only friends of the victim whom he'd met. He said he last heard from Teresita when they chatted by phone about two weeks before her death. "Everything seemed fine then. She appeared to be in high spirits," he said.

Whalen was just saying good-bye to Krauth when Campbell walked in. He went over his account of the night of the murder, recalling how he was awakened by the smell of smoke, and fled from the building. Whalen then showed him a batch of photographs and asked, "Do you recognize any of these men?" Campbell picked out the shot of Robert Knudson.

"He was at one of the parties I attended in her apartment," he told Whalen. "I'm sorry, but I can't recall his name.

He and I were really the only ones there who weren't Filipinos, which is why I remember him. I assumed he was her boyfriend."

"How did this friend of hers act at the party?"

"Fine, if that's what you mean. His behavior was all above board. It was a nice, congenial group."

Whalen then advised Campbell of his Constitutional rights in accordance with the 1966 Miranda decision of the U.S. Supreme Court—the right to remain silent and to have an attorney—after which he asked if he would mind being fingerprinted so police could compare his prints to those found at the scene. Campbell had no objection.

After he'd gone Whalen sat down and typed up a report of his day's activities for the sergeant. As he filled in the date at the top of the page, he realized it was the day after Teresita's birthday.

* * *

On Wednesday, March 16, Ralph Magner drove straight from work to Area 6 headquarters to report for the lie detector examination that had been rescheduled. He knew his way around by now, and went directly to the second floor, where he was met by Chris Grogman. "Cripes," he joked, shaking hands with the homicide detective. "If this keeps up I'm gonna be on a first-name basis with every cop in Chicago."

"Well, if things turn out the way you'd probably like them to this evening, that surely won't happen," Grogman said. "Thought maybe a little change of faces might make things easier for you." They drove over to Eleventh and State in Grogman's car. John Stout, the polygraph technician who had assisted on the previous test, greeted Magner by name.

"See what I mean?" he said. "Already half the cops in town know me, and I haven't done anything."

For the next several hours Grogman sat and chatted with the downtown dicks about the Basa case and other unsolved homicides. Magner, meanwhile, sat wired up to the lie box, not exactly enjoying his controlled conversation with Stout.

110

At the end of the ordeal Stout advised Grogman, "It looks like your man is clean."

"The lie box clears him?"

"Yep. I'll put it all in writing for the record, but basically, it is the examiner's opinion that Mr. Magner is being truthful when he says he has no knowledge of the Basa slaying, other than what he's already discussed with you."

"Well, back to square one," Grogman said, shaking Stout's hand.

"There's one thing you should know," Stout confided. "During our conversation he mentioned someone named Benny, who he said the victim had argued with on previous occasions."

"Thanks, John," Grogman said, turning toward the door. "We'll follow up on that." In the car on the way back, after congratulating Magner on passing the test, he asked about Benny.

"Well, I didn't think of him before or I would have mentioned it," Magner said. "Teresita had a lot of friends. See, I'm a member of a singles group that throws a lot of cocktail parties, and Teresita used to come to them from time to time."

"That's where she met Benny?"

"At some of these parties I would see this Benny guy," Magner continued. "One of the other guys in the group must have invited him, because I didn't know him. But when I think on it, I remember seeing Teresita and this Benny speaking with one another a number of times."

"She and Benny were friends, you think?"

"I don't know about that," Magner responded. "See, since her death I've had several conversations with Bob Knudson, being as how we both knew her pretty well. Anyhow, he mentioned to me that Teresita had a real bad argument with Benny."

"You have no idea what the guy's last name is?"

"No, but I can try to find out for you. I drove him home once, and I remember he lived in the 3000 block of South Michigan Avenue."

"This guy black or white?"

"Oh, he's white. About 38. And—oh, yeah—he's only got one arm."

"Oh, my achin' ass," Grogman moaned.

"Now what?" Magner asked.

"That's all this play needs. A frickin' one-armed mystery man."

CHAPTER 12

THE QUEEN AND THE COMPOSER

England looked so different from the Philippines by air. Teresita was still trying to convince herself it wasn't a dream. Her last days at home were just a blur of activity—shopping for new clothes, saying good-bye to old friends, visiting Dr. Alfredo R. Corpuz, the family physician, for the necessary shots, flying over to Cebu City to see Justino R. Alfafara, foreign affairs officer, about a passport, and assuring her parents a thousand and one times that she was capable of taking care of herself.

On her last morning in Dumaguete City the Basas attended mass in Santa Catalina and prayed for Teresita's safe passage. Her parents accompanied her on the inter-island plane to Nichols Field, south of Manila. From there it was only a short taxi ride to Manila International Airport, still called by the American name of Nielsen Field by many old-timers. There they hugged one another, wept a little, and Teresita took off alone for England, via Hong Kong and Calcutta.

Her last look at the Philippines was of the watery-green rice paddies of Luzon. Below her now were the brownish-green patchwork fields of England, bordered by thick green hedgerows. The Honorable José Romero and his eldest daughter, Tessie, were waiting for Teresita with their chauffeur-driven Mercedes-Benz when she cleared customs at bustling Heathrow Airport.

The Philippine Embassy was nestled in a cul-de-sac at the southwest corner of Kensington Gardens at Palace Green, just off Kensington Road. It was, indeed, within easy walking distance of the Royal College of Music, just a few squares east of Prince Consort Road at Queens Gate, across from the Albert Memorial at the southeast end of the gardens.

"I'll never get used to these strange names," Teresita squealed. "Why can't they have simple names, like Calle Andalucia, or Estrada?"

"Oh, Chita! You'll never guess who they have a statue of in the park," Tessie chirped excitedly, as they took their first walk. "Peter Pan! Cross my heart! This way. I'll introduce you to him." They took the walkway through Kensington Gardens, past Round Pond, which really isn't, over to the famous statue alongside Long Water Pond.

"Amazing!" Teresita exclaimed. "At home we have statues of Rizal, the father of our country, and the English, they honor Peter Pan."

"Oh, you'll see Churchill, too," Tessie explained. "And Richard the Lion Hearted, and knights on horseback. They seem to honor everyone. And they have wonderful names for everything, too. That busy street over there is Bayswater Road, and where you see the Long Water go under the bridge, that's called the Serpentine. And there's even a walkway in Hyde Park—like the one in the Plaza back home—but this one is named Rotten Row."

In the weeks that followed, when not immersed in her piano studies, Teresita explored London in ever-widening circles. She took in outdoor concerts at the bandstand in Hyde Park, that reminded her of the ones in the plaza at Dumaguete. And she bought tickets to the spectacular concerts in Albert Hall, the hundred-year-old circular theater just across Prince Consort Road from the school.

On nice days her walks took her past the Wellington Arch along Constitution Hill to Buckingham Palace.

There she joined the throngs of gawkers gathered around the Queen Victoria Memorial, watching the pageantry of the changing of the guard. "I've noticed something strange at the palace," she remarked at dinner one evening with the Romeros. "Sometimes, when I have gone there, I see two guards in those little sentry-houses outside the gate, and at other times there is only one guard, and the other house is empty."

"More British tradition, Chita," Romero explained. "When you see two guards, the Queen is in. One guard signifies that she is away. Everything here has a reason, usually tradition. England is a slave to tradition."

"I know. Sometimes you can actually feel it," observed Teresita. "When you visit Westminster Abbey you actually feel as though you've been transported into the past. It was like I was in another world. The strangest feeling."

"Did you feel like you were being visited by the ghosts of the kings who had been beheaded?" laughed Romero.

"No," she smiled at her amused host. "I was just filled with a sort of awe as I stood by the burial vaults of the old kings and queens. Even the baby, Princess Sophia. Do you know what it says on her tomb, which is shaped like a crib with the baby princess lying in it? 'A royal rosebud, untimely plucked by death . . .' It gave me the strangest feeling."

"You're an impressionable girl, and a very sensitive person. I've always felt that about you," Romero mused.

"I stood alone in Poet's Corner, where Chaucer's bones are resting, along with Spenser, Tennyson, and Dryden and all the rest. I felt like they were whispering to me," she continued. "It's like if you are with someone close to you, and you don't have to really exchange words. You are sort of communicating without actually speaking. I was frightened, but I didn't want to leave. It was as though the dead were calling to me."

*　*　*

It was several weeks later that Romero dropped his bombshell, and it had nothing to do with ghosts. The family had just finished dinner when he called for some wine to toast Elizabeth II, Britain's new queen, who had been crowned in Westminster Abbey that June.

"Will you get to meet the Queen?" asked Tessie.

"Better than that," he replied, feigning snobbishness. "The Queen wants to meet *me*! Here, read this," he said, dramatically handing his wife, Elisa, an envelope bearing the imprimatur of the Lord Chamberlain. Inside was a card, embossed with a golden crown and the royal monogram, E II R. Mrs. Romero read it aloud.

"The Lord Chamberlain is commanded by Her Majesty to invite the Honorable José Romero and Mrs. Romero . . ."

Romero finished the announcement himself. ". . . to a diplomatic reception in Buckingham Palace!"

"Oh, Daddy," Tessie gushed, wide eyed.

"But that's not all," Romero said, "if you will permit me to continue. It is permissible, at affairs of this magnitude, to bring any unmarried daughters over 18."

"Oh," Tessie gasped.

"And in this case, as far as I am concerned, I have two—Tessie and Teresita."

Romero had played his bombshell to the hilt, and had achieved the desired effect—pandemonium. He let the buzzing continue for a few minutes, until he picked up bits of conversation about shopping at Harrod's, and other such things that make the head of any large family extremely nervous.

"We shall attend as Filipinos, not fashion models," he declared. "The female members of this entourage will wear their very best *balintawaks*."

The week prior to the reception was filled with instructions, dos and don'ts. If you are called on, you bow if you are a man, curtsy if a woman. Someone will announce your name. The Queen makes the first move. You do not extend your hand, and you do not speak, unless she speaks to you. Then you withdraw three paces. You do not turn your back on the Queen.

The day of the reception found Senor Romero wondering whether he was doing the right thing, bringing the young ladies along. And they, in turn, were petrified at the thought that they might twist an ankle and fall during the curtsy. Having ambassadorial status, the Romeros were whisked by limousine to the very door of the Victorian palace. Guests of lesser import had to park in the mall and approach on foot, past a line of gawking tourists.

The reception was held in the palace garden, the most luxurious in all Britain. As Teresita looked over the array of greenery and flowers, she thought how her mother would love to have been there in her place. There were two long tea tents, or marquees, erected on the green. One was for the royal party, and the other for guests.

At exactly four o'clock the band struck up "God Save the Queen" as Elizabeth appeared, magnificent and alone, on the palace portico. She was wearing a pale blue chiffon dress with a matching hat.

Then, surrounded by a group of solemn looking gentlemen known in England as "white slaves," she made her way slowly across the garden to the royal tent. Every dozen or so steps she would stop and chat with someone. Some of the "chosen ones" had been selected days earlier for the honor, and stood nervously waiting as Her Royal Majesty approached. Others were drawn from the invited guests at random by one of the white slaves, and brought forward to be presented to the titular ruler of all England.

Elizabeth was nearing the Romero party now, nodding self-consciously to guests as she passed down the aisle politely cleared through the throng by the Beefeaters. She exchanged brief handshakes with some, and with others she chatted for several minutes or more. It seemed to Teresita that the royal monarch was ill at ease, performing a chore she evidently did not relish.

Teresita suddenly found herself on even ground. The Queen of England was as nervous as she was—probably having the same thoughts, hoping that nothing would go wrong.

The young Filipina had her eyes on the Queen, oblivious of everything around her, when she felt a gentle tug at her gloved hand. "May I present you to Her Royal Highness, Mum?" a voice said softly next to her ear. Startled, Teresita looked at the distinguished white slave, not knowing what to say.

"What is your name, Miss? Where are you from? Do you have an occupation?" The questions came quickly, and Teresita found herself whispering crisp answers, as though in a dream.

Queen Elizabeth II was approaching. She nodded and smiled at the Romeros as the white slave gently guided Teresita slightly forward, and whispered a few words to Her Majesty. Teresita drooped her eyelids and curtsied. Then she slowly raised her eyes. The 24-year-old child of Dumaguete and the 28-year-old Queen of England stood face to face.

"You have a beautiful name, Teresita Basa."

"Thank you, Your Majesty," she replied softly. The queen's hand was warm. The appearance of nervousness was only external. The handclasp conveyed confidence.

"Are you with the Embassy?" Elizabeth asked.

"I am staying there with my godparents while I study piano at the Royal College."

"Perhaps I will hear you play sometime."

"I would be honored, Your Majesty."

The Queen relaxed her grip, and Teresita accepted the signal. She stepped backward and curtsied. The white slave was already approaching to announce the name of the next guest. "The honourable . . ."

The Queen's husband, Prince Philip; her mother, Queen Elizabeth the Queen Mother; and the Duchess of Kent all made similar progressions through the throng. Philip stopped and chatted for nearly five minutes with Romero about the tiny horses of the Philippines. Teresita saw and heard none of it. She did not come out of her reverie until a uniformed caterer offered her a cup of tea and a piece of white-frosted cake.

Teresita felt Elisa Romero's gentle touch at her elbow. "You can come back to earth and join us now, if you like."

She turned to Mrs. Romero and whispered, "She's a girl. Just like me."

* * *

Teresita was graduated from the Royal College of Music with a certificate in pianoforte. She was preparing to return to the Philippines when the Romeros prevailed on her to join them on a tour of the Continent. Romero had just been accredited Minister to Norway, Sweden and Denmark. They would wind up their vacation in Paris, with Socorro flying over to join her daughter there. Teresita and her mother would then fly back to Manila, while the Romeros proceeded to Scandinavia.

Homesick for the Philippines, Teresita at first hesitated to make the extended trip. The Romeros pleaded with her, however, and she was never sorry afterward that she had given in to them—even though the decision would, indirectly, one day lead to her death.

* * *

In Vienna, accompanied by a guide from the embassy, Teresita visited Ludwig van Beethoven's birthplace, where again she experienced the eerie feeling of communing with the past. She felt it again in the Stadt Park, just off the famous Ringstrasse, where she meditated for an hour beneath the towering white statue of the young Wolfgang Amadeus Mozart. In the evening she took a wild Viennese taxi ride through the dipping, winding streets to Grinzing, where she sat and sipped a tiny glass of white wine in Beethoven's vineyard at the house where he died.

Salzburg, in the shadow of the Alps, was even more enchanting. There were daytime walks through the old part of the city, across the picturesque Salzach River, to the six-story yellow stucco building of Mozart's birth. And at night, in exotic Mirabell Palace, she and the Romeros attended a candlelight piano concert in the very room where Mozart entertained as a youth. By closing her eyes, Teresita could actually feel the young composer's presence.

But it was in Paris, quite unexpectedly, that Teresita underwent an experience that would influence the course of the rest of her life—and ultimately her death. She met Alexander Tcherepnin.

Along with the Romeros she attended a concert at which the famed Russian-born composer took over the keyboard to perform his own "Piano Concerto in A-Minor," which he wrote in 1923 at the age of 24. Through Romero's influence the party was invited backstage afterward for a brief social gathering. In Tcherepnin Teresita did not find the brooding, introspective Russian she had imagined, but a cheerful 54-year-old dynamo of warmth and magnetism.

When he learned of her own interest in the piano the maestro, speaking in crisp English, invited her to his apartment the following afternoon. "I would not only like to discuss your future with you, but also have you meet my lovely wife. She is a fine concert pianist, like yourself, I am sure," he added.

Teresita accepted his card, and talked the matter over with her mother when she returned to the Philippine embassy, where the Romero party was staying in Paris. Socorro, tired from the long flight from Manila, had decided not to attend the concert. "If you have been asked to visit the maestro at his home, by all means, go," she advised her daughter. "It is an opportunity that few people are offered, and that you might never have again." The following afternoon Teresita took a taxi to Tcherepnin's studio apartment in Rue Furstemberg.

The tall, slender, habitually slouching composer greeted her in person when she rang the bell. "Come in, come in," he said, holding the large wood-paneled door open for her. "My dear, this is Miss Teresita Basa, the young lady I said you would have to meet. Miss Basa, may I present my lovely wife, Ming Lee?"

As the slightly-built woman of 37, who was decidedly Oriental, extended her hand to the guest, Tcherepnin answered the question he guessed must have been in Teresita's mind.

"We met in Shanghai. Ming Lee was giving a concert, and I fell madly in love with her. I followed her to Paris, where she came to study on a scholarship, and we were married. Those three imps you see peeking around the corner are Peter, who is 14, Serge, our 12-year-old, and Ivan, the baby. He's 10."

When Teresita admired the apartment, with its antique furnishings, the composer explained, "This is our vacation home, where we spend our summers. We actually live in Chicago, during the American school year."

"Chicago? In the U.S.?" Teresita asked, somewhat astonished.

"Since 1949," Tcherepnin said. "We are both on the teaching staff at DePaul University, and we also give private lessons at our home. Ah, ha! I know exactly what you're thinking! Rat-a-tat-a-tat. Bang-bang. Al Capone. Am I not correct? Of course I am."

"You must also be a mind reader," Teresita smiled.

"We had great reservations about going when Alexander received the invitation," Mme. Tcherepnin explained. "We invited Mary Garden to tea and asked her counsel, because she had been everywhere."

"Mary Garden, the soprano?" interjected Teresita.

"Is there any other?" asked Tcherepnin.

"Not to hear my mother talk," Teresita answered. "She, too, is a fine soprano. When I was a child she would put Miss Garden's records on the Victrola and sing along with her."

"An angel," the composer said. "Mary Garden is an absolute angel. We asked her about Chicago and she shouted, 'Go! Chicago brought me luck. It will do the same for you!' And it did. Let me tell, you, it did. But that is not what we are here to talk about. Come, Miss Basa. We would both like to hear you play."

Teresita tried modestly to beg off, as Tcherepnin took her by the arm and guided her to the grand piano while she looked helplessly to Mme. Tcherepnin for support.

"The maestro does not take no for an answer," his wife smiled.

Teresita played Tcherepnin's own "Symphony in E-Flat," which was on the music rack on the piano. When she had finished she turned to him and said, "Your work is so beautiful. I cannot do it justice."

"You did well, my dear. You are a fine pianist, and you can be great. You can stop where you are, with your excellent credentials from London, and be a recognized pianist for the rest of your life. Or, you can continue your studies and become a truly great one. Have you thought about that?"

"No, I really haven't," Teresita confessed. "Right now I don't know what I want to do, except I would like to go back home for awhile."

"Then think about it," Tcherepnin urged. "I mention DePaul University because my wife and I teach there, of course. There is also a fine music college at Roosevelt University in Chicago. And Indiana University, not far from Chicago, has an excellent music school as well. There are many fine schools. The point is: Do not stop learning."

"When did you decide to become a composer?" Teresita inquired, in an effort to steer the conversation away from herself.

"I composed 'Bagattelles' when I was but 14," he said. "Ah, but remember who I had for a teacher. My father, Nikolai, conductor of the Russian Imperial Opera in St. Petersburg."

"Was it your father who helped you with your composition?" asked Teresita, completely charmed by this man whom, she felt, should be wearing a red cape as he paced back and forth across the room.

"Would you like to know my secret?" he whispered.

"I love secrets."

"Ghosts!" he barked, so loudly it startled her. "Ghosts help me with my compositions, and phantoms." Gesticulating wildly with his long, slender fingers, as though punctuating sentences in the air, he continued, "When I write music I go into another world. Thousands of vibrations surround me, and strange things come to life for me, and I put them into my music. When I am so occupied people fear to disturb me. They tell me that the look on my face when I return to reality is absolutely frightening. Can you understand what I am talking about?"

"Yes, maestro, I believe I can," she said. She described the feelings that came over her in Westminster Abbey, and in the palace hall where Mozart once played in Salzburg.

"Ah, you are more perceptive than I thought," Tcherepnin said. "At first I felt I was strange, myself, for feeling this way but I no longer do. I still look inside myself, but I no longer weep at what I see." He paused, and looked quizzically at the young Filipina. "What a charmer you are," he smiled. "I invited you here to find out more about you, and you have tricked me into prating on about myself. You must forgive me."

"Do not forgive him," Mme. Tcherepnin laughed. "He loves to carry on like this. You have just heard one of his lectures from the university. It may help you to decide whether you want to enroll in one of his classes, if you ever honor us by visiting Chicago."

"Here is our address," Tcherepnin said, scrawling a number on a slip of paper. "We are at number 839 Bradley Place, a lovely neighborhood on the city's North Side, not too far from Lake Michigan." He bowed and kissed the back of Teresita's hand. As she prepared to leave she found herself unconsciously backing from his presence, as she had done in the presence of royalty.

Back at the Philippine embassy she told her mother, "I am absolutely in love with him, Mama. I might never see him again, but I will cherish him whenever I see or hear a piano."

Alexander Tcherepnin was Teresita's first real crush.

CHAPTER 13

███████████████████████████████

RONNIE SPARROW

St. Patrick's Day frowned dark and gloomy over Chicago, provoking one Irishman to gaze disgustedly at the sloppy sky and moan, "This coulda never happened if Daley was here, God rest his soul. The sun wudda shone."

A generation of Chicagoans had known no other mayor than Richard J. Daley. This would be the first St. Patrick's Day parade in more than 20 years without the great Irish Buddha who died the previous December. With "Hizzonor" gone, Daley's four sons led the parade down State Street, flanked by Daley's successor, Michael Bilandic; Ronan Murphy, the Irish consul general; a priest friend of the family; and the boss of the plumbers' union—followed by the Shannon Rovers bagpipers.

They hoofed all the way to Congress Street, following the same route the mayor himself marched on Columbus Day with a beamingly bewildered President Jimmy Carter in tow.

They dye the Chicago River bright green on St. Patrick's Day, and nobody works in City Hall. There are some who say nobody works there other days, either. On St. Patrick's Day, however, the taxpayers seem to understand. In fact, very few people in the Loop do work on this festive day, which Chicago has adopted as its own. Among those on duty this day were the police, including any who happened to be Irish.

The mystery of Benny, the one-armed man, was cleared up by two of them, Philbin and O'Connor, who had absolutely no trouble tracking down a one-armed white man on darkly populated South Michigan Avenue.

Benny turned out to be a nobody. How he ever got on anyone's calling list was hard to understand, but he remembered attending several parties at which Teresita Basa was also a guest. Benny was able to account for his whereabouts on the day of the murder, and was unceremoniously written off as a suspect. It gave him added cause to celebrate St. Patrick's Day.

The investigation into the Basa homicide was beginning to shift into low gear.

*   *   *

March 28 was industriously trying to bring spring to Chicago. Occasional thundershowers rinsed the dirty gray mounds of soot-covered snow that still crowded street corners where the plows had shoved it. Now and then a battered beer can or an empty Ripple bottle protruded as the snow melted and trickled down the nearest sewer grating. This was Chicago's dirtiest time of the year, before the street sweepers had a chance to get out and pretty up the town for the opening day of baseball season. It would be only a couple of weeks before a lot of school kids began reporting sick grandmothers.

Stachula and Epplen clomped down the stairs of the Belmont Avenue station house and climbed into the green unmarked Plymouth. Epplen slid behind the wheel as Stachula eased himself into the passenger seat, notebook in hand. Both men sat on their seatbelts.

"Well, we've got this black kid, Ronnie Sparrow, to check into. That lawyer, Myron Walters, said the kid probably knew Teresita," Stachula droned. "He said Ronnie did odd jobs, and was in the office on at least one occasion when she visited the lawyer to see about becoming a U.S. citizen."

"Yeah, he said the kid swiped checks people mailed in to pay their bills, and he wouldn't put anything past him,"

Epplen recalled, as he flipped on the ignition and gave the gas pedal a goose. "This could be another nothing, Joe. But you never know. Where's the little punk live?"

"Oh, boy! This ain't our lucky day," muttered Stachula. "On Felton Court, right over by Cooley High, just off Orleans Street."

"By Cabrini-Green, the fabulous housing project," Epplen observed. "Why don't we go back for our bullet-proof vests—or maybe let somebody else check out this kid?"

"Why don't we just make the sign of the cross and get it over with?" Epplen suggested, only partly in jest. Police on assignment in the Cabrini-Green high-rise apartment had been the targets of snipers more than once. "It's only March. What the hell? The bullets don't really start to fly until summer time, when the natives get restless."

"The sight of a cop also makes them restless," argued Epplen. "I suppose the quickest way is taking Clybourn over to Halsted, and south to Division Street. That's just a stone's throw away, if you'll pardon the expression." He flicked on the wipers to get some of the crap off the windshield, wheeled out of the parking lot, and headed east toward Clybourn, one of Chicago's many time-saving diagonals spoking northwest from the downtown area.

"The thing I can't figure out, Joe, is how come this Basa broad was still a virgin. You'd think that in 47 years . . ."

"That somebody'd at least give her a mercy hump?" interjected his partner.

"Well, she really wasn't that bad looking, from her pictures," Epplen continued, switching off the wipers.

"I guess you don't know too much about Filipinos," said Stachula, wryly. "That's got a lot to do with it."

"Well, we never studied them at Lane Tech," Epplen muttered, hunching his head down for a better view through the clean arc the wipers had made across the windshield.

"I knew this guy who was in the Philippine Islands in World War II. He said there were mainly two kinds of women there—the pom-pom girls in the whore houses, and the ones you didn't even think about touching," Stachula said. "I guess our Teresita was one of those. Most of those people have got morals you wouldn't believe. You want to take a girl out over there, you know what you gotta do?"

"I'm listening, Joe. I can drive and listen at the same time, honest."

"You gotta meet some Filipino guy who knows her—the guys are Filipinos and the broads are Filipinas—and he invites you to a party, that she's also at, and you look each other over from a distance. Then—watch that light! That son-of-a-bitch went right through the red light! Wouldn't you know it? Not a cop in sight. Where were we?"

"At the party, lookin' each other over."

"Then you gotta write a letter, telling her all about yourself, and have your Filipino buddy deliver it in person, because the mailmen over there read everyone's mail. If the letter turns her on, she invites you over for dinner, and the whole damned family checks you out. Here's Division. Turn left."

"I already got the blinkers on, Mother."

"Then, after everybody looks you over, if they don't throw you out on your ass, you tell the girl's old man you want to take his daughter to the movies. If he says O.K., you set the date and the whole frickin' family goes along, even the cousins, and you have to buy the tickets for all seventeen of 'em at maybe four pesos a copy. You see, Lee, by the time you get to know this chick well enough to hop between the sheets with her, you're probably 47 yourself."

Epplen rounded the corner into Felton Court, a forlorn block of two-story ramshackle homes with broken chimneys on the east side of the street, interspersed with vacant lots filled with the rubble of demolished buildings, broken baby carriages, tin cans, abandoned supermarket carts, and the junk of the world. The houses were covered with imitation brick tarpaper, ripped away in places, exposing the bare, nearly century-old boards. To the east was Wells Street and the backside of Old Town—a world in itself. Just west across another rubble-strewn field was Cabrini-Green, yet another world.

"Oh, my God," moaned Epplen, as he eased the unmarked squad over to the curb in front of the second house from the end. "Do we have to get out of the car?"

"A policeman's lot," grumbled Stachula.

They got out of the auto, pushed the door-lock buttons down, and shoved the doors shut gently, so as not to make a slamming noise and alert the snipers. Looking over their shoulders, they paused a moment, then mounted the rickety wooden stairway to the Sparrow house, shoulder to shoulder. Stachula rapped on the door, as courteously as he could, but loud enough to be heard inside. Epplen stood with his back to the door, looking up and down the street. And across at Cabrini-Green.

"Mr. Sparrow?" asked Stachula, as the door was cautiously pulled open by a stoop-shouldered man of about 45, with a stubble of white whiskers on his dark brown face. He was wearing a heavy red sweatshirt under a plaid lumberjack shirt, open at the front and hanging out of his dark green, oily, work pants. He had a pair of old black loafers, turned up at the toes, on his feet, and no socks. The man said nothing. Nobody had to tell him these were cops, but Epplen and Stachula held up their badges anyway.

"Police officers, Mr. Sparrow. We'd like to talk to Ronnie about something he might be able to help us on. About his job at the lawyer's," Stachula said.

"The boy don't live here no more," the man in the doorway drawled. "You kin come in if you want, but the boy not here."

"Ah, could you possibly tell us where we could find him? We only want to talk to him. He might be able to help us."

"Ronnie really ain't a bad boy. Not like some of the kids around here. Growin' up in a place like this ain't easy, you know. Ain't safe for black or white. He been messin' around with some bad ones and gettin' into trouble. Not real bad trouble. He don't carry no gun or nothin'. That lawyer, he fired Ronnie because he said the boy stoled some checks or something. The po-lice, they been comin' around asking about those checks, but Ronnie ain't here. He done moved in with his auntie on Burling."

"Where on Burling, Mr. Sparrow?"

"Wait right here. Let me get the number for you. It's just over there in the project. His aunt, Ella Mae."

Sparrow retreated into the damp smelling house as Epplen and Stachula exchanged glances, then looked over toward the housing project, named after Mother Frances Cabrini, the Sacred Heart missionary who became America's first saint. Off in the distance, dark rain clouds appeared atop the rows of high-rises. It would be a test of even her faith to have to live there today.

Sparrow reappeared at the door with a scrap of tablet paper. It had 1230 and a telephone number scrawled on it in dull pencil. Stachula copied the number into his notebook. "You've been very helpful, sir. We appreciate it. You have a nice day now."

The two detectives walked gingerly down the steps and strode over to their car in what they hoped appeared to be a leisurely fashion. Stachula pulled the door handle, forgetting it was locked. Epplen got into the driver's side, reached across the seat, and flipped up the button.

"Thanks, partner," Stachula nodded. "It was getting lonely out there. Let's get the hell over to Burling before it gets dark. I wanna be long gone when that sun goes down."

"You'll be right behind me, Joe," said Epplen, seriously.

It took less than five minutes from the time they pulled away from the curb in front of the Sparrow home until Epplen pulled into a parking space in the blacktopped lot next to the yellow brick high-rise at 1230 N. Burling Street, in the heart of the project.

They found Ella Mae's name on a mail box and took the small elevator up to the eighth floor. They considered it their good fortune that the elevator was even working. As they stood outside the apartment door they heard the woman undo three latches from the inside before she opened it about three inches, peered over a security chain, and asked, "What do you want?"

Through the crack they could see part of a woman wearing a heavy blue knitted sweater over a flowered house dress. She was wearing slippers. Stachula told her the same story he'd told the boy's father.

"Ronnie ain't here, either," Ella Mae explained. "He run away when the police started comin' around asking about him. About them stolen checks. He don't want to talk to no po-lice, no how. I don't know where the boy is, and that's the truth."

Epplen didn't wait for Stachula to conduct further formalities. It was beginning to get dark. "Thanks ever so much, ma'am. Sorry we had to bother you."

Back outside the detectives dug into their pockets and gave a quarter to each of four kids, about 10 years old, who swore they watched the car while the gentlemen were inside. Epplen then backed out of the parking place, zoomed directly over to Division, cut right over to Wells Street, and headed back north.

"Lee, what do you say we call the Youth Division at Eleventh and State and put a stop order on this kid?" Stachula suggested. "Might be nothing, or he could just be . . ."

". . . the perpetrator?"

"Where'd you come up with that big word, Officer Epplen?"

"Hell, I watch TV just like everyone else," Epplen explained. "We've got to apprehend the individual who perpetrated the offense, right Joe?"

"I knew I should have let you go into that last joint alone," Stachula said, exhaling laboriously.

"Yeah, but then you'd have been sitting out in the car alone, partner," Epplen laughed. "How'd you like to be the mailman in there?"

"Not in a million years. Cops, at least, carry guns."

"You know, Joe. I think you're right. We oughta have the Youth Division pick this kid up. Look—he'd seen the Basa woman in this lawyer's office, and maybe figured she had dough, right? Now the lawyer says the kid's a thief, and he wouldn't put anything past him. He's what—how old?"

"Sixteen."

"O.K. He could have gotten Teresita's address off the mail in the lawyer's office and went over to her place. He knocks on the door, she recognizes the little fart from the lawyer's office, and lets him in. She thinks maybe he's bringing some legal papers for her to sign for immigration or something."

"I'm listening," nodded Stachula.

"Well, something happens in there. He gets her clothes off her and tries to rape her. She fights him off and he chickens out or gets scared off, or something. But he can't let her go because she knows him. He sinks the shiv into her chest, sets fire to the place to cover his tracks, and cuts out. This might not be a genius we're looking for at all, but a scared-shitless kid."

"Take a right at North Avenue," Stachula directed. "I know a nice quiet place were we can grab a sandwich and a glass of beer. We can go over this whole damned thing one more time, step by step. You could have something here."

"The kid's gotta know something, Joe. Why else would he be hiding out from the cops?" Epplen speculated. "Sixteen years old? He knows he's not gonna get sent up for taking a couple of lousy checks. It's gotta be something bigger."

The rain was coming down again. Epplen reached over and flipped on the wipers.

It was still raining like hell an hour later, by the time each of them had washed down a hot beef sandwich with a mug of Stroh's. While Epplen paid the tab and grabbed a free toothpick, Stachula dropped two dimes in the pay phone by the door to make a routine check with Area 6 Homicide before they ducked out to the car.

He listened to the voice on the other end of the line for a minute, hung up, and turned to his partner.

"Guess what! While we've been feeding our faces, Ronnie Sparrow has been calling the station. He's inquiring about the nature of our investigation—wants to know why the cops want to talk to him. But he won't say where he is or come in for an interview."

*   *   *

On Sunday, April 3, Chicago's Filipino community was rocked by yet another slaying, far more gruesome even than the Basa murder. And, once again, it was a bizarre combination of Filipinos, the medical profession, and violent death. The city still remembered with revulsion the July nightmare of 1966 when longshoreman Richard Speck invaded a South Side nurses' dormitory on a rampage of blood-lust and rape, leaving eight young nurses stabbed to death. Two of his victims were from the Philippines, while a third Filipina nurse saved herself by hiding under a bed during the massacre.

The latest victim was Alicia Agsaoay, a 36-year-old registered nurse at Norwegian American Hospital on the Northwest Side. A friend, Miguel Valdes, 40, had taken her to dinner at a restaurant that Sunday evening. Afterward he drove her to a record store he owned in suburban Melrose Park, and escorted her inside. Then he slit her throat with a straight-edge razor, stabbed her in the chest, washed the blood off his hands, and went home.

The next morning Valdes returned to his shop and spent the next two and a half hours cutting off the nurse's head with a scalpel. Then he amputated the toes from her left foot. He carefully packaged each toe and mailed them to several universities in the United States, to the Society for the Advancement of Science in England, and to the President of the United States. He packed the bloody head in a larger box and mailed it to Agsaoay's brother in the Philippines.

After leaving the postal station where he had deposited his grisly parcels, the troubled Valdes walked calmly into the office of 40-year-old Dr. Jesus Lim on West Fullerton Avenue and took a seat in the waiting room. When it was his turn to be admitted into the physician's private office, he drew a .45

caliber pistol and fired five shots into Lim's chest as the Filipino doctor sat at his desk.

Two hours after the shooting Valdes surrendered to the Federal Bureau of Investigation. He directed agents to the record store where they found the Filipina nurse's headless, toeless body in a pool of blood alongside a knife, a razor and a hacksaw.

Postal authorities intercepted the nurse's head at the suburban sorting station in Forest Park before it could be flown to the Philippines, and the toe addressed to England was also recovered.

Would that all homicides were as easy to solve. Valdes, a Filipino like his victims, falsely imagined there was a love triangle between himself, nurse Agsaoay, and the happily-married Dr. Lim. He was diagnosed as paranoid schizo-phrenic and consigned to a madhouse.

The Agsaoay slaying, however, generated feverish excite-ment among the Basa homicide investigators, and provided them with what seemed to be the hottest suspect yet. Anyone capable of killing the way Valdes did would have had no trouble snuffing out the life of Teresita, for any imaginable reason.

But a thorough investigation into his background and his every movement back in February eventually convinced de-tectives that Valdes knew neither Teresita Basa nor anything about her murder.

* * *

On April 21 Epplen and Stachula were back trying to tie up loose ends in the Basa investigation, to wit—Ronnie Sparrow. They reluctantly returned to the Sparrow home on Felton Court to talk to the elusive youth's father. "Other guys get sent up to Waukegan to hold hands with cute waitresses, and what do we draw? Cabrini-Green," Epplen complained. "Let's see how fast we can talk and get the hell out before dark, Joe."

"I'm with you," Stachula agreed. "You didn't even have to ask."

The elder Sparrow met the two investigators at the door. He said he had not seen his son since Stachula and Epplen talked to him three weeks earlier. "The boy, he called this afternoon, though," he volunteered. "He said he thinkin' of comin' home tonight or maybe tomorrow to spend the night with his family."

He promised to call the detectives if the boy showed up, and they wasted no time getting back to their car. He never called.

Back at Area 6 Epplen and Stachula prepared a "wanted for questioning" message on Ronnie Sparrow to be inserted in the daily Police Bulletin. The message appeared in the bulletin on Monday, April 25.

Task Force officers Michael Herigodt and Joseph Mohan, in checking over the bulletin, recalled processing a youth named Sparrow several days earlier for a curfew violation. They had picked him up in the 1600 block of North Talman Avenue. Returning to that neighborhood, Herigodt and Mohan cruised around until they spotted him. They took the teen-ager into custody and brought him back to Area 6 headquarters. It was Ronnie, all right.

Young Sparrow was questioned by Epplen and John Durkin, a seasoned detective with more time on the job than almost anyone else in his department. The youth was advised of his Constitutional rights, and of the purpose of the investigation. He admitted having worked for Myron Walters, the lawyer, and said he had seen Teresita Basa in Walters' office on several occasions.

Sparrow also admitted that he and a 16-year-old cousin had taken six checks from the lawyer's office, and said his cousin cashed one of them. Five of the stolen checks had belonged to the lawyer, Sparrow said. The sixth had been the property of a client who mailed it to Walters in payment for services. The youth could not recall whether Teresita Basa was the client in question. Teresita had claimed that she mailed the lawyer a check, but Walters contended he never received it.

Sparrow vehemently denied ever having even been near the murder apartment. He insisted the only times he had seen Teresita were at the lawyer's office.

"O.K.," Epplen said. "Now, you knew we were looking for you and wanted to talk to you. So, why didn't you contact us if you had nothing to hide?"

"'Cause of them checks me and my cousin took," Sparrow said, hanging his head. "I knew the police were after me because of them checks."

Epplen and Durkin contacted the Youth Division, and learned from Officer W.M. O'Malley that Sparrow was also wanted on warrants issued the previous year for auto theft and reckless conduct. He was turned over to O'Malley on those charges.

Before Sparrow was taken to a juvenile detention center Sergeant C.J. Dockery, Area 6 Youth Watch Commander, permitted him to be photographed and fingerprinted, so a check could be made against prints found in the Basa apartment after the murder.

The print check turned out negative. Epplen commented to Stachula, "It's funny, isn't it Joe? We go out looking for a killer, and end up nailing a punk kid for swiping a lousy car after somebody else couldn't find him."

"Yeah," said Stachula, smiling wryly. "It happens all the time, some of the time. So we're back where we started. Who in the hell killed Teresita Basa?"

CHAPTER 14

TERESITA'S TARNISHED KNIGHT

The flight back to the land named for King Philip II of Spain more than 400 years before had been a long one, but when Teresita saw the familiar baroque buildings with their elaborate carvings and arches she knew she was home. Dumaguete City was no longer the sleepy town she had left at the end of World War II. It was a bustling community of nearly 50,000, and growing every day, thanks to a healthy sugar industry. Teresita giggled at a small boy, clad only in T-shirt and bare bottom, urinating off a curb. "What would the proper English people say about that?" she laughed.

The Certificate of Pianoforte she had earned in London was hung proudly on her bedroom wall. Much of her time, now, was dedicated to her familiar old piano. With the Basa family money she did not have to work, and wanted to give her mind a rest. Occasionally, accompanied by her parents, she and one of the young men from town would attend a movie in the theater by the market place. Teresita did not take the men of Dumaguete seriously, however. After her world travels, and her audience with Alexander Tcherepnin, they seemed country-dull.

Eventually, after several weeks of trying to get up her nerve, she sat down and typed a long letter to the maestro.

The reply came from Chicago. In it he urged Teresita to come to America to continue her studies, if not in Chicago, at the nearby Indiana University in Bloomington.

"The Russians once promised to make me a millionaire if I would return to my native land, but I told them there is no price on freedom," he wrote in his long, flowing hand. "You have everything you want in the way of monetary comfort, but you are still a young bird who wants to fly."

And fly she did. The late summer of 1957 found Teresita, then 28, aboard a trans-oceanic flight for Honolulu, and then on to the States, where she arrived on August 28. She enrolled in Indiana University 16 days later under the Foreign Exchange Visitors Program. It would require her to return to her homeland for two years before becoming eligible for an immigrant visa, should she want to take employment in the United States at a later date.

In Bloomington Teresita took a small rented apartment just west of the campus on East Fourth Street. She quickly found the small circle of Filipinos at I.U., and became particularly close to Corbillita Astroquillo and Amada Santos-Ocampa, who were in the school of music, like herself. Her tuition was paid by her father, who arranged with Mr. Amado Brinas of the Central Bank of the Philippines in Manila to transfer the necessary funds to a Bloomington bank.

Among her closest non-Filipino friends at the university was Prof. Vernon Kliewer, a music theorist, who taught several of Teresita's classes. Their friendship blossomed through a chance remark he made one afternoon while talking to her after class. He had just remonstrated her for being so moody, when he said, "Well, got to get home and water my orchids."

"Orchids?" Teresita's face lit up as though the sun had just come out from behind a dismal cloud.

"Just a music teacher's hobby," he said, almost self-consciously. "I've got a little greenhouse where I grow them behind my home."

"Professor! Can I come home with you to see them? Oh, please."

"Well, I, ah . . ."

"Please, Professor Kliewer. My mother raises orchids in our front yard back home. It is her hobby, too."

"In the yard, you say?" he asked. They were walking together now, toward Kliewer's home. Teresita was fairly bouncing along. "It's interesting to discover that your mother and I have something in common," he added, groping to make conversation.

"Ah, but I don't think you also sing soprano," Teresita laughed.

"Not even in the shower."

From that day on Teresita was a regular visitor to the Kliewer household, sometimes to discuss music theory with the professor, but always to survey his modest field of orchids. She took delight in bringing the professor and his wife surprise gifts from the Philippines, such as table linens and decorative handmade table mats.

Her new-found association with the professor also seemed to fire up Teresita academically. She attained a 3.5 grade average, and earned bachelor's degrees with honors in both music theory and piano. She immediately enrolled in graduate school, where she won a job teaching undergraduate courses as a graduate assistant in piano. In all, Teresita enrolled in 61 courses at Indiana University, completing 58 of them.

Before finishing her last three she abruptly discontinued her graduate studies and moved to Washington, D.C. The reason was the Romeros.

José Romero had been appointed Washington representative of the Philippine Sugar Association, and opened offices in the nation's capital. Tessie, meanwhile, had married the son of Gen. Carlos Romulo, Philippine envoy to Washington. It was like London revisited. In order that she might be self-sufficient, Teresita took a job as a typist with Romero's Sugar Association.

A pen pal, Robert Krauth of Jamaica Plain, Massachusetts, whom she had met at a ski resort where she had gone with a group of students, provided Teresita with the address of his sister, who lived in nearby Annandale, Virginia. Teresita called on the sister, who helped her get settled on her own. In order to maintain her student status, and remain in America, she continued to do music research at the Library of Congress, while also taking courses at the Arlington Institute of Music.

It was here, in Washington, that Teresita—now a mature woman in her 30s—met the first and only man with whom she wanted to spend the rest of her life.

Her "romance" with the flamboyant Tcherepnin, the composer, was, of course, a fantasy. Edward O'Meara, on the other hand, was attainable. He was tall, flashy, handsome, with gleaming white teeth, and an ability to sweep any girl off her sandals. He could, it would seem, have had any female in Washington. Yet, inexplicably, he made his play for Teresita.

They met at a diplomatic reception hosted by the Romulos, at which she was prevailed upon to entertain at the piano. He came up afterward with a cocktail in his right hand and a glass of white wine for her in the other and smiled, "You play very well, Teresita."

"How do you know my name?" she asked. "I have not seen you before."

"Ah, but I hope you will again," he said, putting his face close to hers. "I know a lot about you, Miss Basa. I'm Ed O'Meara from Chicago. I'm what you call a lobbyist here, for Illinois industry. I get to know a lot of very influential people, and I am not without influence, myself."

To Teresita's surprise, the suave O'Meara called her the following day, a Sunday, and invited her to go for a drive. She hesitated at first, but soon gave in to his persuasive powers. That was the beginning. Teresita never talked of her romance with O'Meara. That was her very most private life. They were seen together often, however, and Tessie and other close friends were soon asking intimate questions.

Teresita gave them all evasive answers.

There was one thing, however, that she could not evade. She poured it out to O'Meara one night over candlelight dinner in her apartment, after he turned the conversation to serious talk of marriage. "You know, Edward, that I am here on a student exchange program."

"I'm aware of that, dear," he said, cupping her hands in his.

"Then I must tell you something very important. If I want to remain here, legally, I must first return to the Philippines for two years. After that I will be permitted to reenter the United States with an immigrant visa."

"Two years? That's forever, Chita," he exclaimed. "I couldn't stand being without you for that long. Isn't there any other way?"

"Not unless you wanted to live in the Philippines, Edward. But what would you do for employment?" she asked. "Two years would be a test of our love for both of us. It would also give me time to think. I have not seen my parents for quite some time. This is something that I would have to talk over with my father and mother. That is our custom, you know. Then, I am sure, they would return with me to meet you."

"This is America, Chita, and you're 36 years old."

"I know, Edward. But I am a Filipina. I would never dishonor my parents by doing anything that they did not approve."

O'Meara proved every bit the gentleman he was reputed to be. They talked for hours, and agreed to do it Teresita's way. In the ensuing weeks she took the necessary measures to close her apartment, discontinue her employment, withdraw from her classes, and say good-bye to her friends in Washington. Leaving the city, and O'Meara, was more difficult for Teresita than cutting the invisible umbilical to her parents when she first went off to school in Manila.

The flight back was long and exhausting, from Washington to San Francisco, to Honolulu, to Wake, and on to Luzon. The Basas met the plane at Manila International Airport, and the trio spent several days with Teresita's uncle in Caloocan before taking the island-hopping plane back to Negros.

While she tried not to show it, Teresita was stunned at the change time had wrought on her father. Pedro Cruz Basa, the robust young lawyer who used to fairly strut along the dusty road to his father-in-law's sugar plantation was nearing 70. He suffered from emphysema, and could no longer walk any distance without stopping to let his breath catch up with him.

Teresita wept inside as she hugged the old man and whispered, "Mabuhay, Daddy." When he finally spoke, she realized that none of the spark of his youth was missing.

"So, you have a young man," he beamed. "How wonderful. For a time I had all but given up hope of ever becoming a grandfather. Chita, you make us both very happy. Come, tell us all about him."

Teresita needed no urging. The wonderful Edward O'Meara was the sole subject of her conversation from breakfast until dusk. In the weeks that followed, even when she tried to immerse herself in her music at the old grand piano, the vision of the dashing O'Meara raced through her mind.

One evening, shortly after the six o'clock church bells, when everyone in Dumaguete stopped to make the sign of the cross and mutter a brief prayer of faith, a red, green and yellow *tartanilla* clip-clopped to a halt outside the Basa home on Colon Street. Pedro eyed it curiously from his wicker chair on the veranda, and rose slowly as a dignified gentleman in a white seersucker suit and straw sunhat jumped effortlessly to the ground and cautiously approached the front gate. He was carrying the biggest bouquet of flowers Basa had ever seen.

"Judge Basa?" the American inquired, extending his free hand. "Mabuhay! I am Edward O'Meara, and I've come a long way—with your permission, of course—to court your daughter."

"Well," said the astonished Basa. "Well, well, well. She'll be so surprised. Let me call her . . ."

"Oh, no. Please, sir. Let me go in and surprise her. I can hear her playing inside."

As the two men entered the room, the music stopped and she looked up from the piano. "You play very well, Teresita," said O'Meara, repeating the first words he had ever spoken to her.

*　*　*

Basa sent down to the small hotel and had O'Meara's luggage delivered to the home. The man from America would stay with them, just as he, as a young lawyer down from Manila, had stayed in the Martinez home when he courted Socorro so many years ago.

The Basas found, in O'Meara, a modern-day swashbuckler who had spanned the ocean to claim his lady love. "I believe I once promised Chita that I would follow her to the ends of the earth, and I have kept my word," he laughed one evening as they all sat on the veranda, watching the setting sun reflect off Santa Catalina across the street.

O'Meara had come to Dumaguete for several reasons, he explained: To meet his cherished one's family; to give the family the opportunity to get to know him; and to be with Teresita for as much time as his four-weeks vacation would allow. "Hang the expenses," he chortled when Teresita chided him over what his dido must have done to his bank account. "I'm only glad you don't live on the moon."

He soon learned, in accordance with Filipino custom, that he and Teresita would have precious little time together. In fact, he spent more time with Judge Basa than he did with his daughter, talking Washington politics, discussing the economic future of their two countries, and even going, with the old man, to his first cock-fight.

The highlight of O'Meara's visit was a gala lawn party and pig roast the Basas held in his honor, so that they might proudly show him off to their most influential friends. Teresita had become the envy of Dumaguete.

About three weeks after his arrival O'Meara announced that he was going to take an after-dinner walk, as he occasionally did while Teresita dutifully put in her time at the piano. "I'm afraid I have fallen hopelessly in love with Dumaguete," he said. "And I want to drink in every drop of its beauty in the setting sun." He patted Teresita's hand, and waved good-bye to her parents, promising to "see you in a little while," as he left the Basa home for the last time.

Several hours later a car drove up, and an old friend of the judge's asked if he could talk to him in private. The two men whispered for a few moments. Then Basa, a look of consternation on his face, walked slowly into the house and told his wife he would be back in a few minutes.

"What is it, Pedro?" she asked, alarmed.

"Don't worry, my dear. Please go and sit with Chita."

"Is it Edward?"

"I'll be back soon," Basa replied curtly, as he and his friend walked to the car. They headed for the waterfront and the city's tacky red-light district, frequented mostly by sailors. As they approached a large bamboo house, with the main living quarters on the second floor and a number of cubicles on the clay floor underneath, they could hear roisterous shouting, laughter, and singing.

"I will not set foot in that place," Basa said, indignantly.

"There are some things a father must do," his friend advised, guiding him by the elbow. "Come, I'll lead the way."

Several of the cell-like cubicles were open, and as they passed they could see the dingy interiors in the candle-light. Each contained an iron bedstead, a dirty mattress with mussed bedclothes, and a small wash stand containing a porcelain bowl of water, and a wrinkled towel. The friend led Basa to the fragile looking bamboo stairway. There was no railing, and he held the judge's arm as the two climbed slowly toward the lantern-lit room above. The noise and singing abruptly stopped as the two old men reached the head of the stairs. Several scantily-clad girls in their teens, who had come forward seductively to greet the newcomers, backed off in confusion when they recognized Justice Pedro Basa. There were scattered chairs around the wall, containing girls in various stages of undress. In the center of the room, under a kerosene lantern, was a large, round rattan table. On it were several whisky bottles—the Filipino brands of Three Roses and Four Feathers—and an array of dirty glasses, some partly filled, and others tipped over and dripping through the woven bamboo floor to the level below.

Seated in a large wicker chair, utterly naked, drunk as a feudal lord, and holding a sensuous brown-skinned girl of about 17 on his lap, was none other than the dashing Edward O'Meara.

"Judge Basa! Judge! Lemme explain," he sputtered, pushing the dark-haired girl to the floor and rising shakily to expose his full nakedness. "Judge, I . . ."

Basa, followed by his friend, was slowly picking his way back down the rickety stairs. "Judge!" the man from Washington called after him. "You rich old son-of-a-bitch! Come back here. I can explain . . . !"

In the car, returning to his home on Colon Street, Basa spoke only once. "I had heard of that creature called the 'Ugly American,' but until this day I had never seen one."

"I am sorry it was I who had to bring you there, Pedro," his companion said tenderly. "Some of your friends have known about this for some time, and we thought it best that you should be told. I was the one who drew the short straw."

When O'Meara appeared on foot outside the Basa home a half hour later the lights were out, and his suitcases were setting on the walk by the curb. In the shadows of the unlit veranda he could see the silhouette of the tired old man. In the quiet of the night air he thought he could hear weeping from within the stucco house, but he could not be sure. His head was clouded, and he needed a drink before charting his next move. He picked up his luggage and trudged toward town.

The next morning a small delegation of Basa's closest friends escorted the American to the airport and ushered him aboard a plane for Manila.

*   *   *

That same morning, after mass at Santa Catalina's, a red-eyed Teresita asked her mother, "Do you think they could still use a piano teacher at the college?" Silliman University, started by an American philanthropist with 15 barefoot boys in 1901, now had 3,500 determined students, a medical center, school of nursing, theology quadrangle, engineering unit, high school and elementary school, and a school of music. To the faculty was added the name of Teresita Basa. Previous experience: instructor of piano, Indiana University, Bloomington, Indiana, U.S.A.

Pedro Basa was never completely well after the incident in the whorehouse. He rarely left the home, except for short walks, frequently interrupted to catch his breath, across the street to the plaza where he used to take Teresita to romp as a child.

When he mercifully breathed his last, he was buried there, across the street, in the cemetery of Santa Catalina.

Not long afterward, in the summer of 1971, Teresita made up her mind to return to America. "I'm not happy here like I used to be, Mama," she said. "Whenever someone looks at me, I feel they must be thinking, 'There is that fool who was taken in by the slick American.' And I tell myself they are right."

"You are going back to find Edward?" her astonished mother asked.

"No, Mama. America is a big place. I'm sure I will never see or hear from him again."

On November 2, 1971, she took the inter-island plane to Cebu City where she applied to Justino R. Alfafara, foreign affairs officer, for a new passport. She was issued Passport No. CEB-04558, for which she paid a fee of 70 pesos—about $35. She listed her home address as Colon Street, Dumaguete City, and her "foreign address" as the School of Music, Indiana University, Bloomington, Indiana. She posed for a new photo, and the passport's "description of bearer" identified her as 5 feet 3 inches tall, black hair and brown eyes, a mole on the right side of her forehead and another on her left cheek. Date of birth: 13 March, 1929, Dumaguete City. Occupation: student.

On the twenty-seventh of November she visited Dr. Alfredo R. Corpuz for her smallpox revaccination and cholera shot. She was issued International Certificate of vaccination No. QU-61286 by the Department of Health, Republic of Philippines. Her non-immigrant visa, which she applied for to American Vice Consul Ralph D. Griffin, while in Cebu City, was issued on December 1.

"Oh, Mama, you'll be so alone when I leave," Teresita sobbed the night before her departure, alone, for Manila. "Why can't you come with me?"

"This is my home, Chita. Here by your father, and my orchids. I'll visit him regularly for both of us. And each day I'll pray for you in Santa Catalina."

Teresita Basa reentered the United States on December 7, 1971, exactly 30 years to the day after Pearl Harbor. She carried $53 in U.S. currency and $345.30 in traveler's checks. She was 42 years old.

CHAPTER 15

THE DOLDRUMS

That condition of inactivity known as the doldrums enveloped the Basa investigation after the Ronnie Sparrow arrest. He and the unfortunate toe-chopper, Miguel Valdes, were the last good leads police had. From time to time, between more active investigations, detectives routinely telephoned Teresita's friends to check on whether they had heard or thought of anything that had not been covered earlier. They turned up nothing. The Basa file was in a state of suspended animation. Or, as one cop succinctly put it, "The trail is colder than Kelsey's nuts."

Stachula spent the entire month of May on a well-earned furlough. With 85 honorable mentions he was one of the city's most decorated cops. Among his citations was one from the Chicago Jaycees, for bravery in rescuing an unconscious man from certain death in a blazing building. Afterward Stachula was hauled away in an ambulance, suffering from smoke inhalation and burns.

Epplen—while the Basa case hung in limbo—was going through the final throes of divorce, working in the garden behind his wife's home on Mulligan, and tending to his part-time job as a security man at the Holiday Inn just west of the Loop. At night he continued to work the usual grab-bag out of Area 6 — the "Ma and Pa" killings, lovers' quarrels that got out of hand, and armed robberies that all too often blew up when a victim resisted.

On Friday, May 27, he ran into another stickler. The brutally slashed body of Abraham Abdullah, a 35-year-old bartender, was found lying in the gutter between two parked cars on Chestnut Street. He had a dozen wounds, probably from a straight razor, on his face, chest, and abdomen. Somebody had worked Abraham over good. At the nearby entrance to the Lakeside Hotel on the corner of Dearborn Street, police found another pool of blood, indicating the man had been attacked in the doorway.

With this to go on, homicide investigators searched the hotel. They did not turn up the killer, but they uncovered a cache of drugs and stolen goods taken in a restaurant burglary and arrested several suspects. As in the Ronnie Sparrow case, while investigating a murder they had inadvertently solved an unrelated crime.

Epplen's divorce became final in June. Rose Mary retained the home and custody of the two children. Shortly after the divorce Epplen took the children on a five-day outing to Wisconsin, with friends. Despite his hectic life, he always found time for his son and daughter.

The Abdullah slaying was cleared up after Stachula returned to duty. A tipster told him and Epplen he'd seen two men leave the murder scene counting the victim's blood-drenched money—$17 in all. Epplen and Stachula tracked down the suspects and arrested them. In the months that followed they worked on 17 other homicides, all solved. Only the Teresita Basa file remained open.

Somehow the Basa case gnawed at the two investigators more than any that had ever challenged them. It was as though something was compelling the spectre of Teresita Basa to remain in their minds, no matter what else occupied their bodies. Teresita Basa refused to go away.

CHAPTER 16

HOME IN CHICAGO

Within minutes after the Boeing 707 carrying Teresita Basa and some 160 other shivering passengers from the Far East touched down at O'Hare International Airport she began to question the wisdom of her decision. The temperature in Manila when she said her last good-bye to the Philippines was a balmy 79 degrees. It was in the low 30s in Chicago, and her incoming plane was pelted with a sopping mixture of rain and snow.

While seated in the airport restaurant, after checking her luggage through customs, she charted her next move. She would finish her studies at Indiana University and obtain her master's degree, but she would accept no more support from her widowed mother. To do it on her own, however, meant she would first have to find a suitable job. The music degree could come later.

Teresita took the airport bus downtown and checked into an inexpensive hotel on Ohio Street north of the Chicago River. The next day she took a cab to the Philippine Consulate on North Michigan Avenue. There, in a high-ceilinged sitting room on the twenty-first floor overlooking Grant Park, where she was graciously served coffee on a tray, she discussed her situation with members of the consul general's staff. They immediately set out to help her find permanent accommodations.

Filipinos comprised perhaps the largest group of Asians in the city. And while there were 60,000 to 70,000 of them in the Chicago metropolitan area, they were not congregated in any "Little Manila" neighborhood. Filipinos are, by nature, minglers, who gravitate more out of economic than social conditions. How much a Filipino might be able to realize from the future sale of a home is a major consideration in choosing an area where he will live.

Teresita, alone in a frighteningly large city, settled in an area that gave her the most personal comfort. With the help of a rental agent recruited by the consul's office, she found a modest walkup apartment on the near Northwest Side. In fact, when she discovered the name of the street she would live on, she could not even be coaxed to look at any of several furnished apartments farther north in the vicinity of St. Alphonsus Redemptorist Catholic Church, which celebrated a weekly mass identical to that said at Santa Catalina's. No, her new address would be 1056 Mozart Street.

"It has a special meaning to me," she confided to the agent. "Do you know, I have been in the very room where Mozart was born? And I have listened to concert music in the palace in Austria where he played. I think it was meant that I should live on his street."

Teresita spent her first Christmas in the Mozart apartment alone, living for the first time without a piano keyboard at her fingertips. There was no market for piano teachers in Chicago at the moment, and she could not even offer lessons at home, since she had no piano. Thanks to her experience in Washington, she was able to land a job as a typist through the classified sections of the newspapers. With the memory of Edward O'Meara still fresh in her mind, she extended little effort to make friends. Each day, after work, she took the bus straight home and settled down with a good book. She joined a Book-of-the-Month club and soon began to fill her apartments with the latest selections.

In the spring, at the suggestion of one of her co-workers, she plunked down six dollars for a Gray Line bus tour of the city.

The guided tour, along with Tcherepnin's earlier recommendation, helped her decide that Chicago would be her permanent home.

After the bus tour Teresita began to emerge slowly from the invisible cocoon in which she had enveloped herself. She made friends carefully, always sure not to become too chummy. She also contacted a distant cousin, Kenneth Basa, a year older than she, who managed a food company laboratory in north suburban Evanston. He put her in touch with another cousin, 37-year-old Ron Somera, and the two helped ease her into the social life of the Filipino community.

In less than a year, thanks to her frugal existence, Teresita had laid in a small nest egg, and decided to resume her schooling. Surprisingly, she decided not to return to music school, but to learn a profession that would bring her a better income than that of a typist. She had developed an interest in interior design, through fixing up the Mozart apartment, and for a time considered study along those lines. Then, as she often did, she thought of her father, and how Pedro Basa's life was cut short by a respiratory illness because he could not get the proper treatment.

In September 1972 Teresita enrolled as a student in respiratory therapy at the Central YMCA Community College, located downtown in the old Sun-Times newspaper building on Wacker Drive.

Midway through the course, on July 25, 1973, she visited Etta C. Enriquez, consul at the Philippine Consulate General office, where she paid eight dollars to have her passport renewed.

Teresita took a total of 70 credit hours at the college, despite the fact she still held her outside typing job. In recognition of her academic achievement she was inducted into the Sigma Sigma Chapter of Phi Theta Kappa, the National Honor Fraternity.

A month after she graduated on June 6, 1974, she went to work full time as an inhalation therapist at Edgewater Hospital. A smiling photo was taken of her in her white uniform, and she was assigned identification card No. 50039. Her starting pay was $6.03 an hour—$11,761 a year, after taxes.

Although there were a number of Filipinos among the hospital's 1,800 employees, Teresita did not fall in with any particular group. It was as if she feared one of them might discover how O'Meara had shamed her in the Islands.

Her closest female friend became the widow Ruth Loeb, an administrative aide to the hospital's medical director. For male companionship she carefully chose people with whom she could feel comfortable, without fear of romantic involvement. Among them were Ray King and Richard Pessotti, the articulate young bachelors less than half her age, and Allan Showery, a black orderly more than 10 years her junior, who was devoted to his white common-law wife.

Now earning what was considered a respectable salary, Teresita longed for a larger apartment in which she could install a piano, and revive her interest in music; perhaps even give lessons to enhance her income. She found exactly what she had in mind in the 21-story red brick and glass high-rise with wrought iron balconies at 2740 N. Pine Grove Ave., across from Lincoln Park. She moved in, with her collection of books, stereo set, and phonograph records on September 15, 1974.

Her cousin, Kenneth Basa, embarked on a piano hunt with her, since she did not know the city that well. He took her to a used musical instrument shop near the Eisenhower Expressway, where he discovered a Teresita he had never seen before. Giggling with excitement as she fondled one battered instrument after another, she suddenly grabbed him by the arm and gushed, "Oh, Kenneth, look at the beautiful old organ in the window."

Before her cousin could discourage her she cast all dignity aside and clambered into the display window, seated herself at the organ, and began to stroke the keys. On impulse she began working the pedals, and the music began to flow. All other activity in the store ceased as customers and sales personnel gathered around the window for the impromptu concert by the sloe-eyed Filipina.

Closing her eyes to shut out the glare of the sun on the dirty store window, Teresita's mind spanned continents and took her to Alexander Tcherepnin's Paris studio, to the Royal College in London, and to the concert stage in Dumaguete as the symphony flowed from her sensitive fingers.

Finally, exhausted from laboriously pumping the pedals, she stepped back down into the showroom. Leaning on her amused cousin's arm for support she chirped giddily to an amazed sales clerk, "I've just had a ball! Now we would like to look at a good used piano."

Needless to say, Teresita test-played every piano in the store. She fell in love with an antique classic that had a $350 price tag on it. "This is the piano I must have, but that is more than I expected to pay," she said. "I can give you $300 right now if you will let me have it."

"You've got a deal, Miss. That concert you just gave was easily worth the extra $50," he laughed.

The piano was delivered to her Pine Grove apartment the following day—the day Teresita Basa came back to life.

"Mabuhay, Teresita," she addressed herself while admiring her new acquisition. "I think it's time to have a party."

It would be the first of many. The new Teresita became a popular hostess and an equally popular guest and entertainer. She enjoyed going to or giving parties, and suddenly became known in her growing circle of friends as a person who really enjoyed life, and enjoyed people.

Her younger cousin, Ron Somera, who was married to a nurse, formed a six-piece band, with Teresita on the piano. Somera played bongos, guitar and did vocals. Dr. John Abella, a pediatrician, played alto sax and also sang. The fun-loving group, which catered to dances, parties and other social affairs in the Filipino community, called themselves the Mahogany Five Plus One. The "Mahogany Five" were the brown-skinned Filipinos. "Plus One" was their Polish drummer.

The versatile group, which played everything from classics to jazz, was booked regularly at Rizal Center, the Philippine community headquarters on West Irving Park Road. Rehearsals were held at the center, because of the availability of a piano, and occasionally in Teresita's apartment, for the same reason.

At the hospital Teresita became known as a good worker, who others liked to be around. A creature of habit, she sat at the same cafeteria table every day, and those who sat nearby could hear her humming, or singing softly to herself. She also became known as a soft touch, ever ready to advance money to anyone who ran short before payday—and she was not always paid back.

She seemed to draw her strength from her religion. She attended mass regularly at St. Vincent's, about 10 blocks from her apartment. Whenever she was downtown she visited St. Peter's in the heart of the Loop, or attended services at Old St. Mary's of the Paulist Fathers, under the "El" tracks on Van Buren Street, where the Reverend Wilfred Brimley, a former CIA agent from the Far East, served as priest.

After she was thoroughly settled in her new surroundings Teresita telephoned Professor Kliewer, now head of Indiana University's Graduate School of Music, and discussed completing work for her master's degree. The classwork was done. All that remained was preparation of her master's thesis.

"I propose that my thesis consider the work of Alexander Tcherepnin," she told the professor, after first inquiring about his orchids, and Mrs. Kliewer, in that order. "As you know, I have had personal contact with him, and have talked with him about his pieces." After she explained how she would approach the subject, Kliewer agreed. Furthermore, he offered to act as her advisor, and said he would grade the thesis himself. The much sought-after degree would be in music theory.

Teresita was getting her act together. In the fall of 1975 her pen pal, Robert Krauth, whom she had met at a ski resort more than 10 years earlier, came to Chicago to attend a design engineering exposition. He called and invited her to dinner. He did not know, until he stopped by the apartment to pick her up, that it was going to be a foursome.

"Oh, Bob, how wonderful to see you again," she said when he appeared at her door. "Please come in and meet my friends. This is Ray King, and this is Richard Pessotti. They are going with us. I hope you don't mind." The two, who appeared to be about half Teresita's age, explained to Krauth, "We kind of look out for her."

Despite her return to the real world, Teresita relied on King, Pessotti and other young men from time to time, as insurance against another Edward O'Meara entering her life. The four of them had a delightful evening together, and Krauth returned to Massachusetts having made two new friends.

Another of Teresita's frequent companions was the 30-year-old Showery, a $3.66-an-hour orderly in the respiratory department at the hospital. He and his German-born common law wife lived in a second floor walkup on Surf Street, just the other side of Diversey. The two workers took the bus home together, getting off at Clark and Diversey. After the usual "See you tomorrow," Teresita turned east while Showery headed north.

Showery enjoyed much the same reputation Teresita did at the hospital—always ready to help someone who needed a friend. A self-described jack of all trades—jeweler, medic, mister fix-it, you name it—he told Teresita on one of their bus rides home that he had once played drums in the Count Basie band. On several occasions he accompanied her downtown to the Federal Building, where she consulted with immigration officials about establishing permanent residency. In the end, however, she needed more than Showery's moral backing, and engaged the services of the attorney Myron J. Walters.

Though Teresita did not drink, she always kept a generous supply of liquor on hand for thirsty guests, and for parties.

The biggest soiree she ever threw was in the summer of 1976 when Socorro flew to Chicago for a visit. "I have made lots of new friends, Mama, and I want to show you off to them," she said. "And I want them to meet the person I have told them so much about."

On the designated evening Socorro wore a blue flowered *mestiza* dress with its distinctive scooped neckline and striking butterfly sleeves. The grand dame of Dumaguete, now in her 70s, sat apprehensively in a straight-backed chair as Teresita serenaded her on the piano, while waiting for the guests to arrive. But nobody came.

At seven o'clock, as Socorro began to wonder about her daughter's capability as a hostess, Teresita turned and said mischievously, "Well, Mama. Are you prepared to meet my friends?"

"Yes, but I don't see any."

"Then come with me, and you shall see."

Teresita took her down the hall to the elevator and up to the roof, which was bathed in the soft glow of decorative lanterns strung between poles, illuminating a large refreshment table and punch bowl.

A hi-fi set, arranged with speakers at opposite corners, was playing recorded music from the Philippines, accompanied by Ron Somera on his guitar. Kenneth Basa, wearing dark slacks and an elegantly embroidered *barong tagalog* hanging loosely outside his pants, stepped forward with both arms extended in welcome. Many of the Filipino guests were similarly attired, while Teresita's American friends from the hospital wore trendy leisure suits, with their silk shirts open to display gaudy jewelry hanging from gold chains across their chests.

Meeting and talking with Teresita's many friends affirmed, for Socorro, that her daughter had indeed found a new life, and was more than capable of making it on her own. On the day she was to return to the Philippines she called Teresita over and asked her sit beside her on the couch.

Opening her purse, she told her daughter, "There are two things, Chita, that I want you to have. Your mother is growing old, as you can see, and I don't know when we will see each other again."

She placed in Teresita's hands a pearl cocktail ring, which she had purchased for herself in Paris 20 years earlier,

A music theorist by international training, Teresita Basa chose hospital work to help others be independent. A co-worker provided the information that led to the arrest of her killer.

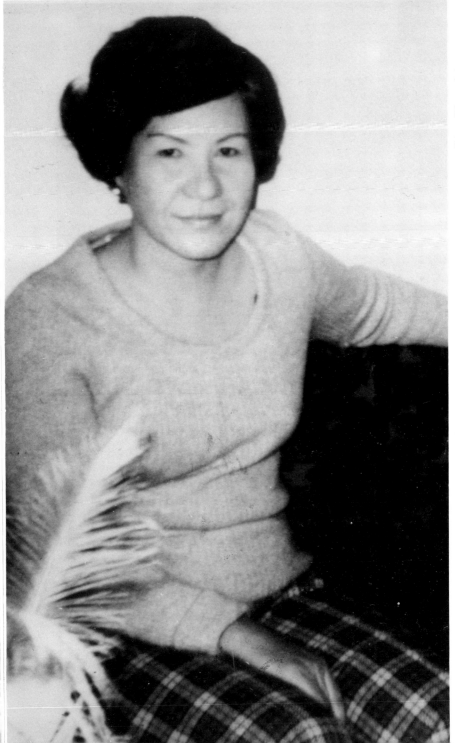

photo by John O'Brien

Lead prosecutor Thomas Organ downplayed talk of ghosts. Despite a mistrial declared because of a hung jury, he still got his man.

Assistant State's Attorney Lee Schoen with the murder weapon. Teresita was already dead from the stab wound when Showery heaped clothing on her body and set it afire.

photo by John O'Brien

and a jade pendant with a scene from the Philippines etched on its flat surface. "The ring you have seen me wear many times," she said. "It is yours, now. Please think of me when you wear it. I want to know, when I am back home in Dumaguete, that it is on your finger."

"Oh, Mama, I can't . . ." Teresita protested, as Socorro slid the ring onto her daughter's finger.

"And this piece of polished jade was given to me by your father, as a token of his love," she continued, "He intended that I some day would pass it on to you. Take it now, so that you will think of him always." There were tears in both women's eyes as Socorro looped the silken cord that held the hand-crafted slab of jade around her daughter's neck.

"I do not need these to think of you and Daddy, but I will have them. They will make me feel even closer to you," Teresita said, holding her mother's hand. "When I wear this ring, and this pendant, you and Daddy will be at my side." She wore them when she accompanied Socorro to the airport where they embraced, and kissed, for the last time.

* * *

In August 1976 Teresita took the "El" to Evanston to help her cousin, Kenneth Basa, celebrate his forty-ninth birthday. It was a small-scale family reunion, and during the gathering a discussion arose over how many Filipinos seem to believe in the supernatural.

"Not me," Basa asserted. "I've never been in a haunted house or seen a flying saucer, although I find reports of UFOs very interesting. But I've got to see one myself before I believe it."

"There are many things, Ken, that can't be explained," Teresita interjected.

"Myth. Mostly myth, Chita," he argued. "Hell, when I was a seaman I spent a great deal of time in the so-called 'Bermuda Triangle,' where so many ships are supposed to have disappeared in the Atlantic. And do you know what? It was a beautiful place. There was no psychic phenomena.

There was nothing strange out there at all. People believe what they want to believe."

"Oh, Kenneth," she teased. "I believe. I've really had strange feelings that I can't explain, and I know of many things that have happened back home . . ."

"Things that are said to have happened," he smiled. "No, I have to have hard data. I'm a scientist. That's the way I'm constituted."

The conversation turned to other things, and the party lasted well into the night. Teresita was one of the last guests to leave. Kenneth Basa never saw his cousin again.

*   *   *

Teresita, meanwhile, finished the first draft of her thesis on Tcherepnin, who had once confided in her that "ghosts" had helped him write his music. She sent it off to Kliewer in Bloomington, and he was pleased.

"It's good, Teresita," he told her by phone. "I would say it is acceptable as it stands. I took it to the hospital and read it to my wife when she had the baby, and she agrees with me."

"No, I can do better," Teresita protested. "I have someone helping me with the language construction, and the final result will be ready for you in a couple of months. I know you will like it much better." The professor would never hear from her again.

In December 1976 Walters, the lawyer, advised Teresita to obtain letters from her employers regarding the quality of her work at Edgewater Hospital, for immigration authorities. Connie Kuehn, technical director of the Respiratory Therapy Department, and one of Teresita's closest friends, told her, "No problem."

In addition to writing a laudatory letter herself, Mrs. Kuehn solicited letters from Dr. Edwin Rayner Levine, medical director of the Department of Respiratory Care, and Dr. Mario E. Oliveros, associate director of the Department of Respiratory Therapy. All three praised Teresita's technical skill, and indicated that Edgewater Hospital would be hard-pressed to get along without her.

That Christmas was one of the happiest Teresita had experienced since the festive childhood marches around Dumaguete with the statues of Joseph and Mary to Santa Catalina. She joined a group of about 20 members of the Filipino Medical Association, who had gathered to go caroling. It was for charity, to raise funds to help defray medical expenses for ailing Filipinos in the city.

Traveling in a caravan of four cars, the carolers visited the homes of influential members of the Filipino community where they passed the hat for contributions, usually in the form of generous checks. One of the homes they visited was that of the Honorable Rodolfo Sanchez, newly assigned Philippine consul general in Chicago, who lived in north suburban Skokie. Sanchez, a slight, perpetually-smiling career diplomat in his late 30s, threw open his door to the sound of "Silent Night."

"Mabuhay, my dear friends. Long life to you," he declared. "Come in, please, and get warm." Stomping the snow off their feet, they gratefully entered and handed their heavy coats to Mrs. Sanchez, who laid them across their bed. Then, for more than an hour, with Teresita at the piano, the entire group, including Mr. and Mrs. Sanchez, joined in singing carols, just as they had done as children back in their homeland. Before they left Mrs. Sanchez prepared salabat, a hot ginger tea, which she served with small sandwiches and potato chips. When Teresita returned to her apartment on North Pine Grove she felt warmer inside than she could ever remember.

Shortly after the first of the year Robert Krauth came to Chicago for another design engineering show. He was not surprised, this time, when Teresita's two "gentlemen in waiting" accompanied them to dinner. He even gave King and Pessotti his home phone number, in case they should ever be in the Boston area.

While they were relaxing in Teresita's apartment afterward, listening to records, Teresita received several disturbing phone calls. On hanging up after the last one she complained, "I wish he'd give up."

"You have a suitor, Chita?" Krauth joked.

"Oh, it's just someone who will not take no for an answer," she replied. It's nothing, really." But the calls, from someone she chose not to identify, put a damper on the remainder of the evening.

Several days later, while Teresita was having lunch with Ruth Loeb, the conversation turned to the subject of psychic phenomena, which was discussed at Kenneth Basa's birthday party. "I've heard of actual instances in the Philippines where somebody died, and their relatives knew about it before anyone came and told them," Teresita asserted.

"Well, I have to admit I'm pretty skeptical myself," Mrs. Loeb said. "But I did have what I would call a mystical experience about 30 years ago—a premonition, I guess you'd call it. Please don't tell anybody I told you this, because I'd feel silly."

"Somebody in your family died and you knew about it?" Teresita guessed.

"Someone I knew," Mrs. Loeb said. "I had a housekeeper, a woman named Amanda Wright. She'd been with me for nine years when she had to leave because of illness. This was back during the war—let's see, it would have been 1944 that it happened, because I was working downtown at the time. I was walking to the 'El' station near my home when I saw some collard greens in the window of a food shop."

"Collard greens?"

"Yep. Collard greens. And they made me think of Amanda, because she had always told me you could only get them on the South Side, and this was way up North. Then, as I was going up the stairs to the train platform, I was suddenly struck with the thought that Amanda was dead."

"Was she?"

162

"She died at almost that very instant," Mrs. Loeb related. "I didn't know it at the time, but when I got downtown my brother telephoned the office to tell me that he had just received word of Amanda's death."

"So, now you are a believer, are you not, Ruth?"

"I don't know. Maybe it was coincidence. But it was strange, I must admit."

The popular band Teresita played with, the Mahogany Five Plus One, disbanded early in 1977. Ron Somera, the leader, had moved north to Gurnee, about 40 miles from the city, and he found it too difficult to get into Chicago regularly for practice. His wife was on the evening shift at St. Therese Hospital in Waukegan, and he had to stay home and babysit.

The group was not out of business long, however. Dr. Abella formed another group. The new combo was 100 percent Filipino, with Jun Pascual on the drums, Joe Laguda playing bass, Nonoy Gangoso replacing Somera on the guitar, Pete Molino tooting the trumpet, and Teresita, of course, at the piano.

The new sextet had bookings even before it had a name, and was signed up to do a benefit performance at the Rizal Center in February. Teresita sold tickets at work and talked the concert up among her friends.

Their final practice session was Sunday evening, February 20th. It was bitter cold outside. It was his wife's night off, so Somera drove down from Gurnee to sit in, just for fun. He stayed around to talk with Teresita in her apartment after the others had left. It was the last talk they would ever have.

CHAPTER 17

THE FINAL HOURS

Monday, February 21, dawned cheerful and sunny. After the bitter cold of the night before, Teresita knew it would be a fine day. She sang aloud as she put on her white pantyhose, white dress, and white shoes and greeted the new work week. It was George Washington's birthday holiday for many in Chicago, but illness never takes a day off, and at any hospital it was business as usual.

Allan Showery joined her table in the cafeteria at lunchtime. "So, how'd the practice go last night?"

"Terrific," Teresita oozed. "We work well together and had a lot of fun. It's really the same group as before, with a couple of new faces. We already have a problem, but we'll work it out."

"What kind of a problem?" Showery asked, between gulps of meatloaf.

"Jun Pascual, our drummer. He's not sure how long he can stay with us. He's got other commitments so we might have to find another drummer."

"Man, I can beat them skins," Showery animated, flailing the air with his hands. "Why don't you give me a chance?"

"Buy a ticket to our concert," Teresita countered. "You can look us over, maybe even sit in for awhile. Then Dr. Abella can see if you're half as good as you think you are."

"Deal!" Showery said, slapping the palm of Teresita's hand with his. "I'm a little short right now, but set aside a ticket for me and I'll get you the bread. Baby, you can tell those Flip cats they got themselves a new drummer—a pro out of New Yawk."

Teresita laughed out loud.

"What's the matter, chick? You don't think I can do a flam-a-doodle? I taught Gene Krupa."

"It's paradiddle, Allan. But that's not what I'm laughing at. I was just thinking. We don't have a name yet, but if you come in it'll be the Mahogany Five Plus One, just like before."

"Plus one?" joshed Showery. "What are you talkin' about? I ain't Polish."

On the bus home that evening, Teresita promised to speak to Abella about Showery's interest in the group.

"Hey, you do that now," Showery insisted. "I'm going to tell the Old Lady I'm going to be a musician again. She'll like that. What you gonna do tonight?"

"Oh, practice the piano and read," Teresita said. "My TV isn't working again. Ron was over last night, but he couldn't make it do anything. I just had it worked on a month ago."

"I'll come by and take a look at it. I'm a television repairman, too, you know. Need help? Call Allan."

"No, that's all right, Allan," she said. "I'll call the shop on Saturday."

"You better let me take a look at it first," he insisted. "Maybe I can save you some money. Repair guys charge as much as doctors to make house calls."

When they parted at Clark and Diversey he said he'd be by in about an hour. He had to check in at home first and make sure everything was O.K.

At five o'clock he knocked at the apartment door and jauntily sang out "Repairman," when Teresita opened it a crack to see who was there. She had changed into a sweater and slacks. After inviting Showery in she handed him a can of beer while he checked over the TV.

"Hmmm. I can see right now what's wrong," he said, after removing the back of the set. "Circuit breaker's upside-down. I'm not gonna touch it right now, though, until I check over my wiring diagrams at home. I don't wanna make it worse."

Showery got Teresita's portable set out of the closet and hooked it up for her. "Leave the big set unplugged until I can check things out," he instructed. "Gotta go now. Yanka's waiting." He drained the beer and breezed out the door. Teresita closed it behind him and snapped the locks. Then she went into the kitchenette and began chopping up some lettuce and a tomato for a salad.

Down in Bloomington Professor Kliewer was working late, trying to catch up on mid-term paperwork. For some inexplicable reason the vision of Teresita flashed through his mind. "By the way," he said, turning to his secretary. "Did Teresita Basa's revised thesis on Tcherepnin ever arrive? It's been a couple of months now."

"We haven't received a thing," she said. "What made you bring that up now?"

"Damned if I know. Ghosts, maybe. Hah! Tcherepnin is big on ghosts, you know. Some of it might be rubbing off onto me through Teresita. Remind me to give Miss Basa a call when we get caught up, to see how her work is coming."

* * *

There is nothing more lonely than a cold winter night in February in Chicago. The holidays are over and there is little else to do but wait for spring.

An inky darkness had settled over the city, and anyone who didn't have a place to go was nestled warmly inside his or her nest. Teresita Basa was settled comfortably in hers. She switched on the stereo and put a record on the turntable.

She received two telephone calls that night—one from Dr. Abella, at 7:10 p.m., and the second from Ruth Loeb, shortly after eight o'clock. Both found her in high spirits, almost childlike in her ebullience.

Abella called to chat about ticket sales for the concert. "Just a minute, Doctor," she interrupted. "There's somebody at my door." Through the receiver he could hear her footsteps cross the room, and the sharp click of the latch as she admitted someone. There was a muffled conversation, and she returned to the phone. "Sorry to keep you waiting, Doctor. I have company. Would it be all right if I call you tomorrow?"

"Anybody I know?" chided Abella.

"I don't think so, but it might be somebody I can sell a ticket to."

"O.K. I wouldn't want to interfere with anything like that," he said. "Do your best, and I'll talk to you later."

They had conversed in a Philippine dialect, and Teresita did not mention the identity of her caller, or even whether it was a male or female. During Mrs. Loeb's call a short time later, Teresita also mentioned that she had company, and giggled mysteriously when her friend asked who it was.

"I'm not interrupting anything, am I?" Mrs. Loeb teased, knowing Teresita's aversion to ever becoming "involved" again.

"Oh, no," Teresita answered cheerfully. "I'll tell you all about it when we have lunch tomorrow."

Teresita hung up the phone, smiled, and turned to face her guest.

Down the hall, in apartment 15G, Mario and Katherine Knazze had just finished dinner and were settling down to watch television. In 16B, directly above the Basa apartment, James Clomey was easing himself into a chair for an evening of relaxation.

At precisely the same moment their nostrils detected the telltale aroma of smoke, and they made for the exits.

CHAPTER 18

TERESITA RETURNS

During the month of July, some five months after Teresita's violent death, strange things began to occur in the department where she had once worked at Edgewater Hospital. They centered around another Filipina, Remebios Chua, a 39-year-old inhalation therapist who worked the midnight shift.

Mrs. Chua had known Teresita only vaguely, having met her during an orientation session two years before. Occasionally they would pass one another, as Teresita was arriving for work and she was preparing to go home, and they would nod. Such chance meetings were generally in the basement locker room where respiratory workers hung their coats.

Because the two women had enjoyed only a nodding acquaintanceship, Mrs. Chua's fellow workers thought it more than a little strange when she began carrying on as though she were Teresita herself. Her unusual behavior first became a matter of note midway through the shift on the night of July 11, when Mrs. Chua went down to the locker room for a break.

She was sitting quietly, alone, when she suddenly looked up in fright, bolted from the chair, and literally ran from the room while her co-workers gawked in amazement. Unable to carry out her duties for the remainder of her shift, she signed out sick and returned to her home in Evanston where her physician husband, Dr. José Chua, was waiting.

She did not tell him, or anyone else, what had happened at the hospital because she could not understand it herself. How could she, an educated woman, explain something like this:

As Mrs. Chua looked up idly from her chair in the rest room she found herself face-to-face with Teresita Basa! The dead woman's apparition stood before her, silent and unmoving, and remained until she got up from the chair and ran.

The following night Mrs. Chua, a slight woman with jet black hair combed tightly back, appeared at work as though nothing had happened. She was cheerful, her bright eyes glistening, and her small red mouth giving her a quality of sensuousness. More talkative than usual as she worked, she chattered about the piano, about classical music, partying— all the things Teresita had talked about when she was alive.

Her co-workers noticed that she seemed to affect Teresita's voice and mannerisms. At lunch time in the cafeteria— though she had never worked the same shift as Teresita—she inexplicably marched straight to Teresita's favorite table and sat at Teresita's regular spot. As she picked at her lunch she began singing softly to herself, as Teresita had always done.

Several employees reported Mrs. Chua's uncharacteristic behavior to her supervisor, complaining, "She's making us uncomfortable." Some even said they were frightened. As her apparent imitation of Teresita Basa continued through the week, co-workers began to question her actions. "What do you mean?" Mrs. Chua asked, puzzled. "I know nothing of what you say. How can you ask such things of me?"

On Saturday afternoon, July 16, which was her day off, Mrs. Chua showed up at Edgewater accompanied by her husband. She walked into the respiratory department, accosted her immediate supervisor, Ted Ellis, and erupted in anger.

"What are you doing here today?" the astonished Ellis asked when he could get a word in. Mrs. Chua exploded into a rage, ranting about her job, complaining about working conditions, and denouncing the people with whom she worked. It was a Remebios Chua none of them had ever seen before. "Look, Mrs. Chua," Ellis tried to reason. "Why don't you go home and take it easy? Give yourself a few days off. This Basa thing has been getting to you, and some of the people here think you could use a rest. Please. Just go home and we'll forget this ever happened."

But Mrs. Chua persisted in her unorthodox behavior until the exasperated Ellis told her, "You are being discharged for gross insubordination. I'm really sorry. Come in Monday and pick up your formal notification."

On the way home the Chuas talked, relieved that at least one problem seemed to be over. Her co-workers had accused Mrs. Chua of acting like Teresita, whom she didn't even know, and she no longer cared to associate with them. Well educated and a registered pharmacist in the Philippines, she would have no trouble getting other employment. The only reason she had taken the hospital job was that she was not yet licensed to practice pharmacy in Illinois.

They would also be leaving their comfortable home in Evanston. They were purchasing a much more luxurious home in neighboring Skokie, and hoped to be in their new quarters by the end of the month. Only three years out of Luzon, the Chuas were doing quite well for themselves.

That evening, however, something happened that would forever cast a pall over the good life they had strived so hard to achieve in their new country. It was a 30-minute nightmare that will be ingrained on Dr. Chua's medical mind until the day he dies.

It had been a trying day, and they were relaxing in their living room after dinner.

Dr. Chua wore a bright blue print shirt, open at the neck, and comfortable slacks. He looked much younger than his 40 years, with a full head of black hair, and rimless eye-glasses curved in dashing aviator style around the side of his face. Mrs. Chua, attractive but on the heavy side for someone of her short stature, had on a loose fitting house dress.

Without explanation, she arose from her chair, a strange expression on her face, and quietly left the room. When she failed to return, Chua went looking for her. The perplexed physician found his wife lying across the bed, eyes wide open, staring at the ceiling.

Chua felt an eerie chill over his entire body as he asked matter-of-factly, "Are you feeling all right, dear?"

Mrs. Chua did not respond. Now standing at the side of the bed, the doctor quickly surmised that his motionless wife was experiencing a trauma of some kind. Bending over so he could look directly into her eyes, he repeated, "What seems to be the matter, Reme? What is it?"

Remebios Chua's lips slowly parted, and she responded in a sing-song voice that definitely was not her own. "Mama! Mama! Are you there, Mama?" The doctor stiffened. His wife never referred to her own mother, who lived with them, as "mama," but called her by her given name, Nananda. His heart quickened and his hands felt clammy as he heard the strange plea from his wife's lips.

"Wha . . . what is this?" Chua demanded softly. "Remebios. Speak to me." He sat on the edge of the bed and gently shook her by the shoulders with both hands. In an attempt to determine whether she was coherent he asked her, "What is your name?"

"Ako 'y Teresita Basa!" came the unexpected response.

"What the devil are you talking about, Remebios?" Chua challenged. "Come on now. Snap out of it! What's the matter here?"

"Ako 'y Teresita Basa." I am Teresita Basa.

Remebios Chua was speaking in Tagalog. The Chuas were from Northern Luzon and often conversed in their provincial dialect. Both were also familiar with the national language of the Philippines, but Mrs. Chua was mouthing the words with a strange Spanish accent which the doctor had never heard before.

"I do not know any Teresita Basa," he asserted.

"I am Teresita Basa," she insisted, still rambling in Tagalog.

Chua, visibly taken aback, began to perspire. His own wife was staring directly at him, insisting she was someone else, in a voice and dialect he had never heard her use in all their years together. He looked around the room as if to make sure of his surroundings. On the wall over their bed was the polished mahogany crucifix he and Remebios had brought with them from their home in the Islands. On the dresser was their wedding picture. Next to it was Mrs. Chua's jewel box, her nail polish and cosmetics. Everything in the familiar room was exactly as it had always been—except that there was an utter stranger on their bed!

"Now, just what the hell is this all about?" he demanded. "What is the purpose of this kind of behavior? Please, darling, let's not joke. O.K.?"

"Doctor Chua, I would like to ask your help." Odd. She addressed her husband by his professional title, rather than his name, José.

"What kind of help?" he asked, trying to collect his thoughts.

"To stop the person who killed me."

"The person who killed you? What is this, Reme? Nobody has killed you."

But the voice persisted. "Ako 'y Teresita Basa. I want to give you information about my killer."

"All right. What about your, uh, killer?" he pressed, totally befuddled.

"You must help me, doctor," she pleaded.

"You're upset, my dear. You've had a bad week at the hospital. The excitement this afternoon. It's been a little too much for you. Just lie there and relax. I'll get something for you."

Chua got to his feet and started toward the bathroom medicine cabinet.

"Call the police," the woman on the bed directed, feebly lifting one arm and motioning toward the phone. "Please doctor. Call the police and tell them who killed me. I cannot rest until they know."

"I don't know who killed you," the doctor answered nervously, suddenly realizing that he was going along with the game. "I can't call the police. Come on, Remebios. Snap out of it."

"I will tell you exactly what to say," she directed.

Dr. Chua stared in consternation at his prostrate wife. He could not fathom that this was really happening. She returned his stare, and her full lips parted anew.

"José? What am I doing in bed? How in the world did I get here?"

"Don't you know?" he asked, placing his hand on her forehead.

"Oh, José. Please get me a drink of water. My throat is so dry. I'm so thirsty."

Chua went to the tap and filled a glass of water. She sat up and gulped it down. Then she returned with him to the living room and sat down in her favorite chair, as though nothing had transpired.

"Do you remember anything about what just happened?" he asked, after a few moments had passed.

"I don't know what you mean," she answered. "Oh, I'm so confused. I must have had a dizzy spell. I don't even remember getting up."

Dr. Chua stared directly at his wife. "What about Teresita Basa?"

"Teresita Basa?" she said in a surprised tone. "My goodness. That's the woman from the hospital who was murdered. Don't you remember? It was on television."

"You mentioned the name—then you . . . fainted," he explained.

"I couldn't have, José. I must have been dreaming."

At about eleven o'clock that evening the phone rang and the doctor answered it. A male voice asked, "Is Remebios there?" He handed her the phone and watched curiously. She answered "Hello" in English. That was the only word she spoke. She listened briefly and hung up, a puzzled look on her face.

"What was that all about?"

"I really don't know," she gasped. "He threatened me. He said he was going to get me next."

"Who?" Chua demanded, rising from his chair. "Who would be calling here at this hour?"

"I don't know who it was," she repeated. "It sounded like somebody from work."

* * *

On Monday afternoon Dr. Chua drove his wife back to Edgewater to pick up her belongings. They talked briefly with Mrs. Kuehn, who advised Mrs. Chua her dismissal was permanent. "You're an outstanding inhalation therapist, and we all thought very highly of your work," she added. "It's so unfortunate that something like this had to happen."

"Oh, don't be sorry, Mrs. Kuehn," Mrs. Chua told her. "Actually I am relieved. I'm scared of some of the people I work with here."

That evening in their living room Mrs. Chua was talking on the phone to a Filipino real estate agent who was helping with the sale of their home. Abruptly she turned and handed the instrument to her husband.

"Teresita wants to come back," she uttered. Then she walked away. The startled Chua, left standing with the phone in his hand, told the realtor he would call him later and went looking for his wife. He found her in the bedroom, lying across the bed, exactly as she had been two nights before.

"Remebios," he said, sitting beside her. "What is happening to you? To us?"

"Ako 'y Teresita Basa," she replied in Tagalog, again speaking the national language with a Spanish accent. The conversation that followed was much the same as Saturday night, except that while the voice had earlier *asked* the doctor to notify police, it was now *imploring*.

"You must help me, doctor. You must!"

Chua, totally rattled, tried to reason with the woman on the bed. At this juncture, however, he was not sure himself whether he was speaking to his wife or to a stranger who had taken over her body. The doctor was not yet licensed to practice in Illinois, and had been working as a surgical assistant at Franklin Boulevard Community Hospital, while preparing to take the state examination. For no particular reason he blurted out in frustration, "These seizures of yours are interrupting my studies!"

"If you help me, doctor, I will help you pass the examination for your medical license," the woman on the bed promised.

"How can I help you?" he demanded in exasperation. "What in the world do you expect me to do?"

"You must go to the police," she insisted.

Chua, a highly educated man who did not believe in the supernatural, knew this would be out of the question. He envisioned himself being laughed out of the profession. "Look, I just can't go to the police. They'll think I'm crazy. When you go to the police, you have to have proof. Don't you realize that?"

"I will give you that proof," she said, grasping his hand. It was "her" first physical contact with the doctor. "I will tell you who killed me, and I will give you the proof you require. Doctor, there is nothing to be afraid of."

After a quarter of an hour Mrs. Chua awoke abruptly from her trance and called her husband by name. She pleaded for water, as before. And once more she professed to have no inkling of what had just transpired. "Perhaps I am just tired," she suggested.

The following afternoon, at about 3:30, Remebios Chua was possessed by the spirit of Teresita Basa for the third and final time. Dr. Chua had just come from the hospital and was still wearing his green surgical slip-on. He found his wife lying on the bed, sobbing into the pillow.

"Mama. Mama. Please help me. Oh, please Mama. Please, Mama. Help me. Help me . . ."

Chua, tears welling in his own eyes, went to his wife's side and took her hand in his. Gently he spoke in Tagalog. "Tell me, Teresita. Tell me everything, and I will do what I can to help you."

* * *

There were two significant deaths that month—one in Chicago by gunfire, and one in the Philippines by a broken heart.

Former Austin Police District commander Mark Thanasouras, 49, an ex-convict, was cut down gangland style by an assassin's shotgun. That same day, in Dumaguete City, on the island of Negros in the Sulu Sea, Socorro Martinez Basa, after five months of grieving for her murdered daughter, breathed her last. She was buried in the Santa Catalina Parish Cemetery alongside her husband, Judge Pedro Cruz Basa, and their only child, Teresita. The little family was now together for all eternity.

* * *

While Dr. Chua pondered how best to cope with his wife's erratic behavior and the information "Teresita Basa" had entrusted to him, police were up to their necks in the murder of Thanasouras, a once-good cop turned rotten.

Thanasouras had risen from patrolman to captain in just six years, and was district commander by the time he was 37. Behind the super-cop facade, however, he was directing shakedowns of bookies and tavern owners. He ended up in the federal penitentiary but got his sentence reduced by testifying against fellow cops who had been in on the scam. He'd been working as a bartender when two shotgun blasts ripped him apart as he stood on a North Side street corner. The trouble with his killing was that police had too many suspects. Between the scores of crooks he had sent to jail, the kinky cops he betrayed, and the underworld characters he ran with, any one of a hundred people had ample reason to gun him down. Virtually every detective in the area had been assigned to the case.

It was in the midst of all this that Dr. Chua and his bewildered wife decided that they would "come forward." The doctor had discussed the incidents at home in vague terms with his superiors at the hospital, seeking guidance, but all he got was shrugged shoulders. "It's a matter for the police," they told him.

And so it was that Remebios Chua, unable to sleep, telephoned Rodolfo Sanchez, the Filipino consul general, at 6:30 one morning and poured out her bizarre story. "You know about the murder of Teresita Basa, don't you?" she asked.

"Of course. She was a guest in my home at Christmas. What a terrible, terrible thing to happen."

"Teresita Basa has entered my body and told my husband who killed her," she blurted out.

The woman on the phone was obviously frightened and confused, Sanchez reckoned. She pleaded with him for police protection. Still drowsy at that early hour, and recalling the faith healing cults in his native country who believed they were guided by spirits, Sanchez patiently asked Mrs. Chua to repeat what she had just told him. After hearing her out for a second time, and determining that he was obviously dealing with a woman of culture, he promised to make some inquiries.

Immediately upon arriving at his downtown office Sanchez put in a call to Felipe Dayoc, a Filipino who worked at police headquarters. He outlined the story Mrs. Chua had related. Dayoc then interviewed Mrs. Chua by phone. Satisfied that he was not dealing with a crank or a crackpot, he advised her to go to the authorities.

Meanwhile Dayoc initiated an investigation of his own. He discovered that three other Filipinos, all working at Edgewater Hospital, had experienced apparitions of one kind or another involving Teresita Basa, all imploring them to help. None of the three was willing to go public, for fear of ridicule, and all begged him to keep their conversations confidential.

The Chuas, however, could not contain the powerful force that had taken over their lives. They took the final step, but in a most oblique fashion. Dr. Chua telephoned Evanston police to complain that his wife had received a threatening phone call. Detective Floyd McKinney was assigned to check it out.

He drove to their home on Oakton Avenue where Mrs. Chua, visibly upset, told him she had received an intimidating call from a male whom she believed was a fellow employee at Edgewater Hospital.

"Well, who do you think it was who called you?" McKinney asked, notebook in hand.

"I believe it was Allan Showery," she said. "I'm terribly afraid of him."

"You're pretty sure, then, that the caller was this Showery person?"

"I do believe it was him," she answered.

"We don't want to blame anybody," Dr. Chua interrupted. "We are just reporting that my wife received a threatening call. She is frightened. We will be moving away soon, but we wondered if it would be possible to obtain some police protection in the meantime."

McKinney explained that this was not possible. Providing protection for everyone who received anonymous phone calls was simply out of the question. He did promise, however, to investigate. Back at Evanston police headquarters McKinney reported the incident to Lieutenant Kip MacMillan.

"Pass it on to Chicago and see if they're interested," MacMillan suggested. "Based on what those people told you, if there was such a call, that's probably where it came from."

CHAPTER 19

![black bar]

FELIPE DAYOC

Felipe Dayoc had just two more hours to work on that muggy August afternoon when the telephone jangled in his fourth floor office in Chicago's central police headquarters building at Eleventh and State Streets. Dayoc had spent six years as a detective on the Manila police force after graduating from college in the Philippines. He had been a good cop. His slight Oriental build, however, had precluded him from meeting the rigid physical requirements of the Chicago police department when he came to the States in 1966, so he did the next best thing. He took a job as a civilian employee in R & D, the Research and Development unit. That way he was able to keep his fingers in police work, and whenever the detectives down the hall had a good case they would come in and kick it around with him.

When Dayoc picked up the phone at two o'clock that afternoon, the first thing he heard was a scream: "Daddy!"

"Arvi? Is that you? What's the matter?"

"I don't know," the frightened voice of Dayoc's 18-year-old daughter echoed through the phone. "I don't know. The drapes—they're going back and forth!"

"You called me at work to tell me the damned drapes are going back and forth?" he exploded.

"Something strange is happening, Daddy," she cried. "The draw-sheers by the living room window are opening and closing, but no one's pulling the cord! I'm all alone and I'm scared."

The girl's voice broke into a sob. Dayoc tried to picture his daughter on the other end of the line. Arvella was a beautiful child, dark-haired and intelligent. Not a teen-aged scatterbrain or a pot smoker who might be seeing things. She had graduated near the top of her high school class, and she and her boyfriend, Andy, were to be married in the fall. If Arvi said the drapes were moving back and forth, the drapes were moving back and forth!

"O.K. Calm down a little, and explain this thing to me. How are the drapes going back and forth?"

"I'm telling you, Daddy," she shouted hysterically. "The drapes are opening and closing real fast. I was talking to Andy on the phone, about that murdered woman you told me about, you know? We were kidding about it, and the drapes just started to open and close, open and close. Daddy, I'm frightened. What am I going to do?"

"First you get hold of yourself," Dayoc asserted. "I'll be right home. As soon as I hang up, you run and get Uncle Pedro downstairs to come up and check things out. Do you understand?"

"I can't get out, Daddy! There's a green thing! Like a cloud. A green wall! It's blocking the door."

"A green wall? What the hell . . ."

"I don't know what it is, Daddy. It's green. It's just hanging there. Oh, God . . ."

"Now listen to me, Arvi," Dayoc instructed. "You hang up so I can call Uncle. I'll tell him to get upstairs right away. You stay put and keep your eyes closed. Do you hear me?"

"Yes, Daddy."

"Keep . . . your . . . eyes . . . closed! When you hear Uncle you go to the door and let him in. Eyes shut!"

"Yes, Daddy," she sobbed, barely able to get the words out.

"Do it," Dayoc said. "Now!"

He hung up the phone, picked it up again, and punched out his wife's brother's number on the touch-tone.

The girl, nearly paralyzed with fright, cowered on the couch in the corner of the room until she heard her relative's footsteps bounding up the stairs. Keeping her eyes clamped shut, she held her arms straight out as she walked, heart pounding, into the green mist. She felt nothing, only terror. When her outstretched hands felt the door she grabbed the knob, but she could not open it. The knob turned, but the door was stuck fast.

Grunting in panic she screamed, "Push, Uncle, Push!" The bewildered uncle hit the panel with his shoulder and the door burst inward.

"What the hell is it, Arvi?" he asked, surveying the room. "Your dad said you were having trouble."

"Look!" she screamed hysterically. "Don't you see it?"

"See what, girl? I don't see a damned thing."

Arvi opened her eyes and turned toward the window. The sheers were open and the bright afternoon sunlight streamed in. There was no green cloud. The girl told her uncle what had happened. He went to the side of the window and pulled the cord to close the drapes. Then he opened them. He looked behind both drapes. He looked at his niece, shrugged his shoulders, and muttered, "Kids." Shaking his head, he trudged back down the stairs.

That evening, over the dinner table, Dayoc reviewed with his wife, Maria, and their daughter what had happened.

Four days earlier he had received a phone call from the Honorable Rodolfo Sanchez. The consul general told him he'd gotten an early morning call from a Mrs. Chua, the wife of a Filipino physician in Chicago. Mrs. Chua, the diplomat continued, claimed that her body had been possessed by one Teresita Basa, a murder victim. She claimed she had gone into a trance, and the dead woman's voice came forth from her mouth, pleading for help, and naming the man who had taken her life. The consul general asked Dayoc how he thought the matter should be handled.

The one-time Manila detective vaguely recalled the Basa homicide. It had caused a stir in the Filipino community because there suddenly seemed to be an ongoing, chilling trend of murders or fatal accidents involving Filipinos in Chicago.

Prior to Teresita's slaying, four other Filipinos—one for each preceding month—had died violently. One man went insane and shot his wife. Another was found strangled in his car. The third died in a tragic elevated train wreck in the Loop. And then there was the woman who was decapitated, and her toes chopped off and sent through the mail.

The Basa slaying, alone, remained unsolved. There had been no progress in the investigation for months, and the case had been all but forgotten. Dayoc understood the diplomat's concern. "I'll take care of it from here," he assured him.

An educated man and a trained police investigator, Dayoc did not believe in ghosts or the supernatural. Yet he knew from personal experience that there were some things that could not be explained. Five years earlier his younger brother, José, died of a cerebral hemorrhage in Chicago at the age of 32. Before Dayoc could cable the shocking news to the rest of the family back in Cabanatuan on the island of Luzon, they already knew of José's death.

The dead man's apparition, wearing a distinctive tan coat, appeared before their younger brother Carlos, 14, in the boy's bedroom. José just stood before the petrified youth without saying a word. The family recognized the sign. It had happened to others. José was dead.

Recalling the incident, Dayoc picked up the phone and dialed the Evanston number Sanchez had given him for the Chuas. After identifying himself, he listened as Remebios nervously repeated her story. "Quit monkeying around and call the police," Dayoc told her. "You live in Evanston. Tell your local police just what happened to you, and if they think it warrants it, they'll follow through."

That night, around the supper table, Dayoc had told his wife and daughter of the incident. The thought of a dead woman's voice naming her killer amused Arvi, who couldn't wait to spill the story to her boyfriend. Now, four days later, a thoroughly shaken teen-ager was telling her father how she and Andy were "joking" about the Basa incident when the drapes began to move, followed by the green mist that blocked the door.

"Look," Dayoc reasoned. "This was just one of those things. It happened, so now let's forget it. It'll never happen again, I'm sure, but I want a promise from both of you. I don't want anyone in this house to ever mention the name of Teresita Basa again."

Dayoc looked across the table at his wife, and then at Arvi. There was a long silence.

Although Dayoc did not know it at the time, Dr. and Mrs. Chua had decided to heed his advice. They had already put in their mysterious call to Evanston police. Fearing ridicule if they told the whole truth, however, they merely reported that Mrs. Chua had received a threatening call from a man she thought sounded like Allan Showery.

CHAPTER 20

███████████████████████████

TERESITA NAMES HER KILLER

The day the drapes mysteriously flung themselves open and shut amid the green fog in Felipe Dayoc's North Side home was the day Chicago police got back into the Basa homicide case.

Lee Epplen had a day off coming, and Stachula was working without a partner on that insufferably hot August afternoon. Sergeant Edward Flynn walked over and casually asked, "What's new on the Basa investigation?"

"Not a damned thing," Stachula said, pulling his wet shirt away from his armpits. "The last entry was April 27, I think. Nothing shaking since then. Every damn lead we had just petered out, and now everybody's out chasing down dead ends in the Thanasouras hit."

"Yeah, well, does the name Allan Showery ring a bell of any kind?" Flynn asked.

"Can't say that it does," Stachula answered. "Is it supposed to?"

"The guy works at Edgewater Hospital in the respiratory department. Same place the Basa woman worked, right? Black dude who calls himself 'Doc'."

"Don't know him."

"Well, there's a Filipino woman up in Evanston, used to work there, too. Now she claims this mope's been threatening her with annoying phone calls."

"Where does this come from?" Stachula asked, arching his eyebrows.

"Evanston P.D. They took a complaint from some people up there and passed it on to us as a courtesy. They're not doing any more with it. Why don't you check it out, just for the hell of it?"

"You mean with half the frickin' cops in town working on the murder of an ex-police commander you're actually asking me to chase up to Evanston to check out a nut phone call?"

"Why not? Might be something."

"Well, I'm not exactly burning up with enthusiasm, but I'd definitely be interested in anything to do with Edgewater Hospital. You say these people are Filipinos?"

"It's a Dr. José Chua and his wife, 2333 Oakton Avenue," Flynn said.

"O.K. I'll run it down and let you know," said Stachula. "Mabuhay!"

"What the hell's that?"

"Just some education I picked up on this case. I learn something new on every one. It means 'long life'."

Stachula checked the North Suburban phone directory and punched out the number for Dr. José Chua on the touch-tone. The operator's voice broke in to report that the number was no longer in service. The detective then called Evanston police, and learned that the Chuas had just put their home on the market and moved away. By checking the suburban criss-cross directory he obtained the telephone of the Chuas' neighbors on Oakton, who confirmed that there was a "For Sale" sign in the front yard.

"Can you read me the name of the real estate firm on the sign?" Stachula asked.

Once he had the name, the detective telephoned the Filipino realtor who was handling the transaction, and obtained the Chuas' new address in Skokie. He tried to get a phone listing from Information, but was told that service had not yet been installed.

The Chuas' move had indeed been fast. Frightened beyond comprehension, they had moved out of their old house without finding a buyer. Stachula wasted no further time. He signed out an unmarked Plymouth and drove out the Kennedy Expressway to Skokie.

It was Friday, the fifth of August, and still light outside when the detective's car pulled up in front of the ranch-style home. It was a rambling brick structure with attached garage on a corner lot. A dark-haired Filipino in surgical greens, looking as though he had just stepped out of the operating room, answered Stachula's knock. He stood in the doorway apprehensively, his hand on the knob ready to swing it shut if necessary, waiting for the visitor to state his business.

Stachula flipped open his wallet and flashed his Chicago police star, No. 13062, as he introduced himself. Dr. Chua swung the door open, backed away, and said, "Come in. Please."

"Nice home you have here," Stachula remarked, as Chua led him across the gold-colored carpeting and motioned him into a gold velour chair next to the piano. Stachula noted the drapes were also gold in color. A truly regal setting. "Just move in?"

"Less than a week ago. The place set us back $90,000," the doctor began proudly.

"Ten years from now, the way people are moving into the suburbs, it'll be worth twice that much," Stachula opined.

Chua took a position on a sectional sofa directly across from the detective. He did not settle back comfortably, however, but rested on the edge of the cushion, clasping his hands together over his knees.

Stachula leaned back into the gold velour, opened a folder on his lap, and asked the doctor a few routine questions —name, age, address.

At that point Mrs. Chua entered the room. The doctor introduced her to the detective, and she took a matching gold chair on Stachula's right. He smiled and complimented her on the new home.

"Oh, thank you," she beamed. "One of the reasons we left our home in Evanston was because we had been receiving annoying phone calls. I had become very frightened."

"I understand you work at Edgewater Hospital. Is that right?"

"I did, but I am no longer employed," she told Stachula. "I was an inhalation therapist."

"I see. Exactly what is an inhalation therapist, if you don't mind my asking?" He was still trying to put his nervous subjects more at ease.

"Well, for example, if a person has pneumonia and has to be given oxygen and medication at the same time," Mrs. Chua explained.

Stachula nodded, and made a notation on his pad. "What about these phone calls you received?" The thought ran through his mind, as it had at the station, that here was an experienced homicide investigator, sitting in a private home in a suburb where he had no jurisdiction, asking foolish questions about crank phone calls. He suddenly felt ridiculously self-conscious.

"We think they were made by Allan Showery," Mrs. Chua alleged.

"Why do you think that?"

"Well, my husband picked me up at the hospital one day and while we were there we heard Allan talking to one of the other employees. My husband agrees that the voice on the phone sounded like his."

"This Showery. What does he do at Edgewater?"

"He's an orderly," Mrs. Chua responded. "He likes to pretend he's a doctor. He even gets mail addressed to Dr. Showery."

"Did you also know Teresita Basa, Mrs. Chua?"

Stachula noticed a quick movement in the doctor's eyes when he mentioned the dead woman's name, but no reaction from his wife.

"I went to work at the hospital in 1975, and met her during orientation week, but that was all. We did not work the same hours," Mrs. Chua explained.

"You mentioned that you're no longer employed. Were you working at the hospital during the, ah, incident involving Miss Basa? I'm curious, because I wonder why I hadn't talked to you before."

"I was a patient at St. Francis Hospital in Evanston at the time," Mrs. Chua responded. "We first became aware of the murder while watching the news on TV."

"I see. Now, getting back to Allan Showery. Doctor, you're sitting all hunched over on the edge of your seat there, rubbing your hands like a Boy Scout trying to start a fire. What's bothering you? Is there something more you want to tell me?"

Dr. Chua looked embarrassed and uncomfortable at the same time. "We are reluctant to become involved," he said. "We would not want to make any unjust accusations. I believe you already talked to the Evanston police, or you would not be here."

"All the Evanston P.D. did was notify us that you possess certain information, but they didn't go into detail," Stachula bluffed. "That's why I'm here. Now relax, doctor. Every time I mention Allan Showery you tie yourself into a knot. You're not the first person who's ever got an annoying phone call."

Dr. Chua leaned forward nervously and stared at his wife for the better part of a minute without saying a word. The only sound was the hum of the air conditioner, and a car passing on the street outside. Stachula waited. He felt the doctor was fighting inwardly with himself, and he didn't want to interrupt his train of thought. Chua slowly turned his eyes on him and said earnestly, "Tell me, Mr. Detective. Do you believe in the occult, or in exorcism?"

It was Stachula's turn to become uncomfortable. He drew a deep breath as Chua waited for his reply—one that the detective knew might be crucial to continuing the conversation. "As a policeman I have experienced many strange things, doctor. Not too much surprises me any more, I can assure you."

A cop learns to give and take with his brain as well as his body. The job demands it, and Stachula had met the test time and again—on the street, in the hostile housing projects, bucket-of-blood saloons, and even in jail. Wherever you have to go to find people with answers to get them to talk. A quick retort often helps, but this time, in the quiet dignity of the physician's suburban home, Stachula was unprepared for his adversary's sudden verbal jab. "A police officer must always keep an open mind," he added.

The answer was the Police Academy's standard procedure in a situation of uncertainty, and Stachula offered it with his best poker face.

Dr. Chua smiled. "Being a physician I, too, have encountered many strange things." His voice was dead earnest. "Over the years I have learned that one must, uh, accept some things; things we in the medical profession cannot, uh, explain." Running a hand through his thick dark hair, he pushed on. "What I am going to tell you now is bizarre. So different, so strange, that you will understand why I have kept silent until now. Officer Stachula, I did not have the nerve . . ."

Chua's eyes were riveted on the detective's face. Stachula felt himself redden but returned the stare, eye to eye, as he nodded. "I understand. I have a feeling that whatever it is you're going to tell me will be very important to both of us."

"All things have a beginning," Chua said slowly. "I will start there. I never knew Teresita Basa, and I knew very little about her, except what was in the papers after her death."

The doctor paused again, as if going over his next sentence in his mind. "By the way, I understand the police are no longer working on the case."

The unexpected statement of fact nearly jolted Stachula from his seat. The Filipino was telling him something that only a tight circle of police were privy to. He made up his mind then and there that Dr. Chua was no individual to play games with. He would level with him, attempt to gain his confidence. "That's true, doctor. There've been very few leads. But I want you to understand that a homicide investigation is never closed. We never give up, believe me."

"What was the date of the last report?"

"April 27," Stachula said, unflinching. "There has been very little evidence to follow up on since then."

"I see," mused Chua. "Well, what I have to tell you pertains to this case. But please understand that I cannot vouch for the accuracy of this information."

"Go on, doctor," Stachula said, continuing his eye contact.

"It involves Allan Showery, and I hope I am not involving him unjustly. That is one of the considerations I had in not contacting the police in the beginning. As I told you, I did not know Teresita Basa, nor do I know Mr. Showery, for that matter. I have nothing on which to base this information except what the victim told me, and what happened to my wife."

"Come again? I'm not sure I got your last remark, doctor," Stachula interjected.

"You will, when I explain. By the way, I have not told my wife all of this, either, because I wanted to protect her. This will be the first time she has heard the details." Remebios Chua, perfectly relaxed, leaned slightly forward in her gold chair.

"Exactly what did happen to your wife?" Stachula asked, as if she were not there.

"She would be doing something around the house," Chua began. "Suddenly she would lose contact with reality, and later remember nothing except waking up and being very thirsty." Chua looked at the detective, anticipating comment. Getting none, he continued. "The first time this happened, I found her lying on the bed. Her eyes were open, and she appeared responsive, so I asked what was wrong. I should explain here that most Filipinos speak at least two languages —our native, or regional tongue, and Tagalog, the national language, which is used in traveling to other islands or provinces. It would be as if you spoke a language called Illinois here at home, and your neighbors to the north spoke Wisconsin. But for purposes of communication, you both also spoke English."

"I understand," Stachula said politely. "But I don't see what that has to do with our conversation at the moment."

"Ah, it has great bearing," Chua emphasized. "You see, when I spoke to Remebios as she lay on the bed, she did not answer me in the familiar dialect we use with one-another. She responded in Tagalog, as though she were a stranger from another island. Moreover, she had a Spanish accent which I had never heard her use before. I tried to determine if she was coherent by asking her to state her name, and she said, 'I am Teresita Basa.'"

The doctor paused. Stachula felt a jolt of adrenaline. He had not expected this. His left eyelid began to flutter as he tried not to show his self-consciousness. He quickly looked around the room to assure himself of his surroundings. In all his years as a homicide investigator he had experienced the worst in housing projects and raunchy saloons in tracking down killers. But here he was on unfamiliar ground, wearing a business suit and sitting in an affluent suburban home, talking to two sophisticated, professional people. "I can't believe this," he told himself. "But there's sincerity here. After all these years, at least I can recognize sincerity."

He jotted some quick notes on his pad and looked at the doctor, signaling him to continue.

"She insisted that I help her," Chua said.

"She?"

"Teresita Basa!" The doctor then recounted in detail the three "visits" his comatose wife had received from the "voice" of the dead Filipina. Stachula took copious notes as Chua recited the narrative of the voice from beyond the grave, and how it had pleaded with him to help bring her killer to justice. "I discovered during the first two visits that if I disagreed with the voice, it would become stronger and more insistent, but if I went along with it, it would eventually weaken and leave my wife," he said. "With that in mind, I decided to cooperate fully during the third visit."

"When was the third visit?" Stachula asked, breaking in to give himself time to catch up on his notes.

"That would have been a little over two weeks ago, on the Tuesday after Remebios lost her job."

"Tuesday the nineteenth? Does that sound right?"

"Yes. The visit came during the afternoon. I came home and found her in the bedroom. The voice was calling, 'Mama. Mama. Help me!' I went to Remebios and sat beside her on the bed and told her I would help."

"Please go on," Stachula encouraged. He noted that Mrs. Chua appeared to be as fascinated by her husband's narration as he was.

"Well, she said her name was Teresita Basa, as I told you, and she asked me to call the police and give them the name of the person who killed her." The doctor cupped his hands in his lap nervously and leaned forward, staring intently into Stachula's eyes. "I asked Teresita Basa, 'Who killed you?' And, much to my surprise, she answered, 'Allan Showery.'"

"She told you Allan Showery killed her?"

"Exactly," replied Chua. "Then she became very emotional. I did my best to try to calm her, but she became more insistent. She kept repeating his name over and over, saying, 'He killed me. He killed me. He killed me.' Then I told her I could not go to the police with information like that. I said you would need evidence to support what she said. Then she explained to me that Allan Showery had taken her jewelry."

"Her jewelry? I can tell you right now that there's no record of any jewelry having been taken."

"I am aware of that," Chua said knowingly. "The voice told me that. She said the jewelry would be the evidence you needed." Stachula was scribbling so fast he could barely read his own notes. He didn't know what to make of Chua's insane story, but he damn well knew that he was suddenly neck-deep in more than a routine crank phone call.

"What were your own feelings while this was going on, doctor?"

"I was convinced that I was talking to Teresita Basa," Chua admitted. "I began to ask her exactly what happened that night. She said she was alone in her apartment when Allan Showery arrived. I asked the voice, 'Why did you let him in?' She answered, 'He was my friend.' She said she had no reason to be fearful of him. I asked the voice what happened next. She said Allan Showery rendered her unconscious and stabbed her."

Stachula was utterly enthralled. He could see the murder unfolding in his mind, yet he could not accept the circumstances "This is too far out," he thought to himself. The doctor was staring at him, waiting for a reaction. He decided to play his ace with a control question—one that would tell him fast whether he was being jerked around.

Knowing that the pathologist had established that Teresita was a virgin—information that had never been made public—he asked casually, "And then, did this voice indicate to you that her killer raped her?"

"Oh, no. She did not," Chua said, not flinching. "She only said she had been stabbed."

"Tell me, doctor," Stachula said, trying to control his own excitement. "Have you ever heard of anything like this before—you know, anyone having this kind of experience?"

Chua bristled, and without hesitation responded, "I have never come upon anything like this before, here, in the Philippines, or anywhere else. Officer, I am not a superstitious native!"

"I wasn't inferring anything of the kind, doctor," Stachula put in quickly. "I've never encountered anything like this, either. You can't fault me for asking."

"I understand," Chua said. "Now, I guess, you can see why this has not been easy for me to tell you."

"I certainly can. Now, you said this voice mentioned jewelry."

"Teresita Basa's voice told me that Showery had taken her jewelry and given half to his wife, and the rest to some friends."

"What kind of jewelry are we talking about here?"

"That is the very question I put to the voice. How would the police know which jewelry was hers? She told me her relatives would be able to identify it. She said the jewelry included a pendant, purchased by her father for her mother in the Philippines, and a cocktail ring her mother bought in Paris and passed on to her. The mother wanted Teresita to have it in the event she died."

"A pendant from the Philippines and a cocktail ring from Paris?"

"Yes, sir. Those were the main items. I told Teresita Basa the police would not know where to look for the jewelry, and the voice said that Allan Showery's wife had it."

"Tell me, doctor. Did you ask Teresita who any of these relatives might be who could identify this missing jewelry?"

"I did. The voice mentioned several names. I can only recall one right now—the last name, Somera."

"Do you know that Teresita Basa had a cousin named Ron Somera?"

"No, as I told you, I had never met Miss Basa, and I know nothing about her except what was in the papers."

"What else did the voice tell you, doctor?"

"That is the sum and substance of it. What I have just told you. Each time the 'voice' visited Remebios the session lasted fifteen minutes to a half hour."

"A half hour?"

"Yes. I learned that if I agreed with the voice, Miss Basa would weaken and subsequently leave my wife. You can see now why I was reluctant to inform anyone what was happening. I would feel utterly foolish. I mentioned a little bit about it to my immediate superior at the hospital. He suggested I write an anonymous letter to the police. How seriously would they have taken that?"

"So, you called Evanston police?"

"At first we did nothing. But after the voice began to come back, we started getting these phone calls. That's when we notified police." The doctor paused and took a long, penetrating look at the detective. "Tell me now, do you believe what I have just told you?"

"I can't say that I do," Stachula answered honestly. "At the same time, doctor, I am not prepared to say I do not believe your story. Nothing like this has ever come up before. I'll have to go over it with my superiors."

In an effort to direct the conversation from himself, he turned to Mrs. Chua and asked, "What do you think of all this?"

Unabashed, she declared that she knew nothing about any of it—only what her husband had told her. Stachula then terminated the interview, and indicated other authorities would probably want to question the couple after he made his report. Dr. Chua said, "We expect to have our phone hooked up any day now. Just have the officers call first to make sure we're home."

"One more thing," Stachula said, standing in the doorway. "Has Teresita Basa returned since you contacted the police?"

"She has not," Dr. Chua emphasized.

Joe Stachula's orderly Marine Corps mind was reeling as he drove back down the now darkened Edens Expressway. Dr. Chua was afraid to come forward because he feared he might be ridiculed. He knew how the Filipino felt. Stachula now possessed information police had been unable turn up in nearly six months of investigation. He also knew quite clearly that if he put what Chua had told him in a report he'd be laughed out of the station house. The whole thing was nuts. He wanted to stop the car and kick his own ass for going to the Chua home without a witness. Why did Epplen have to be off today, of all days?

He didn't know what to believe. Yet—in his mind, at least—the Basa case was alive again. Alive. The word suddenly seemed haunting. But he had information he didn't have before, and regardless of how it was obtained, it would sure as hell be checked out.

A couple of things puzzled him. If the jewelry was stolen, why hadn't someone noticed it was missing? And Allan Showery. If he worked at Edgewater, how in the hell had every cop on the case missed him with all the questioning and requestioning of Teresita's friends and, supposedly, everyone who had known her?

When Stachula got back to the squad room he pulled the Basa file. There, among the list of Teresita's personal effects, was the cryptic note police found in her apartment on the night of the fire: "Get tickets for A.S."

"Jezus Christ," he muttered aloud. "Allan Showery."

He and Epplen, along with other investigators, had pored in vain over that scrap of paper with Teresita's handwriting on it—probably the last thing she ever wrote. They thought possibly she might have been reminding herself to get tickets for a musical event. They tried all manner of combinations, such as "American Songfest" and things connected with her musical life. But they were never able to connect the initials with a name.

Stachula settled behind the Olivetti at the most inconspicuous desk he could find and made a snap decision. He'd be damned if he'd type out a report for every asshole in the department to read and make fun of. Instead, he reduced his interview with the Chuas to a confidential, undated four-page memorandum, which he hand-delivered to his commander, Julien "Jules" Gallet.

The seasoned lawman read the memo and looked up at Stachula skeptically. "Well, what do you make of it?" he asked.

"I'm not quite sure I believe myself how this information was obtained," Stachula said. "But I was there, and everything here is completely true, as I heard it with these two ears. We're both probably thinking the same goddam thing, but this is what I came up with. And—dammit—I'm inclined to believe those people. We're always dealing with half truths and reluctant witnesses, but these Chuas, they somehow ring true to me."

"Let me think on this awhile, Joe. Meanwhile, take a peek at this," Gallet said, tossing Stachula a Xeroxed piece of paper. "When the Evanston P.D. first called, the day guys ran a routine check on Allan Showery after the woman complained he had telephoned her. This came back while you were out."

Stachula recognized the sheet of paper. It was a typical arrest sheet, with front and side mug shots at the bottom of a black man with a goatee.

It was the arrest record of Allan Showery, male/Negro, age 31. He was first picked up by New York police on 5 February 1964 at the age of 18, for burglarizing a store and possession of burglar tools. In 1966 he was busted in New York for possession of stolen mail, and in 1971 Evanston police charged him with theft.

"It gets better," said Gallet.

"Phew," Stachula whistled. "Arrested for rape twice in 1972—both times on the North Side, once in the 18th District, and once in 20."

"Notice where our boy lives," Gallet said.

Stachula read Showery's last known address—445 W. Surf Street—an easy walk from the murder scene.

Stachula's eyes met Gallet's. "Maybe this ain't so nuts after all," he said.

"Maybe it is, and maybe it isn't," Gallet said. "Let's sit on this ghost stuff for awhile. And let's do something else. Let's get somebody's ass over to talk to this Allan Showery. Like we should have done in the first frickin' place. I can't frickin' believe this!"

CHAPTER 21

THE SUSPECT

Finding Allan Showery was more easily ordained than accomplished. The hospital orderly Teresita Basa's ghost supposedly named as her killer was suddenly the man who wasn't there. Showery had not gone into hiding, and he had no reason to believe police were looking for him. He just consistently seemed to be somewhere else, no matter where they looked. A goateed will-o'-the-wisp. Little wonder he had somehow fallen through the cracks in the investigation.

For one thing, police were not looking too hard for the suspect. Showery was hardly the subject of an all-points bulletin. Police don't issue such directives on the word of a mysterious voice, real or imagined. Nor was he even a murder suspect per se. Police work on facts, and these were the facts on Allan Showery at the moment:

- He had been a co-worker of Teresita Basa's at Edgewater Hospital.
- He had a police record of arrest for sex crimes.
- He lived within walking distance of the murder scene.

For those three reasons, and no others, it was decided to bring him in for routine questioning, since this had not been done earlier. Police, at this point, were not even considering the fourth fact: They did not know Showery existed until Teresita's "voice" gave Dr. Chua his name.

Regardless of fact four, and the highly irregular manner in which they had acquired his name, they had enough to go on to pick him up.

Stachula and Epplen drove directly to the Surf Street address, listed on the arrest sheet, on Monday evening—their next working day—only to discover no one was at home. They checked the hospital and learned that Showery was working the day shift. The next morning a day crew was dispatched to the hospital to bring Showery in. It turned out to be his day off. The following day the cops were busy with something else. On Thursday evening, August 11, with Showery still unaccounted for, Sergeant Richard Sandberg tossed Stachula's original memo into his lap and ordered, "Go out and talk to this guy."

"What's the matter?" Stachula grinned sheepishly. "Nobody else wants to work on this thing?"

"Look, Joseph," Sandberg said with exaggerated patience. "This is your baby! You came up with this gent's name all by yourself, due to your amazing investigative ability. The commander thinks it best that you follow it up."

"So, what am I supposed to do if I find him?"

"You can always sneak up behind him and say, 'Boo!'" Sandberg laughed.

Stachula smirked and picked up the confidential memo he now knew must have been circulated around the building.

The 24-hour clock in the squad room said 1930—half past seven at night. He and Epplen checked out a car and headed again for the house on Surf Street. The weather, for a change, was delightful—65 degrees under a fair sky, with good visibility. A soft breeze out of the southwest promised good sleeping when they got off duty.

The Surf Street address turned out to be a bummer. Someone was home this time, but it was not the suspect. The guy never heard of Showery. "He musta moved away a long time ago," he told the detectives.

Stachula and Epplen drove over to Edgewater and checked with the personnel office. The record showed that Showery had lived on Surf at the time of his last arrest, but had since moved to Diversey Avenue. The two detectives looked at one another and shrugged their shoulders. No one else had even come up with this. It was basic police work, and even they had slipped up on it. "I'm starting to see why that ghost decided to give us a lift," Stachula quipped, as they piled back into the car and headed for Diversey.

Showery's personnel folder indicated he lived on the third floor, apartment D. They hiked up, stopped for breath at the top, and knocked loudly on the door. No one answered, but their knock aroused a tenant across the hall. "Who ya looking for?" he demanded, opening his door a crack.

"Allan Showery?"

"Showery? Oh, you mean the doctor? The doc's gone. He moved out a coupla months back."

"Any idea where? It's important that we get in touch with him."

"Naw, he didn't say. You know how those doctors are. They like to keep their personal life private so patients don't bother them at home."

"Ain't it the truth," Epplen agreed. He and Stachula clomped back down two flights of stairs, into the darkened street, and got back into the Plymouth.

"Edgewater?" Epplen suggested, switching on the ignition.

"Edgewater," nodded Stachula.

It now became a matter of investigative pride. One way or another, Stachula and Epplen were going to find Allan Showery before the night was out. The ghost story was already setting Stachula up for the jerk-of-the-month award and Epplen felt for him. By turning up the elusive Showery, when no one else could, they would at least be able to check him out before anyone else tried to make a big deal out of the "voice from the grave."

Back at Edgewater Hospital they talked to employees in the respiratory department, and let everyone know they weren't kidding around. Their stern attitude helped, but not a hell of a lot. Co-workers who earlier kept mum about Showery reluctantly admitted they knew him. He was supposed to be living somewhere around Schubert Avenue and Clark Street.

The detectives parked at the corner of Clark and Schubert and looked around. The neighborhood was more than familiar, and each knew what the other was thinking. "Basa's place is right over there," Epplen said, pointing toward the east. "Not even a block away. You can see the building from here."

"She lived at 2740," Stachula observed. "Schubert is 2700 north, Diversey is 2800 and Surf is 2900. He could have walked over to her place from any one of those addresses with no sweat, no matter which one he lived at on the night of the murder. They were neighbors."

They began to work their way west on Schubert, Stachula carrying a flashlight and Epplen using his cigarette lighter to check names on doorbells. Half way up the block on the north side of the street, opposite the Chicago Transit Authority carbarn, Epplen found what they were looking for. "Over here, Joe," he whistled.

It was a two-story red brick building with an aboveground English basement, an unusually well-kept structure in an area of run-down buildings. The red wooden steps had been freshly painted, and the double-door was newly varnished. A big 630, painted in foot-high black numbers on the wall, clearly heralded the address.

Stachula aimed his flashlight at the mailbox, where the name Showery was written in red grease pencil. It reminded him of those gag "Think Ahead" signs, where the last letters run off the edge. There was a big letter "S" with the rest of the name getting smaller, until the "y" was barely legible.

Epplen pushed the doorbell. There was no need for discussion. The two had worked together long enough to know what they would do next. The lights leading to the second floor went on, and a door at the top of the stairs swung open. There, barefoot, wearing a white T-shirt and a pair of rumpled slacks, stood the man pictured on the police rap sheet.

"Yeah," he called down.

Identifying themselves as homicide investigators as they held up their badges, they moved casually up the stairs, not wanting to scare their quarry back into his apartment. "Hyah," Stachula said cheerfully. "We'd like to talk to you, if you don't mind."

"Is this about Teresita Basa?" he asked, still in the doorway. "Come on in. If there's anything I can do to help . . ."

Stachula caught Epplen's eye. Again, they were both thinking the same thing. They had not mentioned Teresita Basa. It was as if Allan Showery had been standing there, waiting for them, for the past six months.

"Well, what can the ol' doc do for you gentlemen?" Showery beamed.

The detectives' eyes made a quick search of the room. They found themselves staring at a figure sitting cross-legged on the dining room floor amid a stack of books about psychic phenomena. It was Showery's woman, a Teutonic blonde with high cheekbones, sensuous round eyes, and her bright hair tied back. The fact that she was wearing a maternity gown did nothing to detract from her appearance. Showery casually introduced German-born Yanka Kalmuk. They nodded politely and returned their attention to him.

"We were wondering if you could come down to the station to talk," Stachula explained. "It would be a lot easier, you know. All our records are down there. Stuff like that."

"Gimme a couple of secs to get some threads on," Showery said, fairly bubbling with cooperation.

The two investigators followed him into the bedroom, making idle chatter while he pulled on his socks and shoes, and put on a sport shirt. As Showery passed to go back into the dining room Epplen patted him down. "Just routine," he apologized. "I didn't want to do this in front of your wife. She might think something was wrong."

"I get you," smiled Showery. "I'm not carrying. I don't believe in that crap. No gun. Not even a knife. If you're not carrying, you can't ever hurt anybody." Turning to Yanka he added, "I'm goin' with these two gentlemen. Be back in a little while. Wait up for me, O.K.?"

Neither detective spoke during the 12-minute drive to Area 6 Headquarters. They wanted Showery to sweat a little, after all they went through in finding him. He finally broke the silence himself. "Wonderful woman," he remarked. "Teresita didn't have an enemy in the world. She was one of those unique people who was just plain nice, you know what I mean? We were so shocked when this happened to her. I mean that. I was one of her best friends. Been hoping you fellows would come by. I don't know what I can do, but I'm here to do whatever I can."

The car swung into the parking lot behind headquarters, where the sprawling Riverview Amusement Park stood from 1904 to 1967. How many slick-haired dandies with their over-rouged girls in short skirts, popping bubble gum, had walked this ground where police now brought their murder suspects for interrogation? This was the home of the Bobs, the original killer roller coaster; the Rotor; the Freak House; the Chute-the-Chutes; and the giant carousel, now at Six Flags over Georgia. For some inexplicable reason Stachula suddenly thought of The Dip, a game where patrons threw baseballs at a metal bulls-eye and tumbled a black man into a giant tub of water. The black would climb back onto a little bench and hurl insults at the honkies while they bought $5 more worth of balls to throw.

What kind of a game would they have with Showery? Would he and Epplen be able to dump him into the tank, or would he succeed in making fools of them?

They escorted Showery to one of the small interview rooms and left him there. The idea was to leave him alone with his thoughts, give his imagination time to work as he stared at the pair of handcuffs chained to the cinderblock wall. It worked with some people. Others relaxed and fell asleep.

Epplen and Stachula let Showery stew for nearly 15 minutes, and he grew more apprehensive with every passing second. He had come down to talk, that's what the cops said. But they were leaving him sit. What the hell were they up to? When they finally sauntered into the room he was so relieved he stood up to greet them.

"O.K. if we call you Allan?" Stachula asked. "I'm Joe and this is Lee."

"Cool with me, Joe," Showery answered cheerfully.

The two policemen took chairs at the table opposite Showery. In the cool fluorescent glare they got their first good look at the man Teresita's voice claimed had robbed her of her jewelry and her life. Allan Showery did not fit the mold. He had a pleasant face, warm brown eyes, a short Afro haircut, and neatly trimmed mustache and beard. He was the sort of person one could easily come to like, with a face that projected, "I want to be your friend." The tin can ash tray on the formica table top was half full of cigarette butts he had nervously puffed while left in seclusion.

"All right, my man," Stachula began. "First we have to advise you of your Constitutional rights. You understand that. You have the right to remain silent. If you do not remain silent, anything you say can and will be used against you in a court of law. You also have the right to have an attorney present, and if you cannot afford an attorney one will be appointed for you by the court. If you do decide to answer any questions, you can stop answering them at any time. Now, do you still want to talk to us?"

"Right," Showery insisted. "Like I said before, man, if I can help, that's what I'm here for."

"O.K. For the record, now, what is your full name?"

"Allan Showery."

"Middle name?"

"Don't have one."

"Your date and place of birth?"

"I was born March 25, 1946, in New York City. Came to Chi-town in '69."

"And you currently reside at 630 W. Schubert Avenue with your wife, er . . ."

"Yanka Kalmuk. Ah, she's not really my wife, if you know what I mean. It's a common-law marriage, and there's a li'l papoose in the oven."

"I noticed," Stachula smiled. He had made up his mind not to fool around with this individual. Sometimes you edge into a subject slowly. But Showery had brought up Teresita himself. He knew why he was there. No need to be cagey. "Allan, what Lee and I want is to get your story down. We've talked to a lot of Teresita's friends, and we're putting all these stories together. Now, how well did you know Teresita Basa, and when was the last time you saw her?"

"We worked at the hospital," Showery explained. "I'd say we were very good friends. It was a platonic association. We rode the bus home together, and sometimes she'd have me over for a beer. That's all. She liked to have people around."

"When was the last time you saw Miss Basa, outside of work?"

"Oh, I'd say about six months before," Showery answered calmly.

Epplen, laid back until now, shot from his chair and exploded, "Aw, cut the shit, Allan. That's a goddam lie and you know it. Your fingerprints were all over her joint. Are you trying to tell us a fastidious person like her hadn't dusted her furniture in six months? Get off it!"

It was a wild bluff. Had Showery's prints actually been found in the apartment police would have pounced on him long ago. With his past record for theft and rape his prints were already on file, and he would have been an early suspect.

"Let me think a minute," Showery said, slightly flustered. "Yeah, yeah. You're right. I had been there more recently than that, I remember now. I was wrong about that. I'm sorry."

"Let's get out of here, Joe," Epplen snarled. "If he's gonna bullshit us I'm leaving." He stormed out of the room. Stachula followed him out and slammed the door. It was another one of their techniques to keep a subject off guard. As they stood outside the interrogation room they heard a knock on the other side of the door.

"What?" Stachula yelled in the surliest tone he could muster.

"I want to talk to you," Showery's voice came through the door.

The detectives returned to their seats at the table, but promised to leave if Showery lied again. Then Showery began to ramble about his "platonic" relationship with the dead woman. He reminded Stachula of a swimmer treading water.

The poor bugger was doing his damndest to keep afloat, and he knew the other two men in the room were out to dunk him if they could. As Showery unfolded his story Stachula began to detect discrepancies—some relatively minor—but he decided to play them to the hilt.

Showery had said he only knew Teresita from work, but later mentioned how he helpfully accompanied her downtown to the immigration bureau, a good Samaritan helping her become a U.S. citizen. He denied having been near her apartment prior to the slaying, but admitted under questioning that he went there to look at her television set around 6:30 on the night she died.

"I promised to come back later that night and fix the set, but I forgot about it, and when I tried to call her the line was busy," he added. "I spent the entire evening at home, fixing the electric wiring. Yanka can verify that."

"Allan, first you tell us one thing, and then you tell us something else," Stachula said in mock disgust. "Lee was right. You're playing games with us. The hell with you." He and Epplen again left the room, banging the door behind them, leaving Showery alone to think it over.

"Look, Lee," Stachula suggested. "I know this might sound goofy, but don't laugh. The whole thing that put us onto this guy is goofy, but he's looking better all the time. You agree?"

"He's not leveling with us, that's for sure."

"Right. Now, just suppose that what the 'voice' told that Filipino doctor is true—that Showery does have some missing jewelry that we don't know anything about. And he gave it to his girlfriend. So, what do you say we go back and ask this Yanka to show us what she's got—see if there's anything with an Oriental flavor to it?"

"What have we got to loose?" Epplen shrugged. "I'm with you, Joe."

They asked Sergeant Sandberg to keep an eye on Showery, still stewing in the interview room, while they returned to his apartment on Schubert. Yanka Kalmuk answered their knock and invited them in, despite the late hour. The last time they'd seen her she was seated on the floor. Now they could see that she was about 5 feet 7, strikingly attractive, and very, very pregnant.

They got right to the point. They explained that they had reason to believe Allan might have been involved in Teresita Basa's homicide, but said he told them she would be able to clear him. "Would you happen to recall where he was on the night of February 21?" Surprisingly she could, despite the fact it was now nearly six months later.

"I remember because we heard the sirens," she explained crisply. "I was home waiting for Allan, and he came in around eight o'clock. After Allan arrived I went out shopping, and he stayed home. Later we saw on television that the woman had been murdered right in our own neighborhood."

"Did you have any problem with the electricity at the Surf Street apartment, Mrs. Showery?" Stachula queried.

"No, not that I know of."

"Well, do you recall Allan working on the electric wiring that night?"

"No, he never worked on the electricity there," she said.

"You're sure of that?"

"Of course. Why do you ask?"

"You're being very helpful," Stachula said, without answering her question. "Now we'd like to ask your cooperation with one more thing. If we're on the wrong track here, I know you'd like to see Allan released. He's already told us he has nothing to hide, and we're sure you don't, either."

"Well, what is it you want of me? If it will help Allan . . ."

"Would you object if we were to look over your jewelry?"

Yanka went into the bedroom to get her jewelry. While she was gone Stachula called Epplen's attention to the collection of books on the dining room floor. All dealt with extrasensory perception, psychic phenomena, or ghosts. When she reappeared, carrying a large jewelry box in both hands, Stachula inquired curiously, "Whose books are those?"

"Oh, those are all mine."

"Are you interested in that kind of stuff?"

"Yes. I like to read about it."

"Some day, Mrs. Showery, I'll tell you about a psychic experience I became involved in," Stachula said, only half joking.

"Hmmm," she said, showing interest. "Well, here is my jewelry box. Would you like to look through it?"

"Not here, if you don't mind," Stachula said. "Let's take it down where Allan's waiting. He's been telling us some stuff that you might be able to help straighten out."

Back again at Belmont and Western, Showery's common-law wife was directed to a separate interview room with her box of jewelry, and offered a cup of hot coffee. Neither Stachula nor Epplen bothered to look at the jewelry, since they had no idea what to look for.

While Epplen made small talk with Yanka, Stachula telephoned Ron Somera up in Gurnee, and asked if he could drive down to the station. Teresita's cousin agreed, but said he was baby-sitting while his wife worked, and could not leave until she got back. Realizing time was of the essence, Stachula tried to call another cousin, Kenneth Basa, in Evanston. No answer. He then got out his notes and decided to go down the list of Teresita's friends, in hopes that one of them might have been familiar with her jewelry. Number one on the list was 21-year-old Richard Pessotti.

"Yes, I knew some of Chita's jewelry because it was so unique," he told Stachula over the phone. "I can come right over."

Pessotti strolled into the familiar squad room 10 minutes later, accompanied by Ray King. Stachula explained why they needed him, and led him to the room where Epplen was still jawing amiably with Yanka. As they entered, she was sitting comfortably with her hands on her lap. Pessotti grabbed Stachula by the arm and whispered, "I've got to talk to you in private."

"What's up?" Stachula asked, after they had retreated into the squad room.

"That woman is wearing Teresita's ring," Pessotti said. "The one with the large pearl."

"Are you sure about that?"

"Positive! That's the cocktail ring her mother gave her last summer. She bought it in Paris."

Epplen emerged from the room and looked at Stachula quizzically.

"We hit paydirt, Lee," Stachula said softly. "Guess what? Richard here recognizes that ring she's wearing."

"Jeez! The ghost scores again."

"Just a private joke," Stachula remarked, noting the look of surprise on Pessotti's face. "You and Ray go into that little room with Lee, here, and see if you can spot anything else in the jewelry box. I've got to make a couple of phone calls."

While Teresita's former escorts picked through the box of necklaces, rings, and baubles under Yanka's critical eye, Stachula tried another call to Kenneth Basa in Evanston. This time he was home, and agreed to come right down. While awaiting his arrival Stachula joined the small group around the interview room table. King confirmed Pessotti's identification of the pearl cocktail ring, but they were unable to recognize anything else as having belonged to Teresita.

"How did you come by this ring you're wearing, Mrs. Showery?" Stachula asked curiously.

"From Allan. It was a belated Christmas gift."

"Yeah? When did he give it to you?"

"It was around the end of February."

"I see," Stachula said. "Well, we're going to have to con-
fiscate your ring, at least for the time being, Mrs. Showery.
Would you please remove it from your finger? We'll give you a
receipt."

Bewildered, Yanka handed the detective the ring. While
Stachula was trying to think of something reassuring to say,
Kenneth Basa arrived.

"What's coming down?" asked Sergeant Sandberg, who
had ushered Basa to the interview room.

"The whole bit," Stachula said. "And I ain't laughing
about ghosts right now, either." He briefed the sergeant in
hushed tones as Teresita's cousin from Evanston carefully
went over the array of jewelry laid out on the formica table.

A look of deep concern came over Yanka's face as she
watched Basa's eyes. He immediately spotted the pearl cocktail ring, which Stachula had put back with the other jewelry.
He also picked out a jade pendant. "I believe this was hers, also,"
he said, handing it to the detective. He pointed out several items
as "possibly" having belonged to his murdered cousin.

After Basa, King and Pessotti were dismissed, Showery
was brought wide-eyed into the room. Stachula held up the
pearl ring and stared at him knowingly. "Where did you get
this ring, Allan?"

"That ring? Oh, let me see. I bought it from some guy on
the street. Yeah. Gave him 28 bucks for it."

"Who was this guy you got it from?"

"Just a guy on the street," Showery shrugged. "I didn't
know him, man. Wouldn't know the dude if he walked in
right now."

"That's not good enough, Allan," Stachula said gently. The
phony gruffness was gone now. No need to pretend. He and
Epplen had Showery by the balls and they knew it. "It's all over,
Allan. Yanka's wearing Teresita's jewelry. It's been positively
ID'd. You're involved, Allan. You know it, and we know it."

Yanka began to sob in the drab stillness of the room as
the two police officers gathered around Showery and glared
down at him. He sat hunched over in the yellow plastic chair,

studying his hands, opening and closing his palms. After a prolonged silence he said softly, without looking up, "Yeah. Well, let me tell you what happened."

* * *

Yanka Kalmuk was left alone, with her jewelry and her tears, while Stachula and Epplen escorted Showery back to the adjoining interview room. Stachula read him his rights from a card he pulled from his shirt pocket, and Allan went into his monolog without further prompting.

"Well, like I told you, I did it," he said, almost matter-of-factly. "I'd been to Teresita's on numerous occasions, and on the way home from work that day she said something about having trouble with her TV."

Showery paused and lit a cigarette. "How about a cup of coffee, Allen?" Epplen asked.

"Please," said Showery, shaking the flame off his match. He took a long draw, blew the white smoke slowly from between his lips, and continued his narrative. "So, when we got off the bus at Clark and Diversey, I walked home with her to take a look at it."

"About what time was this, Allan?"

"Around five o'clock." Showery looked up as Epplen came back into the room and set three paper cups of coffee on the table.

"Go on," Stachula encouraged.

"Well, I looked inside the set, and right away I noticed that the repairman had placed a circuit breaker upside-down. I told Teresita I had to go home and get some wiring diagrams, so I wouldn't goof anything up. I sat around and had a couple cans of beer while we talked, and then I walked back to my place."

"Which was where?"

"About three minutes away, over on Surf—445 West Surf."

"O.K. After you got home . . ."

"I read up on the set, and then around 7:30 I headed back to Teresita's. That's when I got the idea."

Showery paused, anticipating a question from one of the

detectives, but they just waited. Things were flowing too smoothly to interrupt. They sipped silently on their coffee and waited for him to pick up the story.

Normally Stachula considered himself in the driver's seat in situations like this, in complete control, skilfully manipulating the suspect with carefully phrased questions and interjections. This time he experienced a strange uneasiness. Showery had assumed control of his own interrogation. He was doing all the talking.

I decided to rob her. Whenever I did anything for Teresita, I did it for money. If I ran an errand for her, or took her someplace, she always tipped me five or ten. I figured she probably kept a lot of money around her place. I was a couple of months behind on my bills, really hurting, and she had all that money, just for the taking. I figured out what I was going to do while I was walking over there. She let me in when I tapped on the door, and then she went to the phone where she was talking to someone. She hung up, and when she went back to lock the door I grabbed her from behind and gave her a choke hold, what I call a Japanese Full Nelson. She went limp.

"I laid her down on the living room floor, and went through her purse. She only had $30. Then I went into the bedroom, looking for valuables. I tossed things around, to make it look ransacked, and grabbed some of her jewelry. Then I went back into the living room, picked her up, and carried her into the bedroom and put her on the floor. After that I removed her clothing."

"Can you tell us what she was wearing?" Stachula asked. It was a typical control question, to determine whether the suspect had really been there, or was 'fessing up to something he'd read about in the press.

"Slacks and a sweater," Showery answered. "And pantyhose underneath. After I undressed her I went into the kitchen and got a knife out of the drawer. I went back into the bedroom and stabbed her, in the sternum."

"Was she alive when you did that, Allan?"

"Yeah. She was subconscious. She didn't feel anything."

"What happened then?"

"Well, I searched the bedroom one more time, but I couldn't find anything of value. I searched the rest of the apartment. There wasn't anything there, either. Only the $30 I got out of her purse and the jewelry you already know about. So I went back into the bedroom. I found a paper bag and rolled it up, and lit it with a match. Then I turned the mattress over on Teresita and set it on fire with the paper bag. As soon as it got going, I got out of there and went home."

Stachula extracted the police photos of the dead woman from a manila folder and handed them to Showery. He stared silently at the grotesque photographs of the naked Filipina, lying on her back, legs wide apart, with the wooden knife handle protruding from between her small breasts.

"Did you do that, Allan?"

"Yeah," said Showery, handing back the pictures.

"After you undressed her, when you had her naked like that, did you have intercourse with her?" It was another control question. Only the coroner's pathologist, police investigators and the killer himself knew that Teresita had not been sexually abused.

"I didn't do anything. I didn't molest her or anything like that. I undressed her so it would look like a sex crime, but I didn't touch her." There was a long pause as Showery looked across the table at his accusers.

"You're lying to me, Allan," Stachula said deliberately.

"The fuck I am!" Showery leaped from his chair and stamped his foot on the floor. "I'm not lying to you," he literally screamed. "You're trying to frame me! You cops are trying to frame me!"

"Take your seat," Stachula said icily. "We have to make sure we're getting this straight. How about her jewelry, now? What did you do with that stuff?"

Showery took a deep breath and slumped back into his chair. "O.K. I took it home with me, and the next morning on the way to work I tossed it. I threw most of it in the park near Diversey and Sheridan. I kept the green pendant and the ring and gave them to Yanka. I wasn't able to give her anything for Christmas, so that was it."

"A belated Christmas present?"

"Yeh."

"This the pendant you're talking about?" Stachula asked, holding up the items that had been confiscated from Yanka's jewel box. "And the ring?"

"Those are the ones. That's all I kept."

That was it. Stachula and Epplen miraculously had a confession. But they weren't calling the state's attorney yet. Not only were the two detectives perfectionists in what they did, this was a case different from any either had ever worked on. They wanted to hear it all one more time, from the very beginning. Once again they went through the entire story with Showery, tying up loose ends. Stachula and Epplen, sliding in a question now and then, and Showery calmly pushing back the answer. At no time during the long interrogation did they mention Mrs. Chua's story, or give Showery any indication as to how they happened to zero in on him.

"I know you, Allan," Stachula remarked afterward. "You've been living by your wits too long."

"Yeah, you're right," Showery agreed, now totally relaxed. "I've lived by my wits all my life, and nothing has worked. Not even this."

"We're going to call an assistant state's attorney to take a formal statement, Allan. That agreeable to you?"

"Yeah. But first I gotta talk to Yanka. Is that all right?"

Stachula nodded to Epplen, and all three got up to go over to the room where Yanka was waiting. It was well past midnight. Cool breeze or not, there would be no sleep this night for the two detectives who would normally be off duty by now. On the way to the other room Showery spotted Pessotti, still hanging around the squad room with King out of curiosity, and stopped abruptly. The two men stared awkwardly at one another, and then Showery spoke softly.

"Richard, I don't know what to say to you. I know Teresita meant a lot to you. I really didn't mean to do what I did. I know that if I had asked Teresita for money she would have given it to me."

Pessotti stared blankly at the pathetic orderly for a moment, turned, and left the room, followed by King. The detectives took Showery by the arms and guided him into the adjoining room where Yanka was waiting. "Allan is cooperating," Stachula explained. "He told us everything. Now he has something he wants to say to you."

Showery gently took the weeping woman's hand in his and looked softly into her face, as Stachula and Epplen discreetly stepped back out of earshot.

"Honey, you are a wonderful woman, and you are going to have my child," he said, looking into her face. "I did something terrible, and I want you to start a new life without me. Yeah, I was responsible. You know what that means? You're going to have to start a new life for yourself. No, don't cry. Don't talk. Listen. I want you to sell the furniture and find someone decent to take care of you."

"Allan, I want to help you," she sobbed.

"No," he pressed. "Listen to me. I won't be with you when the baby comes. I love you, honey, but I won't be with you any more. I'm probably going to be gone a long, long time. Do you understand that? I don't want to see you again. Don't visit me in jail, please. Forget I ever existed."

The tall, forlorn woman looked completely devastated, her handsome features contorted into a map of pain. Epplen touched her elbow and gently guided her out of the room. Yanka was given a receipt for her jewelry and driven home. As Stachula and Epplen walked her to the front door of her building she turned, wiped the dampness from her eyes, and asked, "When will he be going to court? When can I see him?"

"That I can't say, Mrs. Showery," Stachula said. "It won't be for a day or so. But we'll let you know first thing."

She turned and walked up the stairs, head held high. The two men waited on the sidewalk. In the stillness of the early morning they heard the door close. Then the muffled sobbing.

CHAPTER 22

CLEARED/CLOSED BY ARREST

Neither man said a word for several minutes as they drove back to the station, the car windows rolled down to let the breeze whip through their sweaty clothes. It was Stachula who finally broke the silence.

"God-damndest thing I've ever seen."

"I can't believe it myself," muttered Epplen.

"I felt completely surrounded in there . . . surrounded by an invisible pressure. There isn't any other way to explain it," Stachula confided. "It was like Teresita Basa wrote the script. Every fricking thing came down, just exactly the way *she* said it happened."

"Now you're talking like you believe in ghosts, Joe."

"I'm saying I don't know what the hell to believe. I just know we got our confession and we didn't twist anybody's arm. We knew exactly what to ask him, that's why. But I still can't believe it really happened."

"He didn't help himself any," Epplen noted. "My old man used to tell me if you tell one lie you have to tell ten more lies to cover up the first one."

"Yeah," said Stachula. "He just couldn't explain away that jewelry. That's what nailed him. The jewelry. And we didn't even know the shit was missing until Teresita told us—told Dr. Chua, I mean—that he swiped it. Hey, how about swinging by McDonald's?"

"I'm for that, partner. I'm so hungry I could eat a maggot. Haven't had anything since lunch."

Epplen wheeled into McDonald's parking lot and stayed in the car while Stachula went inside. He was back in less than five minutes with a cardboard tray holding three large coffees and a sack of Big Macs. "That poor bastard's got to be as hungry as we are," he explained, when Epplen eyed the extra coffee cup.

When the two detectives reached the top of the stairs back at Area 6 they were met by Paul Linton, a bright young man in an impeccable business suit who looked like he was going nowhere but up. Called out in the middle of the night, the young assistant state's attorney looked like he'd just emerged from a refreshing shower—in sharp contrast to the rumple-clothed, sweaty investigators. An attractive brunette, who was obviously a court reporter, was relaxing at one of the empty desks.

"The sergeant says you guys have got a good one," Linton beamed.

"We'll leave that up to you, counselor," Stachula winked. "What did he tell you?"

"Not a hell of a lot. Just that they needed a prosecutor to take a statement. He said you'd brief me."

Cute, Stachula thought. He's gonna let me be the one to tell him about the voice from nowhere, and be the laughing stock of Chicago. No way, José!

"Ah, I'll take the sandwich and coffee to the prisoner while you fill the gentleman in," Epplen volunteered, excusing himself before Stachula could protest.

"O.K., sit down while I grab a bite and I'll give it to you in a nutshell," Stachula agreed. "I won't bore you to death with all the police work involved—months of it, in fact. I'll just lay out the nuts and bolts. You can take it from there."

He then briefed the prosecutor on the Basa homicide and Showery's admission, carefully omitting any reference to

Dr. and Mrs. Chua, or to Teresita's reputed voice from beyond the grave. He wolfed down his hamburgers while the two of them talked, washing them down with the McDonald coffee. Then, after answering a few pointed questions on details the lawyer wanted to nail down, he and Linton joined Epplen and Showery in the interrogation room.

"Allan, this is Assistant State's Attorney Linton," Stachula explained. "He is here to take a formal statement from you. But before we do that, he'd like you to run through just what you told us, so he'll have a better idea of what we're all talking about."

"One more time, eh?" Showery smiled, shaking his head. "Encore! Encore! And thanks for the burgers. They hit the spot. I feel a lot better now. You get anything to eat yet?"

"Don't mention it," Stachula said stiffly. "Yeah, I ate at the same restaurant you did."

The prisoner grinned at Epplen, then went into his monolog. He was prompted occasionally by one or the other of the detectives as he rambled on, in an effort to keep the string of events in some sort of chronology. He told Linton essentially the same story he'd told Stachula and Epplen. After 35 minutes had passed the prosecutor nodded and said he was satisfied.

"Now, Mr. Showery, I'm going to bring in a court reporter to take this all down for the record. Do you understand that?"

"Yes, sir. I know what you have to do."

Blanca Lara was summoned and quietly set up her Stenograph shorthand machine. It was agreed that Epplen would remain during the taking of the formal statement, while Stachula made out their report and started putting together the necessary paper work required by the court.

It was 2:35 a.m. Friday, August 12. Linton began by establishing, re-establishing, and buttoning down as firmly and legally as possible the fact that Showery was making his statement of his own volition and without coercion.

As Blanca Lara's fingertips tap-danced across the miniature keyboard of the Stenograph the lawyer began. "Mr.

Showery. You recall that you had a conversation with myself and the investigator a little while ago. Do you remember that conversation?"

"Yes, I do."

"Do you also remember earlier tonight, before you talked to myself, you had a conversation with other investigators?"

"Yes, I did."

"All right. At the conclusion of your oral statement, which was approximately 10 minutes to 2 this morning, you indicated you would give a written statement going over the matters that we covered at that time. Do you recall that?"

"Yes, I do."

"Do you wish to do that?"

"Yes, I do."

"Before we go into that I wish to re-advise you of your rights and go over some other preliminary matters, O.K.?"

"All right," Showery answered patiently. He lit another cigarette and waited.

"First of all, do you understand you have the right to remain silent?"

"Yes, I do."

Linton excruciatingly took him point by point over the Miranda decision and the Constitutional rights of an accused party, with Showery mechanically answering "Yes, I do." each time he was asked if he understood.

Epplen was getting uneasy. If Linton continued to hammer away at what the prisoner did and did not have to do, Showery might just say the hell with it, and six months work would go down the drain. The young prosecutor was being super cautious. He had seen iron-clad cases blow up in court before when a defendant claimed he had not been properly advised of his constitutional rights.

"Did I also explain these matters to you before we had a conversation earlier this morning?" he continued.

"Yes, you did."

"Did you understand them at that time?"

"Yes."

"And did you nevertheless give a statement at that time?"

"Yes, I did."

"Were you also advised of your rights earlier by the investigators?"

"Yes."

"Did you understand them at that time?"

"Yes."

"You also talked to them at that time?"

"That's correct."

"Do you understand what all your rights are at this time?"

"Jeez, get on with it, before he tells us all to go screw ourselves," Epplen muttered under his breath as he rolled his eyes at the ceiling.

"Yes, I do," Showery answered.

"Do you wish to give a statement relating to what happened in February of this year?"

"Yes."

"Thank God!" Epplen mumbled.

"Would you please state and spell your name?" the prosecutor asked.

"My name is Allan Showery. A-l-l-a-n S-h-o-w-e-r-y."

And now it began. After painstakingly establishing that what Showery would say was being done on his own volition, Linton led him point by point through events leading up to the night of February 21, 1977, when he plunged the blade into Teresita's breast.

At the end of the narration, Linton again established, for the record, the voluntary nature of the confession. There would be no repeat of the celebrated Heirens case three decades earlier, where the accused slayer confessed and collapsed in a stupor after six days of around-the-clock police badgering.

"While you've been here tonight have you been given coffee and food?"

"Yes, I have."

"Do you feel alert at the present time?"

"Yes, I am."

"Have the police officers and myself treated you satisfactory?"

"Yes, they have."

"Have you given this statement freely, of your own free will?"

"Freely, and of my own free will," Showery repeated.

He exhibited no remorse, as is often observed in such cases. He just seemed grateful it was over. Blanca Lara went to another room to transcribe her notes while Showery sat alone, puffing on cigarettes. The confession came to a total of 13 pages, double spaced. When she had finished the sheets were stapled together and presented to Showery by Linton.

Showery read each page carefully and, on Linton's advice, initialed the bottom of each page, "A.S." He signed the last page in his flowery hand, "Allan Showery." Lee R. Epplen and Paul Benjamin Linton autographed the final page as witnesses.

On Linton's recommendation, Showery was charged with murder, felony murder, armed robbery, and arson. Stachula and Epplen took the prisoner downstairs to the first floor lockup. There he was photographed, fingerprinted, and allowed to make the customary phone call. He telephoned Yanka to tell her, one more time, that he loved her and was sorry about what had happened.

Stachula split off from Epplen on the way back to the squad room, grumbling, "Damned coffee goes right through you." Linton was in the men's john when Stachula burst in. He had just finished drying his hands.

"I wish every case was as well prepared as this one, Joe," he said. "If all the cops were like you, we'd have a 100 per cent conviction rate. How'd you ever get onto this bird in the first place?"

"You wouldn't believe it if I told you," Stachula said.

The lawyer shook his head, pulled open the door, and walked out. Stachula ran the faucet, dried his hands, and went back to the squad room to finish typing out his report, omitting any reference to the Chuas and the "voice" that pointed police in the right direction.

"Therefore, due to the arrest, confession and formal charging of the perpetrator responsible for this incident, it is requested that this investigation be classified as CLEARED/CLOSED BY ARREST," he concluded. He presented the report to Sergeant Sandberg who signed it and rubber-stamped it:

CLEARED
HOMICIDE 6
CLOSED

* * *

The sun was coming up over Lake Michigan like a fiery red ball reflecting off the deep blue water as the two emotionally exhausted detectives walked out of the building.

"I don't know about you, Joe, but I could use a snort."

"What time do the joints open, Lee? I don't think I've ever been up this early."

"Let's check the Slammer and find out."

CHAPTER 23

![black bar]

ALLAN SHOWERY

Allan Showery spent the rest of the day in the district lockup. He slept right on through, as if the problems of the world had been siphoned out of his brain.

While Showery was off in Dreamland, Stachula and Epplen were busy scheming over their early morning beers across the street in the Slammer. Before calling it a night the two detectives concocted a believable story that could be released to the press, through their commanding officer, with no mention of the "voice from the grave." The yarn appeared in the morning *Tribune* on August 13. It was considerably longer than the article that ran when Teresita was murdered:

NOTE LEADS
TO SUSPECT
IN MURDER

By Philip Wattley

A BRIEF NOTE that a North Side woman had written to herself so she wouldn't forget an errand led police to the man now charged as her killer.

"Get concert tickets for A.S.," Teresita Basa had written to herself last February. Investigators discovered the note when the 45-year-old woman was found stabbed to death Feb. 21 in her apartment at 2740 N. Pine Grove Av.

Her body had been covered with a mattress which had been set on fire in an attempt to destroy all evidence. Police who found the note in the charred apartment also discovered that several pieces of her jewelry were missing.

AFTER NEARLY six months of investigation, they arrested Allan Showery, 31, of 630 W. Schubert Av., Thursday on charges of murdering Miss Basa.

Showery is the "A.S." mentioned in the note, according to homicide Lt. Julien Gallet, who said Showery admitted the killing.

Investigators Lee Epplen and Joseph Stachula were credited with uncovering the identity of A.S. Because they lacked other clues, the two set out to trace the initials.

THE FIRST big break came when they established that Miss Basa, a respiratory technician at Edgewater Hospital, and Showery, a therapist-technician at the hospital, had known each other well enough that she might have bought tickets for him.

Police said the clincher leading to Showery's arrest was the discovery that he had given a ring and pendant as gifts to another woman shortly after Miss Basa's death. Relatives of Miss Basa identified the jewelry.

*　*　*

The story was simple. It made sense. And it had the ring of truth. They had also decided, mercifully, to leave Yanka Kalmuk's name out of it.

The same morning the story appeared Showery was taken in a sheriff's squadrol to the Criminal Courts building at Twenty-sixth and California for a preliminary hearing in felony court. Judge Maurice Pompey routinely ordered a continuance to give the defendant time to find an attorney, and Showery was remanded to the Cook County Jail without bond.

He was logged in as inmate No. 7707061. In jail code that meant he was the 7,061st guest of Cook County in 1977. He was assigned to a fourth-floor cell, which he shared with a convicted armed robber who went by the alias of Willie Chester. Chester was really 22-year-old Bernie Wheatstoon, but who ever heard of a black named Bernie?

A forlorn Showery spent his first day staring absent-mindedly out of his dreary fourth-floor window across a four-foot walkway. The rust-flaked yellow bars seemed to simmer in the searing August heat, and he wondered whether they would burn his hands if he could reach out far enough to wrap his fingers around them.

"Twenty-Sixth and Cal" was how Chicagoans possessively referred to the infamous Cook County Jail at 2600 South California Avenue—a scandal since the day it was built with $7.5 million in taxpayers' hard-earned money. Designed to hold 1,302 prisoners in one-man cells five feet wide and eight feet deep it had been overcrowded from the day its iron doors clanged open for business 49 years earlier. On this day it boasted an inmate population greater than San Quentin.

More than 2,000 of the roughest men around, 85 per cent of them black and one in every 10 infected with venereal disease, paced like caged animals behind the gray stone walls, crammed into 34 tiers of 30 cells each.

There was a small dayroom on each tier where prisoners could huddle in front of a small-screen black and white TV when they weren't watching heat waves squiggle up outside the window. Tiring of that they could always grab a smoke, count the days, play cards until the deck rotted, bugger their bunkmates, perhaps, or watch a group of Blackstone Ranger street gang members cornhole some smooth-faced honky whose friends and family couldn't come up with the trump to get him out on bail.

In addition to the countless poor bastards who had been beaten to death, kicked to death, stabbed to death, burned to death or hanged themselves in their cells over the years, the windowless basement of the drab compound housed the ghosts of 65 men—killers all—who rode 1,900 volts out of there in the homemade, black wooden electric chair.

This would be Allan Showery's home for the next year and a half.

* * *

Teresita Basa's murder had been marked "solved" to the satisfaction of almost everyone concerned. The two exceptions were Lee Epplen and Joseph Stachula. Whenever they finished a case they liked to tie it up into a neat little package, but this one still had a couple of loose ends hanging out: Namely, who *was* Allan Showery, and how had he managed to escape the attention of all the cops involved in the investigation until Teresita's "voice" put the finger on him?

"Showery's not the killer type, Lee," Stachula told his partner. "We've put lots of killers away, but he doesn't fit the pattern at all. A rapist, maybe, but not a murderer. I'm thinking he knocked her out, took off her clothes, but got cold feet and didn't want to go through with it. She'd been too good to him."

"That's gotta be it, Joe. But he couldn't take a chance on her blowing the whistle on him when she came to, so he had to kill her. It was his only way out."

"Let's start at the hospital and work backward. See what we can turn up on this dude."

Now that he was safely behind bars, a different picture began to emerge of the man known as "Doc" Showery. The detectives learned he'd been having affairs with a number of women at the hospital, both black and white. Some were in love with him, while others feared compromising their marriages, so they all kept his name out of it when police made their inquiries about people who had been close to Teresita.

There was also the matter of jewelry. From time to time Showery offered rings and watches to fellow employees at bargain prices. In several instances the jewelry had been traced back to hospital patients.

One of the rings Showery offered for sale had been slipped off the finger of a dying woman. The detectives determined that co-workers who had purchased hot goods from Showery feared that if they implicated him in the Basa case, they might be drawn into the net as buyers of stolen property.

The hospital's security chief, Captain Robert Webster, told Stachula and Epplen that several employees had come to him after Showery's arrest and said they had received gifts from him that they suspected had been taken from patients' rooms.

A week after Showery had been charged with Teresita's murder the two detectives received a visit from Richard Pessotti. He gave them a yellow metal ring with three white stones, which had been turned over to him by a woman who worked at Edgewater Hospital. "She said Allan gave it to her, and now she thought it might have come from Teresita's apartment, but she was afraid to give it to you herself," he explained.

Pessotti reluctantly gave the detectives the woman's name, and they talked to her, determined to find out everything about Showery that should have been turned up in the first place. "Allan seemed like such a nice person. He gave me the ring for my birthday in March," she explained. "I didn't think any more about it until Allan was arrested. Then I remembered. It was right after the murder that he gave me the ring. I didn't know what to do, so I gave it to Richard, because I knew he was a friend of the murdered woman."

Before leaving, Stachula and Epplen had extracted from her the name of another woman, a 35-year-old nurses' aide, who had also been involved with Showery. Reached at her North Side apartment, the divorcee produced a white metal ring with white, green and blue stones, which Showery had bestowed upon her. Because it resembled the description of some miscellaneous jewelry relatives thought was missing from the Basa apartment, they took the ring and gave the woman a receipt.

Webster, the hospital security chief, had given Epplen and Stachula the name of a West Side housewife who complained that someone had slipped into her mother's room at Edgewater earlier in the year and taken a diamond ring, with smaller diamonds and blue and green stones. When shown the ring surrendered by the nurses' aide, the woman positively identified it as having belonged to her mother. As had happened twice before in the case, while investigating one crime the detectives had solved another.

They were also learning a lot about Allan Showery, who turned out to be—among other things—a monumental liar.

Legal papers filed in connection with one of his earlier court appearances indicated that Showery, born March twenty-fifth, 1946, in New York City, was one of four children of Shirley Showery, an employee of the New York Police Department. After graduation from Manhattan Technical High School in 1962 he spent five years studying at New York University, Rutgers and Utah State University, where he majored in psychology and sociology. A Viet Nam vet, he was briefly married to Lucy Bright, with whom he had one child. His police record dated back to 1964, when he was arrested for burglary and possession of stolen United States mail.

That was Showery's official biography. What Epplen and Stachula discovered about his true past was quite another story.

Fresh out of high school the glib-tongued Showery landed a job as a "youth recruiter" for the Harlem Youth Organization. He indeed enrolled in New York University, but dropped out within a year. He then got a job as a dorm leader on a Job Corps construction crew in New Jersey. Rutgers University professors occasionally offered lectures to the Job Corps workers, which was as close as Showery ever got to Rutgers. He was subsequently transferred to a Job Corps facility in Utah, which he embellished to a claim of having studied at Utah State University, according to his court testimony under oath.

Showery and Lucy Bright lived in Battle Creek, Michigan, where the Job Corps took him in 1967 as a $150-a-week dorm counselor. He quit the Job Corps and moved with his wife and infant child to Mobile, Alabama, and took a job as a dock worker a year later. He never served with the military in Viet Nam, as he had often boasted to fellow workers at Edgewater Hospital.

Instead, after six months in Alabama, Showery abandoned his wife and baby and came to Chicago. He moved into a West Side flophouse, and after two weeks of walking the streets landed a $135-a-week job as a compounder in a detergent factory. In December of 1969 he was injured while cleaning a mixing vat at the detergent plant, and spent several months in a hospital. That was where he picked up what he knew about the medical profession.

After his release from the hospital Showery worked as a free-lance photographer, snapping the flower children and assorted weirdos in the Old Town neighborhood along North Wells Street. That was where he discovered the statuesque Yanka, and they set up housekeeping. Not long afterward he was awarded a $12,000 settlement for his detergent vat injuries.

Showery blew the twelve grand on a new car, fancy clothes and photographic paraphernalia, and when the money was gone he decided to enter the field of medicine. He held short-term jobs at Henrotin Hospital as an orderly, Northwestern Memorial as a dietary aide, and Grant Hospital as a file clerk in radiology. It was during this period that he bestowed the title of "Doc" upon himself. A friend eventually lined him up with a $3.65-a-hour orderly's job at Edgewater—and he met Teresita.

"You can believe one thing about this guy," Epplen laughed. "He's sure one hell of a liar!"

"A card carrying shit," Stachula added. "Thank God he isn't our problem any more." He was wrong about that.

*   *   *

Showery, meanwhile, received an unexpected visitor in the county jail. "I'm Bill Swano," the stranger said, extending his hand. "I'm with the public defender's office. The judge appointed me to be your lawyer."

Showery eyed the visitor, a medium built white man, maybe three inches taller than himself, and about his own age. His blond hair was fully fashioned around the ears, and he had a mustache. "What's happening?" he asked, accepting the lawyer's hand suspiciously.

"Well, for starters, you've been indicted by the grand jury. Murder, arson and armed robbery."

"Indicted!" Showery spat.

"What do they have on you?" Swano asked.

"What have they got on me? I don't know," Showery responded. "That's what's puzzling me."

"Well, you'd better tell me all about it," Swano said, pulling a yellow legal pad from his portfolio.

"I was sitting at home with my wife and these two cops just knocked at the door," Showery began. "They said they wanted to talk to me about Teresita Basa . . ."

At the end of the defendant's long recitation Swano looked puzzled. Something just didn't gel, but he couldn't put his finger on it. "Yeah, but what led them to you?" he asked pointedly.

"It was the jewelry, I guess."

"No. They didn't see the jewelry until after your wife brought it to the station. What made them go to your home in the first place?"

"Well, that's a puzzlement to me, too. But they sure got me."

"Maybe they did, and maybe they didn't" argued Swano, who had built a brilliant record as a defense lawyer. "The law protects you from police just walking into your home and arresting you without a reason. They have to show what is called probable cause. And right now I don't see one scintilla of probable cause. We're going to plead not guilty, and go in with a motion to show probable cause. That means they've got to explain how they got onto you."

"Not guilty?" the astounded Showery asked.

"Not guilty!"

*　*　*

Thomas Organ, a 34-year-old member of the prosecutor's staff, was assigned by State's Attorney Bernard Carey to prosecute the case, which was a hot potato. Every member of the large Filipino community was watching it. Organ's "second chair man" would be Lee J. Schoen, with whom he shared a tiny office on the second floor of the Criminal Courts Building.

Organ had tried some 50 felony cases since being sworn in as an assistant state's attorney five years earlier. Affixed to the wall over his desk was a bulletin board listing "Wins" and "Losses"—mostly wins. The office, decorated in what he described as "disgusting yellow," was where he and his partner would spend many nights plotting strategy in the Basa case while his wife, Ruth, kept dinner warm in their suburban Elk Grove Village home.

The 30-year-old Schoen would have no such problem. He was single, and lived in the same New Town neighborhood where Teresita had. An avid skier, he looked forward to winter weekends in his home town of Minocqua, Wisconsin, where his late father Herb had run the local saloon.

At the moment, however, Organ and Schoen were concerned about the same thing that had puzzled Swano: What led police to Allan Showery? Easy enough to find out. Just consult the arresting officers.

"My God, we've got serious problems, Lee!" Organ confessed to Schoen after Stachula sheepishly recited the unpublished details. "The obvious question is whether the cops had probable cause to arrest this guy based on a mysterious 'voice' of some ghost. That's the first thing the defense is going to nail us on. What the hell are we supposed to do? I have no intention of bringing in psychics to try to convince the jury this voice business could be for real. No way."

"Well, was it a bad pinch or wasn't it?" asked Schoen, trying to be logical.

"Hell, based on the information a copper gets, he has to check it out. He can't ignore it just so he won't look like an asshole. And these two dicks, Epplen and Stachula, are solid guys. They aren't anyone's fools."

"So, what are we gonna do?"

"Dammit, I'm going to talk to some psychics. No shit! In strictest confidence. I don't know whether to believe this crap or not, but I want to get a feel of what they think. Not to use in court, just to get my own thinking in line. The defense will be doing the same thing. There's no way we can prosecute this matter if we don't believe it ourselves."

*   *   *

August drifted muggily into September, and summer stepped aside for fall. And on the last day of September, 1977, one more man in Teresita Basa's life—the man who had influenced her future more than any other—joined her beyond the pale. Alexander Tcherepnin, pianist, composer, professor, died in his Paris apartment at the age of 79. It was he who had taught Teresita that it could be exciting, believing in the spirit world.

CHAPTER 24

JUDGE BAR-B-Q

Justice in Cook County moves not with leaps and bounds but with squeaks and groans. Allan Showery sat disconsolately in the county jail, contemplating his fate, while Yanka gave birth to his son. He spent Christmas behind bars. He celebrated his 32nd birthday in his cell. And Easter. Through the walkway window of his tier he had watched as autumn transformed into one of the bitterest winters in years. And he witnessed the arrival of spring, as always in Chicago, cold, sloppy and miserably wet.

His case was eventually assigned to 58-year-old Judge James Emmet Strunck, a creature of the powerful Cook County Democratic machine. Curiously, at the very moment Showery was being arrested for the murder of Teresita Basa, Strunck was in the Philippines to address the Conference on Law of the World in Manila.

Showery was still awaiting trial when the secret of what put the cops on his tail became public knowledge on March 5. The *Chicago Tribune,* in a world scoop, asked in a headline stretching across the top of page one:

DID VOICE FROM THE GRAVE NAME KILLER?

The copyrighted story, under the by-lines of John O'Brien and Edward Baumann, was picked up and banner headlined by newspapers from coast to coast.

The reaction was instantaneous. Stachula and Epplen became the cruel butts of department jokes. Paper clips would fly out of nowhere and land on their desks, and they would find their mail boxes at Area 6 headquarters stuffed with notes to call people who had been dead for years. Eerie hoots and spooky moans emanated from various corners of the room where their fellow detectives—some smarting at the page one publicity—snickered around the water fountain. "Hey, Joe. Talk to any dead people today?" became a familiar greeting when Stachula walked into the room.

The two detectives let the boys have their fun. Both knew it would have to come out sooner or later. They stood their ground, banking on the state's attorney's office to exonerate them.

Prosecutor Organ sat tight. The next move would be up to Swano. Organ did not have long to wait. In April Swano went before Judge Strunck with a motion to suppress Showery's confession on the ground that there had been no probable cause for police to arrest him in the first place. "Allan Showery was not in the process of breaking any laws at the time of his arrest," Swano argued. "The state must prove, your honor, that the police had cause to arrest the defendant."

Showery's mother, Shirley, flew in from New York for his court appearance. Swano made an impassioned plea that she be permitted to visit her son in the lock-up adjacent to the court, saying the woman was ill. Strunck gruffly denied the request. He granted no special favors in his court. Swano then declared that he intended to ask for a change of venue to another judge, due to "prejudicial pre-trial publicity."

Secretly the lawyers on both sides reveled in the notoriety they hoped the Showery trial might attract. A so-called "publicity trial," with attorneys performing before a jammed court and the press, can often lead to a successful future. Even a loser who performs well can attract the attention of a high-powered law firm recruiting new blood.

Showery next appeared before Strunck on June 12, exactly 10 months after his arrest, for the purpose of hearing routine motions. None was heard, however, because the defendant became ill in the lockup and asked to be hospitalized for a lung condition. "Is Mr. Showery sick in the County Jail, or just when he has to appear in court?" Organ asked snidely when Swano petitioned for a delay. Already the lawyers were taking pot-shots at one another.

Because of the "voice from the grave" publicity, Showery's court appearances were beginning to attract more than the usual amount of attention. The court was receiving inquiries from throughout the world, and out-of-town papers and news services were trying to make arrangements to move in their big guns to cover the trial.

Swano, meanwhile, had done his homework and decided it would not be in his client's best interest to go to bat before the unbending Judge Strunck. Strunck had the reputation around the building of being a "prosecutor's judge," and defense lawyers felt he tended to give the state's attorney the benefit of the doubt. Furthermore, Organ had been assigned to Strunck's courtroom for the past two years, and knew all of the judge's idiosyncrasies.

Clearly the prosecution would have the advantage under the circumstances, so Swano decided to take a draw and see if he could come up with a "defender's judge."

He planned his move carefully, going into court with his motion while Strunck was on vacation, so as not to ruffle his feathers. He and his assistant, Daniel Radakovich, appeared before a downstate jurist who was sitting in for Strunck, disposing of routine motions. Swano shrewdly invoked a legal technicality that permitted him to request a "substitution of judges" without listing his reasons.

Organ, naturally, was furious that the case was about to slip out of his own back yard, but he was powerless to do anything about it.

Neither lawyer, however, was prepared for what was about to happen next.

The normal procedure was to send the case back to the presiding judge, Richard J. Fitzgerald, to be re-assigned to another court. Either the visiting judge was unfamiliar with the routine, or he didn't give a damn. Or, as Stachula cracked afterward, "Maybe Teresita whispered into his ear." He promptly granted Swano's motion for substitution—but instead of sending the case back to Fitzgerald he reassigned the case himself, to Judge Frank W. Barbaro, one of the toughest on the bench.

The 55-year-old Barbaro, another creation of the Democratic machine, was known among county jail inmates as "Bar-B-Q Barbaro" because of the heavy sentences he handed out. Coincidentally, Chicago newspaper columnist Mike Royko had just done a column on "Bar-B-Q" in which he quoted one lawyer as saying, "When he gives out sentences, he uses such big numbers that you think he's announcing a lottery." Prison sentences of 100, 200 and even 300 years were not unusual for defendants found guilty in Bar-B-Q's courtroom.

Swano's jaw dropped so hard you could almost hear it bounce off the courtroom floor when Showery was re-assigned to Barbaro. As he strode dejectedly from the room Radakovich turned to him and moaned, "He sure cleaned our clock." Organ, who'd been doing a slow burn only minutes earlier, could hardly believe his luck.

Though a tough jurist, Barbaro was not without a touch of humor. Earlier, when a burglary suspect appeared before him clad only in a smile, Bar-B-Q ordered the court cleared of all spectators, and instructed the court clerk to sit with her back to the naked defendant.

Showery appeared before Barbaro on August 30, wearing a brown and white polka-dot shirt, neat brown slacks, and highly polished dark brown shoes. He affected the air of a scholar, wearing wire-rimmed glasses.

He sat cross-legged at the defense table, neither smiling nor frowning, while he carefully avoided the eyes of Stachula on the other side of the room.

The purpose of the hearing was a defense motion to quash the arrest and suppress the evidence—the jewelry and the confession. It was Swano's latest ploy to force Organ to play the cards he didn't want to lay out. Swano hoped to make the prosecution admit in court that police had arrested his client on the say-so of a ghost.

Swano called Showery as his first witness. After raising his right hand and swearing to tell the truth—"so help me God"—he took the seat on Judge Barbaro's right.

Showery was on the stand only seven minutes, calmly responding into a hand-held microphone to questions put to him by his lawyer. Under Swano's guidance he recounted his arrest at the hands of Epplen and Stachula more than a year earlier.

"I was getting ready to go to bed. I told them I was in no shape or condition to go with them. I said, 'Could it wait another day? I need a lawyer.' They said, 'C'mon downtown.' It was my opinion that I was under arrest, so I went."

Under cross examination by Organ, Showery admitted that neither officer drew his gun, and he was not handcuffed.

The star witness at the pre-trial hearing was Stachula, who was obviously less than delighted at being put into the spotlight under the circumstances. If the detective decided to hold back what he knew, it would not be the first time a Chicago police officer lied under oath in order to achieve justice as he perceived it. Neither Swano nor Organ had any doubt as to what Stachula would testify to, however.

He was on the witness stand for the next five hours.

Seated self-consciously to the right of Judge Barbaro's dais, Stachula testified that he was able to solve the murder of Teresita Basa after talking to Dr. José Chua and his wife, Remebios, in their Skokie home.

"Dr. Chua indicated that on several occasions his wife had been possessed by the spirit of the victim, and that from his wife's body came certain information which he detailed to me," Stachula related. He then went on to detail each of the three "visits" Teresita made to Mrs. Chua's body, as recounted by her husband, and how Teresita's "voice" named Allan Showery as her killer.

The worst over, Stachula then calmly supplied the details of Showery's arrest and the identification of the jewelry Teresita's "voice" told the doctor had been stolen from the murder scene.

"When he was confronted with the jewelry, Mr. Showery told us he was responsible for Miss Basa's murder, and wished to tell us what transpired," he continued.

Asked by Organ whether Showery specifically admitted killing Teresita Basa, Stachula answered in his matter-of-fact voice, "Yes, sir. He did."

The day's hearing ended with Stachula. At Swano's request, Judge Barbaro continued the hearing until Friday, September 1, at which time Swano said he expected to introduce a rebuttal witness.

* * *

It was Yanka Kalmuk. All eyes were upon the mother of Showery's infant son as she took the stand as a witness for the defense. Her bleached blonde hair, combed straight back and gathered at the neck, hung several inches below her shoulders. Her eyes were pale gray, her cheekbones high and pronounced, and while not overweight, she was somewhat thickly-built to European standards. She wore a blue denim dress, and two-inch high heeled shoes.

Courtroom spectators' eyes were explicably drawn to her jewelry, since earlier testimony had revealed that it was her collection that had led to Showery's admission of murder. She wore a gold heart-shaped object on a thin chain around her neck and three rings on the fingers of her left hand.

Yanka looked at Allan but he did not return her gaze. She fidgeted with her fingers, and stroked her Adam's apple.

"We were living together then," she answered, in response to questioning by Swano's partner, Radakovich.

"And what is your relationship with Mr. Showery today?"

"Presently, none."

"Now, as to the evening of August 11, 1977. Do you recall anything unusual transpiring on that date?"

"Two plainclothesmen came to the door, which was ajar. I stood behind the door, but could not hear their conversation. Then Allan started to dress, and said to me that he had to go with the men for questioning."

"Do you recall, Mrs. Showery, what you were doing when the police arrived?"

"We had been playing chess when the police arrived. Allan was calm and relaxed up until then. When the police came he was tense and nervous. I was very, very upset."

That was Swano's rebuttal witness. Hardly a bombshell. Yanka left the witness stand, head high, and strode from the courtroom, eyes straight ahead, without as much as a glance at the father of her child.

Now Swano tried to pull another trick from his magic hat, but the sleight of hand failed, due, in part, to Dr. José Chua's monumental ego. The defense attorney wanted, more than anything else, to wind up the hearing with Chua on the witness stand. He wanted to make him testify, under oath, that the voice of the long-dead Teresita Basa had come out of his wife's mouth.

Instead, he and Radakovich could only stand before Judge Barbaro and shrug their shoulders.

A subpoena is the ultimate weapon of the court. Even top echelon members of the crime syndicate know better than to ignore one when it is served on them. They might refuse to testify on grounds of self-incrimination, but they never fail to show up. Dr. Chua did.

He had sent word to Swano that he was "busy in surgery" and would be unavailable until the following week. The Filipino physician was not yet licensed to practice in the United States, and was working as a surgical assistant in a nearby hospital. Any qualified nurse could have filled in for him.

Judge Barbaro was on the bench. Allan Showery was in court. The prosecution and defense batteries were at the ready. But the witness, Dr. José Chua—whose testimony was crucial—was represented by an empty chair.

It is not unusual for a judge, in such cases, to dispatch a sheriff's deputy to pick up and deliver the reluctant witness to the court forthwith. Barbaro wisely decided, however, that he would do nothing to antagonize the star player in so sensitive a case. He continued the hearing until the following Tuesday.

* * *

"Get Showery!" Judge Barbaro commanded, after convening court on the morning of September 5, with a minimum of pomp.

"Showery! Allan Showery!" boomed the bailiff, scurrying from behind the judge's bench to the bullpen, where a dozen prisoners were awaiting their turn to appear before Judge Barbaro.

Presently the calm, erect figure of the much-talked-about defendant marched into the room, and paused at the bench looking at Barbaro for some direction. "Over there," nodded the judge, toward the defense table, where Swano and Radakovich were already seated.

Showery trudged over and took the third chair. "I didn't get any cigarettes yesterday. I think the guards keep 'em," he whispered to the tall, thin Radakovich, a product of South Chicago's Croatian community. "Friends say they give cigarettes for me to the guards, but I never see 'em."

"I'll look into it," Radakovich nodded.

"O.K. counsel. You got another witness?" asked Barbaro, himself anticipating the appearance of the elusive Dr. Chua.

"Yes, your honor," replied Swano, glancing in the direction of the jury box, which was empty save for three television sketch artists and half a dozen newspaper reporters. "The defense would like to call Investigator Floyd McKinney."

It wasn't Chua at all, but Detective McKinney, brilliantly attired in a three-piece plaid business suit, who strode confidently to the witness chair. As he took his seat, after uttering the customary "I do" to the truth-swearing oath, he glanced in fascination at the artists, whose hands were busily racing across the lap-held sketch pads. Photographers were still not permitted in court in Cook County, under the assumption that they might intimidate a witness. Artists, on the other hand, were objects of fascination whose presence almost seemed to flatter a witness into thinking he was sitting for a portrait.

"Coven years I've been a policeman—18 months a detective," McKinney testified, after introducing himself for the record. Radakovich then called upon him to explain how it came about that Evanston police got word of Allan Showery, which they passed on to Chicago authorities.

"I was assigned to check a suspicious telephone call which our department received a complaint on July 15, 1977. I got the case on the afternoon of the seventeenth. I interviewed the complainants, a Dr. and Mrs. Chua, on the phone, and later in their home," he related.

"She—Mrs. Chua—said she feared for her life and that a man named Allan Showery, whom she worked with, was calling her. She believed it was him. She said he was employed with her at Edgewater Hospital. Dr. Chua told me he thought the caller was a black male. He said he spoke with Showery the day after the call."

McKinney concluded his piece by pointing out that he passed the information on to Sergeant Edward Flynn of Area 6 Homicide.

There was no cross-examination. Organ moved to have all of McKinney's testimony stricken from the record because it did not relate to the motion at hand. Judge Barbaro agreed.

With McKinney's testimony thrown out, Swano had the accounts of only three witnesses on the record—Showery, Stachula and Yanka Kalmuk. "The defense calls Dr. José Chua," he announced dramatically.

It was 10:50 a.m. The doctor had been waiting for more than an hour in the witness room, where persons waiting to testify are isolated so they won't be influenced by what others might say. Chua had spent part of the time chatting amiably with newsmen. "You know, since this story came out I've had to spend a lot of time answering my telephone and front door," he chuckled. "One guy came to my house all the way from Germany."

The Chuas had hoped to keep their psychic experience a secret, particularly from the medical community, but the cat was already out of the bag. Now the world was about to hear the inside story right from the source.

Dr. Chua strutted to the witness stand, colorful as a Philippine fighting cock, in his blue leisure suit and light blue print shirt, masculinely open at the neck. His rimless glasses curved dashingly around the side of his face. He was cool and in complete control as he testified he had been in the United States for five years and first spoke with Stachula in early August 1977.

"I called the Evanston Police Department for protection," he explained. "We received an anonymous telephone call during the night of July 15."

Swano: "Prior to that, had your wife had any psychic premonitions during the summer of 1977? Did your wife experience an unusual possession?"

Chua: "I think so."

His answers were crisp, short and occasionally vague. He said the three "possessions" occurred within three or four days, lasting from a few minutes to as long as 15 minutes. The first intrusion into his wife's body by Teresita Basa took place before the anonymous call, he said. The second and third, after the call.

Swano: "Would you call them possessions?"

Chua: "Uh, more or less."

Swano: "Had you ever met Allan Showery?"

Chua: "Only once, at Edgewater Hospital. The next day, after the call."

Swano: "Did your wife tell you she did not like Showery?"

Chua: "Uh, I don't think so."

The doctor said there was no mention of Showery's name during the first two "possessions," but it did come out during the third time Teresita took over his wife's body. He added that, upon awakening, Remebios "did not recall a single event."

Swano then asked Chua to describe the three possessions.

Possession I: "I asked my wife, 'What is your name?' She answered me, 'Teresita Basa.' So I was really surprised and scared. At no time before the possessions had we ever discussed the Basa murder. She said, 'Doctor, I would like to ask your help.' I asked, 'What kind?' She said, 'I want to give you information about my killer.' My wife then awoke, The voice was not hers. It was different. It had a Spanish accent."

Possession II: "It was more or less the same thing—asking for my help. She was really pleading for me to help her solve the murder. I asked how I could help her. I have no proof or leads. Who did the murder? She told me I have nothing to be scared of."

Possession III: "That was the time Teresita Basa came out with some proof. She was really pleading, and crying, 'Mama, Mama, please help me.' She gave me proof to tie up this case. She mentioned the jewelry taken by Allan Showery. 'How can the jewelry be identified?' I asked. 'My relatives can identify it.' 'How come you let Allan Showery get into your apartment?' She told me, 'He was a friend of mine.' The voice told me the jewelry was in the possession of his common-law wife."

Dr. Chua testified for less than an hour. Then Swano offered his motion. He asked that Showery's arrest be quashed on grounds the investigators had no sufficient reason to go into his home and confront him in the first place.

Prosecutor Organ argued, "The only issue is whether police had probable cause to arrest the suspect." It was a point, he asserted, that was supported by the evidence, and did not concern defense claims of a bizarre psychic phenomenon.

Judge Barbaro clasped his hands pensively, paused while he studied the two sets of apprehensive attorneys standing before the bench, and declared he would withhold his ruling until the following morning. It would guarantee one more day of headlines.

* * *

On Wednesday morning, September 6, Judge Frank "Bar-B-Q" Barbaro did not keep the lawyers, the defendant, or the press in suspense. He announced right off, as soon as court was called to order, "Motion denied." He refused to dismiss the charges, and ordered Showery to stand trial for murder.

The judge said he found "no misconduct" on the part of either Stachula or Epplen in meeting with and questioning Showery, after receiving "certain information" concerning him from Dr. Chua. He added that he was satisfied that, once at police headquarters, Showery was informed of his legal right to remain silent. Then the detectives not only took a statement from Showery in which he admitted the murder, but found jewelry in his home that had been taken from the Basa apartment. Barbaro emphasized that police did not file the murder charge against Showery until after he had admitted he had killed Teresita.

At no time during his recitation did Judge Barbaro mention psychic phenomena or the "voice from the grave." The closest he came was when he asserted, "I see no reason to restrict the investigatory power of the police. Whether they believed the information or not, they had to check it out."

Showery's trial was scheduled for Monday, October 2, 1978.

Several hours later Organ was seen passing out cigars in the criminal courts building—not because he had won his argument, but because his wife, Ruth, had just given birth to a 12-pound 9-ounce son.

CHAPTER 25

![black bar]

THE TRIAL

It's a rare day, indeed, if any event comes off as scheduled in Cook County's dinosaur system of criminal justice. Out-of-town newsmen, trying to make arrangements to cover the "voice from the grave" murder trial, soon found that the October date was little more than an "X" on the judge's calendar. Trials must often be put off until another day when a judge finds himself faced with previous matters yet undisposed of. Prosecutors ask for continuances to give themselves more time to locate necessary witnesses. Defense attorneys often find themselves needing more time to prepare their strategy, or to seek out their own witnesses—or to collect their fee.

Many never intend to go to trial, because of the expense. They string things along in hopes the prosecution will offer a deal in return for a guilty plea. Other times, lawyers find themselves still on trial in another court on a different matter, and have to plead for a continuance because they can't be two places at once.

Also, juries are historically lenient around the Christmas holidays, so prosecutors try to avoid lengthy trials that might extend into the festive season.

It was for any or all of the above reasons that Allan Showery's trial did not get under way until January 8, 1979—

nearly 23 months after the death of Teresita Basa, and after 17 months of sitting in jail where he was "presumed innocent." By Cook County standards, everything was right on schedule.

Organ had spent much of his free time since the previous hearing interviewing and re-interviewing Dr. and Mrs. Chua. He had to know, for his personal satisfaction, whether they were for real. He had no intention of calling them as prosecution witnesses, but at the same time was not about to have a widely-publicized case blow up in his face because two of the main characters turned out to be phonies.

On one occasion he and Schoen brought Stachula along when they went to the Chua home. The detective, who used his "open mind" tack to draw the information out of the couple during his original visit, now changed to the tough, skeptical cop tactic.

"Look, doctor. You're going to have to prove your story somehow," he attacked. "I just don't believe it, and I'm not about to swallow this 'voice' baloney."

Chua calmly shrugged his shoulders. "O.K. Then let's forget the whole thing, if that's the way you feel."

In the end Organ and Schoen were as convinced as Stachula had been of the Chuas' sincerity. They decided to press Showery's prosecution to the limit.

Judge Barbaro's courtroom was on the fifth floor of the criminal courts building on Chicago's nearly inaccessible Southwest Side. There were three other courtrooms, a snack stand operated by a blind man, and the usual foul-smelling public toilets on the same floor. The water fountains in the corridor did not work, and the marble walls, everywhere, were adorned with graffiti.

The short, swarthy Barbaro, the son of an Italian day laborer, had spent his entire life in the politically heavy Bridgeport neighborhood of the late Mayor Richard J. Daley. He was but one of hundreds of obedient Democrats put on the bench by the late mayor. Since getting the nod in 1965 he had spent his entire judicial career at criminal court. Twenty-Sixth and Cal was considered a legal Siberia to many, a dumping ground for jurists who couldn't hack it, or who had offended the Daley machine. Barbaro, on the other hand, found the unending flow of accused felons "fast moving . . . very stimulating . . . exhilarating."

In his 13 years on the bench he had heard some of the county's biggest cases, but this would be the first to pull him into the national spotlight. The doors through which jurors would pass into his court were carved with the names of the "Insane Disciples" and "U.K. [unknown] Killers" and other street gangs.

A new defense lawyer also passed through those doors, to join Showery's team of Swano and Radakovich. She was 27-year-old Karen Thompson, a thin blonde with a quick smile—who just happened to be the kid sister of Governor James Thompson. In fact, Thompson was inaugurated for his first four-year term as governor of Illinois on the opening day of Showery's trial.

Thompson, who reveled in being called "Big Jim," got his start as an assistant state's attorney, right out of law school, in this very building. But Sis was playing on the opposite team.

It was bitter cold in Chicago, with seven inches of powdery snow on the ground, as the prosecution and defense lawyers began the painstaking task of selecting a jury to hear evidence in the case. Midway through the process during the first morning a prospective juror bolted from her seat and ran from the courtroom screaming, "I'm sick! I'm sick!" Up to that point Barbaro had asked each member of the venire whether he or she knew any of the lawyers, the defendant, or the victim, Teresita Basa.

After the unnerving scene of the woman who ran screaming from the room, however, he shifted gears and began asking each potential juror, "Have you ever heard of the 'voice from the grave' case?" The room grew pin-drop quiet at his question. Any prospective juror who had not recognized the names of principals in the case up to now suddenly knew why he or she was there.

It took two full days to select a jury and fate—or was it Teresita Basa?—played one more trick as testimony was about to begin on Wednesday, January 10.

Three weeks earlier police seeking a missing teen-aged boy had gone to the home of John Wayne Gacy, a ne'er-do-well building contractor, just northwest of Chicago. Before leaving they had unearthed the bodies of 28 young men and boys from under Gacy's home, and found the bodies of five more of his victims elsewhere. The likeable, 34-year-old builder, who liked to put on a clown suit and entertain at children's parties, was catapulted into the headlines as the biggest mass murder suspect of civilized times. The avowed homosexual who said he lured young boys to his home with promises of jobs was charged with 33 counts of murder.

On the morning of January 10, he was being arraigned before Chief Judge Richard J. Fitzgerald in the courtroom directly below Barbaro's. The out-of-town newsmen, wire service and television reporters sent to cover the "voice from the grave" murder trial instead flocked into Fitzgerald's courtroom to get a first-hand look at the little man people were calling the "monster from the house of horror."

And the trial upstairs of the man accused of murdering Teresita Basa opened quietly, and with dignity.

* * *

Day 1:

It was below zero outside. The windows on the east side of Judge Barbaro's courtroom were coated with a layer of no-see-through frost as the eight men and four women filed into the jury box. Three of the men and one of the women, like the defendant, were black.

Showery, wearing a maroon knit shirt, dark trousers and dark colored shoes, was already seated at the defense table with his troika of attorneys. He appeared remarkably calm, resting his arms on the arms of the wooden chair, and his legs crossed nonchalantly at the ankles. As the trial was about to begin he leaned over and whispered something into Karen Thompson's ear, his lips brushing her fair, blonde hair.

"This is a case about murder," Organ declared, introducing the case for the prosecution in the most fundamental way.

"And that man, Allan Showery, murdered and robbed Teresita Basa, and set fire to her apartment to cover it up."

In calm, direct tones he went on to describe the discovery of the body by firefighters. "Teresita was lying on her back, naked and badly burned. A large kitchen knife was stuck in the middle of her chest. Her apartment was in shambles." He told the jurors that no fingerprints were found on the knife, an ordinary kitchen instrument with a wooden handle and a nine-inch blade, made in Japan. The only prints found in the apartment, he said, were lifted from two Budweiser beer cans, but they could not be traced. The motive, Organ said, was robbery.

He pointed out that Showery, a friend and co-worker of Teresita's, had confessed to the murder, which he said he committed because he needed money. "The evidence will convince you," he concluded, "to return a verdict of guilty."

At no time in his opening statement did the prosecutor refer to the mysterious "voice" that had incriminated the defendant. Nor did he mention either Dr. or Mrs. Chua.

But Radakovich did. It was he, not Swano, who fired the opening salvo for the defense. In a surprise move, the tall, awkward-appearing public defender whisked Teresita Basa's ghost right out of the closet.

"There is no doubt that Teresita Basa was brutally murdered," he agreed, grinning boyishly but trying to be serious at the same time. "But there is also no doubt that Allan Showery was not the murderer. We are going to prove Allan Showery innocent."

Then he laid it all out—what he characterized as the "unbelievable" story of the possession of Mrs. Chua's body by Teresita Basa. "The police investigation was stalled when the unbelievable happened," he said. "And, yes, the 'voice' named Allan Showery."

The young defender argued that Showery's wife was pregnant, and insisted that Showery confessed "under police coercion" to spare Yanka from being arrested along with him "and giving birth to their children in jail." He acknowledged that Teresita's jewelry was found in Yanka's possession, and charged that police had threatened to jail her as an accessory unless Allan confessed.

"Mrs. Chua was in the process of being fired from her job at Edgewater Hospital when she was visited by the mystery voice," Radakovich concluded. "She had personal problems."

Yanka was not present in court, but another woman was. A middle-aged black woman in a red cloth winter coat, she identified herself to reporters only as "Naomi," and said she worked at Edgewater Hospital. She would be there every day of the trial, and occasionally Allan Showery would toss a smile in her direction.

The first witness for the prosecution was James Frankenbach, the police lab technician. He identified the murder weapon, marked "People's Exhibit No. 1."

Teresita's cousin, Ron Somera, who had moved to San Diego, flew back for the trial. He told the jurors, "She and I played in the same band. I last saw her February 20 at band practice. When I next saw her in the morgue she was lifeless. She was dead."

Balding, red-haired Fire Lieutenant Warren Whelan was next in the parade of witnesses. He told of discovering the body while fighting an apartment fire at 2740 N. Pine Grove. "We all crawled in. One man with an axe pole broke out the patio window to ventilate. We started to put water on it while we were on our hands and knees. Another fireman smashed the bedroom window. As the smoke lifted we started to take the mattress out of the bedroom. There was nothing left to it but the springs. Then I noticed what appeared to be a large pile of clothing. As I picked it up I found the body of a woman wedged between the bed and the wall. I noticed a large knife stuck in her chest."

The prosecution witnesses were led through their testimony by Schoen. There was no cross-examination at this point. The defense was not contesting the fact that Teresita Basa had been murdered, and they were doing nothing to interrupt the flow of the trial that might antagonize the jury.

The sooner the prosecution wound up its presentation, the better.

Two more witnesses were called before court recessed for the day. Crime lab technician Robert Reese told of photographing the body, and of placing plastic bags over the victim's burned hands to "preserve" them for fingerprinting.

FBI Agent Robert M. Reilley, who was a Chicago crime lab technician at the time of the murder, told how he took Teresita's fingerprints as she lay on a basement embalming table in the funeral home at 1706 W. Jackson Boulevard. "I took prints from her left hand. Her right hand was severely charred."

*   *   *

Day 2:

The weather on Thursday was almost a carbon copy of the day before—a typical, cold, mid-winter day that was lulling Chicagoans into a false sense of security.

Allan Showery walked into court wearing a gray ski sweater, black necktie and dark trousers. He took his seat between Swano and Karen Thompson. Among the spectators who came out in the cold to see the man accused by Teresita's ghost was Judge Barbaro's wife, Rosemarie.

It was another day of nuts-and-bolts testimony—establishing for the record the undisputed fact that someone had once been vibrant and alive was now dead, and the change was not due to natural causes.

The first witness was the slightly built Dr. Tae An, the Korean pathologist who performed the post mortem examination on Teresita at the morgue. "The cause of death is stab wound lacerating the heart, and strangulation," he recited.

"Did you have a problem removing the knife?" Organ asked.

"It was stuck in tightly."

For the remainder of the day the witness stand was occupied by Joe Stachula. Wearing a conservative gray business suit and vest, the slender Stachula looked more like a mild-mannered accountant than the ex-Marine cop who, by way of a route he could not explain, had found the key to the mystery case. After being discreetly advised by the judge not to go into Showery's prior criminal record Stachula, led through the paces by Organ, recounted with little visible emotion the story he had told so many times before.

Since the defense lawyers had already brought the Chuas into the case, in Radakovich's opening statement to the jury, Organ thought it best to lay everything out first, rather than risk being accused by Showery's side of withholding the real story. His line of questioning deliberately led Stachula to the Chua's front porch in Skokie.

"Upon being ushered into Doctor Chua's home and being seated, the doctor started the conversation by saying he did not want to unjustly accuse anyone . . . that his wife was possessed by a spirit not her own," Stachula testified.

"A voice identified itself as Teresita Basa and said she had been murdered, and that Allan Showery was responsible."

The ghost of Teresita was now out but good. The jurors had heard Radakovich describe the incident the previous day. Now they had heard it from the lips of the detective, under oath on the witness stand.

Stachula then told how the "voice" asked Dr. Chua to notify police. "She wanted Doctor Chua to notify police of this information. Initially he was embarrassed and did not want to unjustly accuse Showery. He was reluctant to notify authorities. But the voice became more and more insistent, even commanding."

After hearing the doctor's story, Stachula said he and Epplen went to Showery's home, and found the victim's jewelry. "When I asked Mr. Showery where he got the jewelry, he told me 'Off a guy on the street for $28.'" He then proceeded to tell how Showery ultimately confessed to the murder.

Showery sat motionless, staring straight at the policeman as Stachula continued. "He grabbed her from behind with a stranglehold . . . and plunged a knife directly into her chest."

"Now, Detective Stachula. Do you see Allan Showery, the man who confessed to the murder of Teresita Basa, in this room?" Organ asked.

Rising easily from the witness chair, Stachula pointed a finger directly at Showery. "That is the man."

Under cross examination, Swano endeavored to build on the fact that Stachula had not filed an official police report on his interviews with the Chuas, but instead left a confidential memo on the "Voice from the Grave" for his commanding officer.

"My decision was not to disregard the information, but to check out what was told to me that evening," Stachula said firmly.

*   *   *

Day 3:

Reporters covering the trial were beginning to wonder where the hell a man who was accused of murdering for $30 could come up with the wardrobe Showery displayed. He flounced into court Friday morning wearing a baby blue denim suit, cut Western style, and neatly pressed. He had on a white shirt, flower-print necktie, and vest.

As court convened a group of 24 high school students from Evanston trooped in, wearing their heavy winter coats and galoshes. Their teacher explained that they were from a class in consumer economics and law. They arrived just in time to hear Richard Pessotti, Teresita's long-time friend, tell how he squired her to dinners, movies and social affairs.

The final witness for the day was Paul Linton, the assistant state's attorney who took the original confession from Showery on the night of his arrest. He testified that Showery's confession lasted for 35 minutes, from 1:15 a.m. to 1:50 a.m., and after being transcribed was signed by Showery at 3:08 a.m.

"He told me he was having severe financial problems, and took $30 from her purse and some jewelry from her bedroom after the killing," Linton related, as the jurors shifted their gaze from the witness to the nattily attired defendant. With a nod from Judge Barbaro, Linton then read the entire 13-page confession to the attentive jury panel.

On Saturday and Sunday, January 13 and 14, Chicago was hit by a severe blizzard, comparable in every way to the "Great Snow Storm of 1967" that paralyzed the city. Fortunately there was no court on Monday, January 15, because of the Reverend Martin Luther King Jr.'s birthday. There was no court the following day, either, because three of the jurors were unable to make their way through the snow.

*　*　*

Day 4:

Al Ballard, the tall, lanky black bailiff assigned to Judge Barbaro's court, bellowed the now familiar, "Showery! Allan Showery!" in his high-pitched voice, and escorted the prisoner into the courtroom.

"Call your next witness," Barbaro said, nodding toward the prosecution table.

"The state rests," Organ announced unexpectedly. There would be no next witness. He wasn't about to put the Chuas on the stand and let the defense lawyers rip them to pieces.

So now it was up to Swano and Radakovich to get their man off the hook. Karen Thompson, who had been ill on Friday, was back at the defense table, and that seemed to cheer Showery up.

Waiting in the witness quarters, both Dr. and Mrs. Chua wore puzzled looks. They had been instrumental in bringing about Showery's arrest, and now they were being told to stand by to testify in his defense. "Only in America," Chua whispered to his wife, shaking his head.

The 40-year-old Remebios Chua—Reme, he called her—nervously sipped coffee from a plastic cup as she read the paper. She was still bundled in a heavy imitation fur coat. Chicago, with its wicked winters, was a far cry from the pleasant Philippine Islands. Dr. Chua, sitting across from her, puffed a cigarette while he leafed through the pages of a golf magazine. It was the only other reading material in the small room.

He rose, walked around the conference table, and stared glumly out the window at traffic struggling along snow-clogged California Avenue. "They don't even have the plows out yet," he grumbled. "Can you imagine? Three hours to get here from Skokie! I thought it would take forever." Mrs. Chua, huddled in her fur, did not bother to reply.

Swano, wearing a gray pin-striped suit, quipped, "This is my convict suit," as he strode into court. Organ and Schoen did not smile. They did not like Swano. Few prosecutors did. He was tricky and, they claimed, given to "misstating some things." The owner of a cunning and devious personality, he was a defendant's dream.

"Is the defense ready," asked Barbaro.

"We are, your honor," smiled Swano, aching to get his performance under way.

"You may call your first witness."

"The bailiff ushered in Petro Lulusa, the janitor. Questioned gently by Swano, Lulusa related that he first met Teresita when she locked herself out of her apartment, and he had to open the door with his master key. On another occasion, he recalled, he helped her move a piano she had sold out of the building in the freight elevator.

"I last saw her two weeks before she was gone," he testified, avoiding the word "murdered." "She was in the lobby with a man, white and bald, about 45 or 50. I had the impression they were arguing about something."

Swano held up a photograph of Robert Knudson and asked whether that was the man who had been with Teresita.

"That is the man in the lobby," Lulusa nodded.

"Ever see this man?" Swano questioned, holding up a photo of Showery. The witness shook his head. Swano then turned and pointed to the defendant in court.

"I never saw him," Lulusa asserted.

Swano next called Ralph Magner, in a subtle effort to point suspicion at him in an attempt to confuse the jury. The handsome Magner, with his thick, sandy hair, admitted having socialized with Teresita on a number of occasions. He acknowledged having talked to police twice, at their request, and like Lulusa said he had never seen Showery, at Teresita's apartment "or anywhere else."

Schoen, on cross examination, asked Magner, "You didn't confess to this crime because you didn't kill her. Is that correct?"

"That's correct," Magner answered, almost amused.

The third defense witness was the tall, lean, and scruffy Arthur Shields, the one-time janitor in the Pine Grove building. He appeared in work clothes, and said he now managed a liquor store on Broadway. He testified that he had known Teresita for about two years, but had never met Showery. He pointed out Magner as the man he had seen knocking on Teresita's door in the afternoon on the day of the murder.

"I saw this man knocking on her door and told him there is a building policy to challenge anyone walking around on the floors," he said. "All he said was he wanted to see if she was home."

Outside the courtroom during a brief recess, Magner quipped to the press, "I'm the guy he identified, all right. But I still wasn't there."

The recess had been called while Swano and Radakovich decided what to do about their next witness. Swano intended to call Ronnie Sparrow, the teen-ager who at one time was a hot suspect in the slaying. Sparrow had agreed to testify that police abused him and threatened him when they questioned him during the homicide investigation. Swano's game plan was to give the jury the impression that authorities had used similar coercive tactics on Showery to get him to confess. At the last minute, however, Swano discovered that his witness was not in the witness quarters, but in the prisoners' bullpen behind the courtroom.

"What the hell is he doing in the bullpen?" he demanded.

"I just found out," Radakovich said. "They tell me he went to the home of Myron Walters, the lawyer he used to work for, and shot him in the head."

"Oh, Jesus Christ," moaned Swano.

"Yeah. There goes his credibility. No way are we going to vouch for his character now," Radakovich pointed out.

"Never in a million years," agreed Swano. "The prosecution could tear the son-of-a-bitch apart."

"O.K. then, let's go with the Chuas," Radakovich suggested.

"The defense calls Mrs. Remebios Chua," Swano announced when court reconvened. Organ leaped to his feet.

"Your honor, we object to this witness being called," he declared, approaching the bench. "The Chuas have no relevant or material testimony to offer as to the guilt or innocence of Allan Showery."

"Your honor," Swano argued. "While I, myself, do not believe the Chuas' story, the defense would like to put them on the stand to show the three comatose episodes might have been fabricated."

"All right," Barbaro agreed. "They may testify. Since this might be a lengthy witness, the court is going to adjourn for lunch, rather than have her testimony interrupted. We will hear your witness when we return this afternoon."

At exactly 1:50 p.m., after Showery had been led into court by the bailiff and seated at the defense table, Judge Barbaro turned to Swano. "You may call the next witness."

"Remebios Chua," said Swano.

"Remebios Chua," called the tall, lanky bailiff as he strode across the room to the witness quarters. Al Ballard knew that at the moment all eyes were on him, and he relished the cameo role he was playing in the unfolding drama. "Remebios Chua!" he called once more, just for effect.

Ballard escorted Mrs. Chua into the room, and helped her up the step into the witness box. She settled into the chair nervously as he handed her the hand-microphone. She did not look comfortable in the bulky knit beige sweater with the cowl neck, and her long, flared beige skirt. She wore full-length brown leather boots, and had her black hair combed tightly back.

Now, for the first time ever, Mrs. Chua would be asked to tell how Teresita Basa possessed her body. Under oath.

Swano, hoping to open the door to potentially damaging testimony that might discredit the witness around whom police based their case, began slowly, gently, to probe. "Yes," Mrs. Chua testified, she had worked at Edgewater Hospital from the summer of 1975 until July 1977, "when my job was cancelled." She said she knew Teresita only slightly, because they worked different shifts. "She worked days, and I worked 11 p.m. to 7 a.m. Only during orientation did we work together."

"How about Allan Showery? Did you work with him?"

"Showery worked nights with me twice a week."

She also testified that she earned extra money selling jewelry to fellow employees. On one occasion, in the summer of 1976, she recalled, she sold Showery a man's diamond ring on a trial basis. The price was $250, but Showery could only come up with a $50 deposit. "He returned the ring to me three months later and I returned the deposit," she said. Swano then hit her with the two pieces of jewelry police took from Yanka—the jade pendant and the pearl cocktail ring.

"Did you sell this cocktail ring to Allan for $28?" Swano asked dramatically, holding up the state's evidence.

"No," Mrs. Chua responded nervously.

"And this jade pendant, didn't you sell it to Allan for $100?"

"No."

Swano then moved to the anonymous call, which Mrs. Chua said she believed came from Showery. "It was just one call, about eleven o'clock on a Friday night. It was July 15, 1977. My husband answered the call. We were still living in Evanston at the time."

"Did you tell police you thought Allan Showery was responsible?"

"Yes."

"Did you tell police you thought Allan Showery was going to harm you?"

"Yes."

Up to now Swano was only toying with the witness; getting her accustomed to answering from the stand. Now he moved into the so-called "possessions."

"Did you have three psychic seizures, or possessions, in which Teresita Basa spoke through your lips?"

"Yes," she responded, as the wail of a lone fire truck forging through the snow-clogged street below pierced the eerie quiet of the courtroom. Mrs. Chua then related, under Swano's guidance, the three times Teresita Basa "spoke through my lips"—on July 16, July 18 and July 19.

"Do you remember Teresita's voice?"

"All I remember was hearing the name Al," she said.

"Al? As in Allan Showery?"

"Yes," she responded softly, nodding her head.

Asked what else she remembered about the visits, she said, "I felt cold and thirsty. I remember nothing."

On July 30, she said, she and her husband moved to Skokie.

Organ made his cross-examination brief. He intended to ask nothing that might lay the groundwork for additional questions by the defense.

"Did you kill Teresita Basa?" he asked.

"Nooooo," she wailed loudly.

Mrs. Chua stepped down, thoroughly shaken, as Swano called her husband, and turned the questioning over to Radakovich. Dr. Chua, wearing a gaudy sports coat of dark and light blue checkered squares, and trousers to match, sniffled as he marched to the stand. He was fighting a miserable cold.

The doctor took the oath, assumed a relaxed position in the chair, and waved the microphone casually in front of his face as if to say, "Let's go so I can get the hell out of here."

Dr. Chua then retold the story he had related so many times before, of the three "possessions" of his wife's body by Teresita Basa, how Teresita's voice named Showery as her killer, and how she asked the doctor to help bring him to justice.

There was no cross examination. Dr. Chua was excused, and Judge Barbaro recessed court for the day.

* * *

Day 5:

Thursday, January 18, found Chicago in the midst of the worst snow disaster in the city's history. The day was sunny and cold, with a forecast of up to nine more inches. Traffic was snarled from one end of town to the other, but help was on the way in the form of caravans of heavy duty snow removal equipment from as far away as Canada. Judge Barbaro, who himself had no easy time getting out to Twenty-Sixth and California, gazed warily from the courtroom window as the snowflakes wafted down upon the already near-paralyzed city, and nodded to Swano, "Call your witness."

It was John Redmond, the police evidence technician. Showery, wearing his fashionable blue denim outfit, watched with interest as the 11-year police veteran, in uniform, marched briskly to the stand. Questioned by Karen Thompson, he described how he lifted several latent fingerprints from the three empty beer cans found in Teresita's apartment after the fire. "The cans were all bent. Someone had crushed them," he pointed out.

Redmond was followed by another police evidence technician, John Olejniczak, who said one of the prints on a beer can was Teresita's. He could not identify any others.

Then a third police evidence technician, Dennis O'Neill, was called. Swano was using the time-honored tactic of wearing down the jury with trivial testimony—over-killing them with minuscule data. He was also wearing down Judge Barbaro, who made no secret of his irritation. Unperturbed, Swano insisted that each witness, under oath, outline his qualifications in detail. The prosecution had offered to stipulate to the qualifications of the Chicago police officers, but Swano elected to travel the nickel-and-dime route as Barbaro frowned down from the bench. The judge loudly shifted papers, and twirled in his swivel chair, giving the witness his backside and closing his eyes as O'Neill droned out answers to Swano's seemingly unending line of questions.

The gist of his testimony was that he had checked fingerprints on the beer cans with those of Allan Showery, Ralph Magner, Richard Pessotti and Ray King, and none matched.

Next came yet another evidence technician, James Dunbar, who took the oath to tell the truth as Barbaro appeared to be counting the falling snowflakes outside the courtroom window. After stating his qualifications, he testified that he had found five strands of hair on Teresita's left arm as her body lay in the Cook County morgue.

Enter the brothers Palenik—Mark and Samuel—who were introduced as Chicago hair experts. The snow continued to pile up outside as Mark, a man in his late 20s, described how he picked, pulled, and combed three hair samples from Allan Showery's head on January 12, while Showery was having lunch in the prisoners' bullpen. "I accomplished this by reaching through the bars," he said.

Next Swano called Samuel "Skip" Palenik, the older of the two hair experts, who sported a drooping mustache. He testified that he had studied hair since the age of eight, had been collecting it since he was ten, and said he was a "hair adviser" to the Royal Canadian Mounted police.

Palenik rattled on so fast the court reporter had to interrupt his testimony to ask him to slow down. Palenik said he examined the hair strands Dunbar had removed from Teresita's arm in the morgue, and determined that they belonged to neither Showery or the victim. He described the strands as four to seven inches in length, and treated with bleach, or dye. He also disclosed that Teresita dyed her hair.

Much to Barbaro's obvious relief, the hair experts were excused and Swano called his final witness of the day, Mrs. Joanne O'Hara, an attractive woman of about 30, who said she was a bookkeeper for the property management firm that collected rent for the Surf Street building where Showery had lived with Yanka Kalmuk. Armed with records for the building, Mrs. O'Hara revealed that the third-floor quarters had been leased in Yanka's name for $225 a month.

She testified that, while Yanka owed as much as $560 in back rent on February 1, 1977, the sum was reduced to only $130 two weeks later, through payments of $125 on February 1, $125 on the ninth, and $180 on the fourteenth.

Swano had elicited her boring testimony to dispute the part of Showery's confession in which he claimed he killed Teresita because he needed money to pay back rent and the electric bill. Under cross examination by Schoen, however, Mrs. O'Hara said Yanka had been in arrears since September of 1976, and that eviction proceedings had been started in October of that year.

After Mrs. O'Hara stepped down Judge Barbaro swung around in his chair and faced the jury. "Ladies and gentlemen," he began, referring to the psychic phenomenon testimony they had heard earlier, "the only phenomenon that concerns me at the moment is the weather. Rather than making your way down to the courthouse as usual tomorrow, I would ask that each of you remain at home and await a call from my staff before you attempt to come in. I'm not sure I like what is going on outside."

Barbaro proved very perceptive. By Friday morning two more inches of new snow were on the ground, and the city was being buffeted by high winds and drizzle. He called off court for the day.

* * *

Day 6:

The city was still digging out on Monday, January 22, when the trial resumed. While waiting to be brought into court Showery complained bitterly. "There's no heat in the jail. Some of the windows have been busted out, and not even fixed. They got sheets of plastic strung over the frames to keep out the wind. It's awful bad," he said, between puffs on a cigarette. He was again wearing his blue denim togs—clearly his favorite.

The opening witness was Gilbert T. James, an immense black man who said he worked as a draftsman and sign painter at Chicago's main post office. He said he was also an instructor in the martial arts—karate, judo and aikido. James did not know Showery, but that was not why he had been called by the defense.

Swano wanted him to demonstrate for the jury a "Japanese full-Nelson," the hold Showery claimed, in his confession, to have used on Teresita's neck. James stepped down from the stand and proceeded to demonstrate the hold on Swano, who dramatically yelled, "Ouch!" The point of the demonstration was to show that a Japanese full-Nelson pressed on the back of the neck, not the front, where Dr. An earlier testified he had noted injuries on the fire-burned victim. Thus, one more element of doubt was raised in the state's case against Showery as the giant James, slightly mystified by the whole thing, lumbered out of the court.

"Call your next witness," Barbaro droned, somewhat amused.

Karen Thompson, wearing a dark wine-colored suit, rose from the defense table and called out, "Allan Showery."

Showery, who was sitting next to her, walked calmly to the witness stand and grasped the microphone. Then, led by Miss Thompson, he related his life history, from birth to Yanka. Most of the questions were in the form of facts stated by the defense attorney, with Showery simply responding, "That is correct."

Finally the governor's sister got down to what everyone was straining to hear: Showery's own, under oath, story of what happened on the night of February 21, 1977.

Showery testified that he knew Teresita, often rode the bus home with her, and occasionally walked by the building in which she lived. He had never been inside the apartment, he insisted, and never "socialized" with her. After work on the day of the murder, he said he stopped off at a pub known as the Roadhouse on North Clark Street.

"I shot two games of pool, drank beer, and left about 6:00 p.m. I went home and had dinner with Yanka." Sometime around 7:30 p.m., he said, he went next door to the home of another couple, Revelle and Kathleen White. He said he brought along a half-filled bottle of Southern Comfort. Actually, it was a Jim Beam bowling pin bottle into which he had poured the Southern Comfort, he explained. Yanka dropped in a short time later to make it a foursome.

Showery told the jury that he and Revelle spent the next few hours "drinking and playing darts," while the women sipped wine in the kitchen. When he and Yanka returned to their own apartment to watch television around 10:00 p.m., he left the empty Beam bottle with Revelle. "He's a collector," Showery explained.

"Did you see anything unusual?" asked Miss Thompson.

"Yes. The news was relating about Teresita Basa's death," he said. "The next day just about everybody in the hospital was talking about it. The police and press were there."

Showery testified that he subsequently read stories about the grisly homicide, which was how he knew what to say when he "faked" the confession. "I had been drinking when the two detectives came. I asked if I need a lawyer, and they said, just come on downtown." Once at Area 6 headquarters, Showery said, "Stachula showed me a picture of her. She was dead, and he kept saying to make a confession. They accused me of killing her."

When Stachula and Epplen brought Yanka in, he said, he agreed to give a signed statement after they threatened to arrest his pregnant woman as an accessory to murder.

"The police said they were going to arrest Yanka and me for the murder. They said I would never see Yanka or the child again, but if I confessed, Yanka would go free. They were telling me to confess, so I said, 'I will tell you anything you want to know.'"

Pressed by Miss Thompson as to why he agreed to confess, Showery reiterated, "Because I wanted to get Yanka out of there that night. She was eight months pregnant and very upset."

He said the two detectives coached him on what to say while awaiting the arrival of the assistant state's attorney. "I never helped her with immigration. I don't even know what immigration is," he interjected.

"Then why did you say that in your confession?"

"I just threw it in."

Again Miss Thompson asked about his mention of felling Teresita with a Japanese full-Nelson. "I just threw it in," Showery said. "I didn't know anything about karate or judo. I just read some books on the martial arts, that's all."

"Why did you say it, then?" asked the lawyer.

"They wanted answers, so I gave them answers."

The governor's young sister then launched into her finale.

"Did you choke Teresita Basa?"

"No, no, no."

"Did you stab her?"

"No, no."

"Did you put a mattress on her body and set it ablaze?"

"No."

"Did you kill Teresita Basa?"

"No, no, no."

It was 3:40 p.m. when she completed her examination of the defendant. After a brief recess the anxious Organ swung into the counter-attack.

Drawing from Showery an admission that he had never attended Rutgers, Utah State, or embarked on a career of study of sociology and psychiatry—as he had testified at a bond hearing after his arrest—Organ began to paint the picture of a consummate liar. He also forced Showery to admit that he lied when he said he worked as a surgical assistant preparing patients for the operating room. What's more, he lied on his job application at Edgewater Hospital when he described himself as "a college educated professional and a karate instructor with a knowledge of electrical work."

How did Showery explain such damaging misstatements of fact?

"I was advised it would be impressive to put things down like that on the application."

"I see," said Organ sarcastically borrowing a phrase from Showery. "You just, 'threw it in!'"

At the end of the cross-examination, Judge Barbaro adjourned for the day. Showery, tense and rigid, left the witness stand rubbing his temples with both hands, as if he were trying to eject a severe headache.

Walking triumphantly back to the prosecution table, Organ commented out of the side of his mouth as he passed the press gallery, "I tore him a new asshole."

* * *

Day 7:

The U.S. Weather Bureau was calling for four to six more inches of heavy snow for Chicago. It promised to be a real sockdolager. Allan Showery arrived in court wearing a tan cotton sports coat and dark trousers.

Dr. John Abella, the Filipino physician who had telephoned Teresita on the night of the murder, was the first witness. Swano called him for the defense in an effort to cast doubt on the prosecution's contention that Teresita was slain immediately after Showery entered her apartment for the second time that evening. Abella, a pediatrician who operated a South Side clinic, said he talked with Teresita "for over ten minutes." He said he placed the call at 7:10 p.m., but he could no longer remember some of the details 23 months later. His testimony was interrupted by frequent objections from the state.

"During the course of the conversation, were there any interruptions?" asked Swano.

"Objection!" shouted Organ.

"Objection sustained," droned Judge Barbaro.

"Did you hear the door buzzer?"

"Yes. She excused herself because somebody . . ."

"Objection!"

"Sustained."

"... she returned to the phone. I heard no other voices," Dr. Abella concluded, ignoring the byplay.

He told the jurors he had met Teresita four or five years earlier, and that they played in the same band. "We planned to set up an orchestra and call it the Professionals."

The pediatrician was followed on the witness stand by Showery's former next-door neighbor, Kathleen White, a tall, 27-year-old brunette. Displaying an academic attractiveness behind dark-rimmed glasses, she wore a large turtleneck sweater, long wool skirt and snow boots. She seemed all legs and well prepared for the elements as she strode to the witness stand. Mrs. White, the mother of two, said that at the time of Teresita's death she worked in admitting at Grant Hospital. She was currently employed as a title examiner for the Chicago Title and Trust Co.

Referring to Allan and Yanka, she said, "We met socially on a regular basis. Playing darts, cards, and drinking." She did not recall the exact night in February that Showery and Yanka were over, nearly two years earlier, but thought it was somewhere around the twenty-first. "I remember the distinctive bottle Allan brought. It was empty and he left it with us. My husband collects empty bottles."

"Was there anything unusual about Allan's clothing on the party night?" Swano asked.

"I don't remember."

"Did you notice blood?"

"No."

The Jim Beam "pin bottle" that Showery had left with Revelle White on the night of the party was introduced into evidence as Defense Exhibit No. 25.

After Mrs. White stepped down, the defense called Connie Kuehn, Edgewater's directory of respiratory therapy. She related the circumstances that led to Mrs. Chua's firing after the confrontation with Ted Ellis, whom she described as a close friend of Showery's. The date of the firing was July 16, 1977—the day of the first "possession" of Mrs. Chua's body by Teresita.

"After you fired her, did she warn you of any physical harm?" asked Swano. The witness never got a chance to answer. Both prosecutors were on their feet objecting so loudly the judge called the attorneys for both sides into his chamber to discuss the matter.

"She will testify that Mrs. Chua called her and warned her, 'You're next.' Such testimony is highly relevant," Swano insisted. "We should be able to bring out that she warned Miss Kuehn, particularly in light of Mrs. Chua's suspect story."

"This conversation, if it indeed occurred, leaves an inference that goes no farther. To allow it would be improper," Judge Barbaro said. "I am going to sustain the state's objection."

"But judge," Swano protested. "Picture the situation. Chua is getting fired. She hears these voices. She tells police Allan Showery is the killer . . ."

"The objection will be sustained," Barbaro repeated sternly.

Back in the courtroom, Miss Kuehn was waved off the stand by an obviously angry Swano. "No further questions," he exclaimed.

"No cross, your honor," Organ droned airily.

After lunch Barbaro's daughter, Carrie, a 20-year-old student court reporter with her father's dark features, showed up with her Stenograph machine for some practice. She took a position near her father, fingers racing over the miniature keyboard, as the trial proceeded.

Karen Thompson called Yanka Kalmuk. Yanka did not look well. She was pale, a condition that accentuated her pronounced cheekbones. Brown shoots were clearly visible in her bleached blonde hair, which sorely needed retouching. She appeared older than her allowed "late twenties." She was wearing a ratty cloth coat with a fake fur collar, of the style generally worn by women much older than she. Underneath was a wine colored dress with matching sweater.

Yanka testified that she and her infant son, Emile, had moved in with her parents on Superior Street. She glanced furtively in Showery's direction as she testified, but he merely fixed a blank gaze on the table before him, refusing to give eye-contact to the woman he claimed he risked his all for by confessing to a crime he did not commit.

Yanka said she was presently working at Grant Hospital. Before Emile's birth she had worked at a realty firm, taking home $100 a week. She quit that job "in early February, 1977"—the month of Teresita's death—"but our financial condition at that time was comfortable."

Miuu Thompson then led Yanka through her alibi story for her ex-lover.

"Allan came home at 6:00 p.m., and we later went across the hall to the Whites' apartment. The men were playing darts and a TV tennis game. Kathy and I talked in the kitchen and had some wine."

"Did Allan ever give you any gifts?"

"When we were lovers Allan gave me lots of jewelry. About 20 things in all."

"Did he give you this pearl cocktail ring?" asked the lawyer, holding up the ring Epplen and Stachula had confiscated.

"Yes, that's the cocktail ring he gave me. He said he bought it at the hospital."

"And this jade pendant. Did Allan give that to you?"

"Yes, the jade pendant, too. But Allan didn't say where he got it."

She was then asked about the night of Showery's arrest, August 11.

"The police came to our house. Stachula and Epplen. I was very much pregnant at the time. They searched through the apartment after taking Allan away. They noticed a book in the corner. It said 'Ghosts' on the cover, and they asked me if I was superstitious, and did I believe in those kinds of stories. I said no."

"One final question. Have you visited Allan in jail?"

"A couple of times."

Schoen conducted the cross examination, making a point of letting the jury know they were dealing with an immigrant. He drew from Yanka the story of her German birth, and how she came to the United States with her parents at the age of nine. He also elicited from her an admission that she had originally told police that, on the night of the murder, she was out shopping and did not know where Allan had been. She now declared that the previous story was incorrect, and the tale of spending the evening with the Whites was the true version.

"Oh, one more thing," Schoen said quickly, is if it were an afterthought. "Did Allan support you, or . . ."

"I paid the bills!" retorted Yanka, showing no shame over who was the keeper and who was kept. "I paid the bills when Allan and I lived together."

Again she turned her eyes to Showery. He did not return her glance.

The next witness was Ruth Loeb, who had since retired from Edgewater Hospital. Her hair was tinted a light red, and she wore a neat, brown print dress. She testified that she telephoned Teresita about 7:30 p.m. on the night of the murder, and spoke to her for 10 or 15 minutes. "At one point I heard the voice of a man speak about 10 words in a normal tone. But I didn't get their meaning, and I couldn't recognize the voice."

The last person known to have heard Teresita's voice was the final defense witness. When Mrs. Loeb stepped down from the stand at 3:30 p.m. Swano rose and announced, "The defense rests."

Organ called Lee Epplen as a rebuttal witness. Among other things, Epplen repeated for the jury the claim Yanka had made of being out shopping on the night of the murder.

Epplen also testified that Showery confessed "of his own free will" after a brief, emotional meeting with Yanka while in police custody. He quoted Showery as telling his woman, "We've had a great seven years, but I am responsible for Miss Basa's death. I don't want you to wait for me because I am not coming back. I want you to sell the furniture and make a good life for our child."

The detective was on and off the stand in five minutes. The testimony and evidence of Allan Showery's trial was at an end.

Judge Barbaro adjourned for the day, after advising jurors that deliberations for a verdict would probably begin the following day.

* * *

Wednesday, January 24. It was time for closing arguments. The snow was falling fast outside.

Schoen went to bat first for the prosecution, summarizing the evidence. On the matter of the "voice from the grave," he told the jurors, "Police would be remiss if they did not follow up on each and every lead furnished by the public, no matter what it sounds like." Clearly the state's attorney was concerned over how the mostly blue-collar jury would take this bizarre aspect of the case.

Schoen also moved to knock down another wall of doubt raised by the defense: Did Mrs. Chua sell Showery the two pieces of jewelry the state said belonged to Teresita Basa? Mrs. Chua, after all, admitted selling jewelry at the hospital as a sideline.

Schoen held up for the jury's inspection both the jade pendant and the pearl cocktail ring. "These are family heirlooms of Teresita and they weren't sold by Mrs. Chua!" he declared. "That man, Showery, killed Teresita for them."

Turning to the confession, Schoen emphasized, "Showery gave it freely and of his own will, after being advised repeatedly of his rights, first by police, and then by Assistant State's Attorney Paul Linton. Look at it this way. Here, on trial, is an educated man in his 30s, not a 16-year-old kid who might be easy prey to intimidation by police. When you decide this case, use your common sense. Don't be misled by a lot of smoke."

Now it was Swano's turn. This would be his only shot, and he aimed to give it with a full charge of powder. Under Illinois law the prosecution gets a chance to plead its case.

Then, after the defense presents its side, the prosecution can make a rebuttal. Swano warmed up gradually.

Standing before the jury he began by referring to the abhorrent weather that had dogged the trial, commending the jurors as "heroic troopers for braving the 'Blizzard of '79' to get to court." Then, swiftly moving into high gear, he asserted, "I say to you this man is innocent, and the state's case is nothing but a fishing boat riddled with many reasonable doubts. That boat won't float."

He moved on to underscore these points:

- Showery's fingerprints were not found on the murder knife or anywhere else in the apartment.
- What about the drunken man seen arguing with the victim two weeks before her death?
- And what about those "mysterious strands of hair" found on Teresita's body? "They weren't Allan's."

He then attacked Stachula, branding the veteran detective an "overzealous officer" whose investigation and story about the "voice" took "one too many short cuts." He charged: "The police broke Allan Showery!"

And, what about that Jim Beam bowling pin bottle? "Thank God for this pin bottle," he declared. "It helped Allan remember where he was that night, and Yanka and Kathleen White also remembered, thanks to this bottle."

The defense lawyer saved his final salvo for Remebios Chua. He portrayed her as a woman possessed, not by spirits, but by paranoia. He pointed out that she had been pregnant and lost a baby around the time of the murder. Then she had her disagreement with Ted Ellis at the hospital. Then she phoned Connie Kuehn, her supervisor, "and warned her that she was going to be the next victim." He also brought out that she regularly sold jewelry at the hospital, and even admitted selling Showery a ring. Ignoring Showery's own assertion that he had brought the jade pendant and pearl cocktail from a stranger on the street, Swano charged that Mrs. Chua had Teresita's jewelry, and sold that to Showery as well.

"She didn't get that information from a spirit," he thundered. "If you believe her, that a voice from Teresita Basa spoke through her lips, and that is how she knew Allan Showery had the jewelry . . . If you believe that story, then don't believe Allan Showery."

It was Swano's final challenge to the jury: Believe in ghosts, or believe in Allan Showery, who was sitting in court before their very eyes.

Last up was Organ, for the prosecution's rebuttal. By now the heat in the courtroom was turned up too high, and several jurors shifted uncomfortably in their chairs. A 250-pound black juror in the front row mopped his brow with a white handkerchief.

Remarking about the weather, Organ began, "I know the elements outside are bad, but I didn't think you'd get a 'snow job' inside the courtroom. He paused to let his snowball at Swano sink in, then continued. "I have no cute stories about fishing boats and pin bottles to tell you. This was a brutal and senseless murder."

Organ then turned to Dr. and Mrs. Chua. "Did Mrs. Chua have a vision? Did Teresita Basa come back from the dead and name Allan as her slayer? I don't know. I'm a skeptic. But it doesn't matter as to the guilt or innocence of Allan Showery. Maybe she heard it at the hospital. Maybe the defendant told her at the hospital. What does matter is that the information checked out. The jewelry was found, and Showery confessed."

Then, reminding jurors that Showery testified that he was "just kidding" when he confessed to the murder, Organ suddenly grabbed the kitchen knife that had been found imbedded in the victim, held it high in the air, and shouted dramatically, "Well, Allan Showery! You weren't 'kidding' when you plunged this knife into Teresita Basa's chest!"

The startled Showery sat wide-eyed in fear at the defense table as Organ stood with the knife poised high. And suddenly the long trial was over. The road the "voice from the grave" had taken him down was near the end.

Judge Barbaro routinely instructed the jurors on the law. He noted that, in addition to murder, Showery was charged with arson and armed robbery.

At 3:55 p.m. the jurors filed out of the courtroom to begin their deliberations, and the wait for the verdict began. Allan Showery's fate was in their hands.

CHAPTER 26

![black bar]

THE JURY SAYS . . .

There is a saying among those who work in the hoary old criminal courts building at Twenty-Sixth and California: "Never bet on a precinct captain or a jury."

Nobody was betting on this one.

The eight men and four women filed solemnly into the jury room behind Judge Barbaro's court to determine Allan Showery's future. They elected James Cunningham, a 55-year-old black juror, as their foreman. Because he was production superintendent at a candy factory, they reasoned he had more organizational ability than anyone else among them.

By nightfall, after rehashing the case for several hours and getting absolutely nowhere, they called it a day. They were driven in a sheriff's bus to the Holiday Inn at Madison and Halsted Streets, just west of the Loop, where they were put up for the night. Coincidentally, this was the same motel where Lee Epplen moonlighted as security chief.

* * *

Thursday, January 25, came and went without a verdict. During their morning session the jurors sent a note entitled "Request for Information" to Judge Barbaro. The judge, waiting in his chambers, patiently mused over the contents and decided to take no action whatsoever.

He returned the missive with a brief one of his own,
saying, "You have heard the evidence. Continue to deliber-
ate." Turning to his bailiff he said, "What do they want? I
don't know. But I won't have a running dialog with them."
The vague note was interpreted by the lawyers present as a
sign the jurors were "playing detective" over inconsequential
matters. The message, which was slipped under the door,
listed eight separate requests for information by number:

1. Lt. Whelan.
2. Beat policemen.
3. Mobile unit.
4. Inv. Stachula.
5. Mrs. White.
6. Unintelligible.
7. Mrs. Loeb.
8. Revelle White.

At 3:20 p.m. a second note from the jury was slipped
under the door to Barbaro's bailiff. The contents were not
revealed. Again, Barbaro ignored the communication.

After a full day behind closed doors, the jurors were
bussed back through the snow to the Holiday Inn for their
second night of playing cards and watching television.

* * *

On Friday, January 26, they resumed their deliberation.
Inside the secluded room a titanic tug-of-war over Allan
Showery's life was going on for the third day.

The panel was evenly divided. The four black jurors, led
by Cunningham, the foreman, were arguing for acquittal.
Cunningham had been convinced from the beginning of
Showery's innocence, and wanted to wrap it up and go home.

Four white jurors, on the other hand, were equally
adamant for conviction. Mildred Schafer, a medical secretary,
was particularly influenced by Showery's admission of the
slaying to Yanka before he even signed the confession.
"Look," she argued. "One doesn't usually lie to someone with

whom he's had an intimate relationship for a period of years. If anything, he would have told her that he DID NOT commit the crime, but had been coerced into confessing."

The other four members of the jury vacillated from one side to the other, between guilty and innocent, turn him loose or give him the juice. One of them, 30-year-old Richard Webber, a machine shop supervisor and Viet Nam veteran, wrestled with his own conscience. "In my heart I feel he's guilty, but in my head there are certain doubts," he said. "Sometimes I feel he's guilty, but then, maybe he isn't."

"The proof is in the pudding," argued 60-year-old Marie Rader, a retired bank vault manager. "The jewelry was found in Yanka's jewel box. And Showery was lying when he said he signed the confession to protect Yanka. Can't the rest of you see that? My God! I wouldn't take the rap for someone else. I wouldn't sign anything I didn't do."

One of the male jurors nervously chain-smoked cigarettes throughout the deliberation. When he ran out, and couldn't get any more, he fished butts out of the ash tray and re-lit them for a few bitter drags.

"I agree with you about the jewelry found in Showery's wife's possession," said Webber. "But that confession. How can we be sure it wasn't coerced? We don't know how long Showery was in custody before they got that confession. Nobody told us, and I think they should have."

"We can't lose sight of the fact that Showery had a clean background before all this happened, and he always had a job," asserted Cunningham. "I'm also impressed with his clean personal appearance."

"Wait a minute! How do we know he has a clean background?" interrupted Schafer. "You're not allowed to bring up previous arrests in a trial. A lot of people aren't aware of that, but it's true."

"Well, the evidence just isn't strong enough," argued Cunningham. "It seems to me that if you are going to prosecute you can't bring in a case in which there is reasonable doubt and expect to get a conviction."

"Hell, the only damn reason they prosecuted Showery is 'cause he's black," interjected one of the other black jurors. "We all know that. This whole damned case was a racial issue, and Allan Showery was the fall guy. That's the way I feel."

"Well, ah, what was this cult they kept talking about?" asked one puzzled juror. "I never did figure out the cult business."

"That wasn't cult," said Schafer, exasperated. "They were saying 'occult.' That was in relation to Mrs. Chua getting a message from the great beyond."

Cunningham grinned. "You just can't believe that the voice of a dead woman could come back from the grave and say this person was the cause of my death. I'm a religious person, and I don't believe this sort of thing. I've never been involved in it, and I don't read those kind of books."

"She's a kook!" laughed another juror. "You can't take her testimony seriously."

"Well, she did appear a bit emotionally distraught, but the mere fact that the Chuas came forward is very courageous, I think," persisted Schafer. "They must have faced an awful lot of embarrassment. No matter how they came by the information, I believe they thought they had a moral conviction to relay it to the proper authorities, and that's what they did. What do you think, Rich?"

"I really don't think I believe she had those 'possessions' she talked about," mulled Webber. "But I can't disprove them, either. Something like that could have happened. Things do happen that are unexplainable."

Marie Rader stared straight ahead without a word. She was thinking about the many times in her youth when she had premonitions, and how they often came true. Twenty-five years earlier her parents had returned to their native Germany for a visit, and one morning while leaning over the ironing board an eerie chill came over her. She had been thinking of her parents' trip, and was anticipating their arrival home for Thanksgiving. She could not describe the feeling that suddenly took over her body. She had never felt it before, or since. But she was unable to continue with the ironing or any other household chore. She was unable to accomplish anything for several hours. At two o'clock in the afternoon the doorbell rang, and the mailman handed her a special delivery letter. It was from her mother. It said her father had died while they were vising her mother's birthplace.

"It is startling how mysterious events reveal the facts," she heard herself commenting.

"What do you mean by that, Marie?"

"Oh, you know. How the name of Showery came out along with where the jewels could be found."

"Hell, I think the very fact that Showery kept the jewelry proves he's innocent," argued another juror.

"Yeah, and don't forget, they didn't have any physical evidence that Allan was ever at the scene of the crime," asserted another. "That Organ tried to bring fingerprints into the case, but it just confused me, because none of them belonged to Showery, that's for sure."

"How come they never tried to lift any prints from the TV sets?" pondered another.

"The TV set business bothers me, too," agreed Webber. "When they showed us those pictures of the apartment, the backs were on the television sets. They didn't look like they were being worked on to me."

"That's another indication the confession was a phony," hastened the black woman member of the group. "I just know the police told Showery exactly what to say. The cops do that all the time."

"Well, I'm impressed with how often he had been informed of his rights," said Schafer. "He had every opportunity NOT to confess, and yet he did. I don't care how much anyone threatened me—I still wouldn't confess to a murder I did not commit. I think he was at the end of his rope and had no other choice. I'm sorry, but I just couldn't believe him as he sat there on the witness stand and said, 'Oh, I just threw that in.' Every time he said that it drove me up the wall."

"I don't see how a guy as little as Showery could have gotten a large woman like Teresita down," shrugged another.

"Nobody told us how big she was," Webber pointed out. "I wish Mr. Organ would have shown us a photograph of her. The only one they showed us was when she was dead, lying there on the floor, and you couldn't even tell what she looked like. She was once a living, breathing, human being and I think the prosecution should have come up with a living picture of her."

"Speaking of the prosecution," grinned Mildred Schafer. "Isn't that Organ just a younger version of Charles Laughton —the way he stood there with his hands on his hips?"

"He does remind you of Laughton, doesn't he," Webber laughed, picturing the noted actor. "His stance. His posture."

And on they went, hour after hour, after hour. From day one of deliberations, through day two, and into day three.

Could you believe Detective Stachula? Was there a conspiracy to frame Showery? Why was Mrs. Chua fired from the hospital? Was Showery responsible for the firing? They never told us! What kind of locks did Teresita have on her door? How come the janitor said he never saw Showery in the building? What kind of security did the building have? Was robbery really the motive? Was Showery in arrears with his rent or wasn't he? That was confusing. What did Mrs. White's testimony prove? Nothing. Why didn't they call Mr. White? Who was Teresita Basa? Did she have money? We never learned anything about her. What about the guy the janitor saw knocking on her door?

"Nobody ever saw this Showery person in her apartment at any time," Cunningham reminded the rest of them. "And look at the brutality of this crime. Teresita and Showery worked together. I just can't see a guy doing what was done to her for a lousy $30 unless the killer was somebody else—a stranger."

Cunningham and the other three black jurors stuck to their guns. No way was Allan Showery guilty of murdering Teresita Basa. Miss Schafer cajoled, argued and tried to reason, but she could convince no more than three of the others of Showery's guilt. Those who were wavering began to tilt toward the "innocent" side, because they had what Judge Barbaro had described to them as "reasonable doubts."

That was the way it stood Friday afternoon. Meanwhile the snow continued to cascade from the sky and pile up on the ground, on the sidewalks, in the streets, and on top of parked cars. Some of the jurors were wondering out loud how they would ever get home once their ordeal was over. One woman, holding out for acquittal, declared, "I'm going to get out of here tonight if I have to feign illness. My husband has been home alone for three days now, and I don't even think he fed the dog. At least he'd better be alone!"

Cunningham, who had taken two secret ballots earlier, without positive results, called for a third. He passed out a dozen slips of paper, on which each juror wrote his or her decision. Then the count was taken once again while all looked on in anticipation. The final vote was seven for acquittal, four for conviction, and one still unable to make up his or her mind.

At 2:30 p.m. they sent Judge Barbaro a note saying they were "hopelessly deadlocked" and unable to reach a verdict. They had been deliberating 13 hours and 40 minutes. Reluctantly, Barbaro summoned them back into court and declared a mistrial.

Bill Swano was ecstatic! A mistrial is almost as good as a not guilty, because it showed him the jurors couldn't make up their minds. He now knew the state's whole case against Showery, he knew what every witness would say, and he knew every bit of evidence the prosecution had gathered, and how the jurors would react to it. "The next time around," he assured Showery, pumping his hand, "you'll be home free."

Tom Organ was utterly crushed. He had done his damndest, but he knew it was the "voice from the grave" story that beat him. He had wanted to keep it out of the trial, but the slippery Swano had maneuvered it into the testimony. It was a story the jurors simply could not swallow "beyond reasonable doubt." He felt the same way himself.

There was an old newspaper saying that dogged the young prosecutor as he walked forlornly back to his office: "Chicago is a not guilty town."

Judge Barbaro ordered that Showery continue to be held in lieu of $500,000 bond, and remanded him to the county jail, where he had been since his arrest nearly a year and a half earlier.

A new hearing was scheduled for February 14—the 50th anniversary of the infamous Saint Valentine's Day Massacre.

CHAPTER 27

SHOWERY STUNS
SWANO

On Wednesday, February 21, the second anniversary of the murder of Teresita Basa, a low, sullen gray cloud hung over the city. Streets clogged with ice and snow only a few days earlier had now taken on the appearance of mountain tarns as the temperature soared to 40 degrees. As the more than 80 inches of snow that fell during the bitterest winter in the city's history began their pell-mell retreat down the sewer gratings, the United States Weather Service issued a flash flood alert for the Chicago area.

Work crews, remodeling the aging facade of the old criminal courts building were laying waste to the celebrated press room, leaving the ghosts of Ben Hecht, Hildy Johnson, George Wright, and the rest of the rough-and-tumble front page rogues of the Roaring Twenties without a place to haunt.

Saint Valentine's Day had come and gone, and the Showery case was consigned a routine continuance while the court disposed of other matters. Swano patted his client on the back and assured him, "You'll be out of this joint in no time, Al. A 'not guilty' is in the bag, my man, and you'll be home free."

Then something strange and unexpected took hold of the case. It was almost as bizarre as whatever else had transpired

in the mysterious "voice from beyond the grave" murder. On
the night of February 21 Allan Showery called his lawyer.

At 11:00 a.m. on February 22 a cast of familiar characters
lined up before the bench in Judge Barbaro's fifth floor courtroom. When Barbaro asked the reason for the gathering, a
totally dejected Swano advised the court that Allan Showery
—against the advice of his attorneys—*insisted on pleading
guilty to the murder of Teresita Basa!*

The judge, somewhat jolted but obviously relieved at the
prospect of getting another in the endless stream of criminal
matters out of the way, looked down curiously at the defendant and inquired, "Is that right, Mr. Showery?"

Showery, looking fit in his freshly-pressed go-to-court
blue denims, simply crossed his arms over his chest and fixed
a blank gaze upon the judge.

"All right," droned Barbaro. "The defendant has asked
for a conference. Actually no agreement was made between
all parties as to what sentence should be imposed. What is
your plea to these charges, Mr. Defendant?"

"Guilty!" whispered Showery.

"There is no commitment by the court. This is a blind
plea. Have any threats or promises been made to you in return
for your plea?"

"No."

A surprised Organ then recited the highlights of the
state's evidence for the court record, and to refresh the
judge's memory, as if that was necessary. The prosecutor, vin-
dicated—but God only knows how it came about—asked for a
sentence of "substantial penitentiary time."

Swano, his case in shambles, could only plead for mercy.
He described Showery as a "fine fellow," with an infant child,
and a 10-year work record.

Barbaro turned his attention to Showery and asked, "Is
there anything you have to say before sentence is imposed?"

"No, your honor." The words came out like cracked ice.

"The court, having considered the charges and the
evidence, and having accepted the plea of guilty, finds that

plea to be the first step toward rehabilitation. That shows some remorse. The sentence is 14 years!"

Fourteen years. It was the minimum sentence for murder that could have been imposed under Illinois law. Barbaro quickly threw in two concurrent terms of four years each for the crimes of armed robbery and arson. He did so without so much as another glance at Showery, prattling legalese much like a station agent calls out the day's train schedule.

Suddenly it was over. The entire session lasted no more than 15 minutes—precious little more than it took to strangle Teresita, plunge the knife into the center of her chest, strip off her clothing, and envelope her body in flames.

A sheriff's bailiff, with a black patch over his left eye like the Hathaway shirt man, tugged at Showery's sleeve and led him back into the bullpen for one last hike through the underground tunnel to the county jail.

There Showery solemnly packed his meager belongings, and was hustled off to the fortress-like Stateville Penitentiary near Joliet.

It was an astounding anti-climax to one of the strangest homicide cases in history. Until the day before—the exact anniversary of Teresita Basa's untimely death—the cocky Showery had it made. He had all but beaten the system. He was in orbit and about to make his re-entry into society. Then, precisely two years to the very night the knife was plunged into Teresita's breast and she left this world, some unknown force made Allan Showery change his mind.

Who, or what, ever possessed Allan Showery to bring *himself* to justice? Was it you, Teresita?

EPILOGUE

Immediately after the story of Teresita Basa's "voice from the grave" made headlines in Chicago, investigators uncovered three other members of the Filipino community who said they were—in one way or another—"possessed" or "visited" by the murdered woman. All had connections with Edgewater Hospital.

None of the three wanted to become involved, or to have their names made public, according to former Manila police detective Deo Dante, who conducted an independent investigation of the matter.

In recent history, records of voices from the dead go back to 1919 in Chicago when Col. Robert G. Ingersoll, a World War I Army officer, appeared every Friday afternoon in the home of the Reverend Jeanette F. Erion, to speak through the lips of Professor Rheaumont, a Milwaukeean who claimed to have been an Indian medicine man. Reverend Erion, curiously, lived at 55 W. Surf Street, a block from where Allan Showery resided when he killed Teresita.

In 1954 Percy Philip, a 68-year-old retired newspaperman from the *New York Times*, told of a "conversation" he had on a park bench in Quebec with Canadian Prime Minister W. L. Mackenzie King, who had died four years earlier.

Philip, who said he was not a spiritualist, was adamant about the incident. "I sat chatting with Mr. Mackenzie King for nearly two hours," he declared. "I don't just think I did it. I am convinced that I did. Our conversation ranged from politics to international affairs."

A closer parallel to the Basa case occurred exactly a half century before Teresita's murder, in El Dorado, Arkansas, a rural community just north of the Louisiana border. In that instance a dead woman reportedly returned to chastise a man who had mistreated their teen-aged daughter.

Mrs. Tressie Glover, who subsequently moved to Detroit, and her brother, Emmett Taylor, who remained in El Dorado, were among those who witnessed the psychic incident. "To me, what happened in that little town was real," Mrs. Glover, a retired Chrysler auto parts worker, told the authors. "Call it a mystery, a coincidence of some kind, I don't know." She was eleven at the time, two years younger than "Sister," the girl who was possessed.

"The girl's mother died shortly after she was born, and as she lay on her deathbed she summoned her cousin, Simon Kilgore, who was my uncle," Mrs. Glover recalled. "Simon was a farmer and proprietor of a little country store." The dying woman elicited from Kilgore a promise to raise her child, and implored him to never, for any reason, physically mistreat her—a vow he kept until "Sister," as she was known, reached her teens.

"My uncle Simon's wife had made the girl a dress that reached all the way down to her high-button shoes. The Sunday after she was given the dress, while the rest of the family was in church, Sister secretly shortened the hem of the gown so it would be more like the dresses worn by other girls her age," Mrs. Glover explained. "That night it was discovered what she had done, and Uncle Simon took a switch to her.

"The following evening, as Simon and other farm hands were sitting on the front stoop chatting, while waiting for supper, a small light came moving across the field toward them. At first it appeared to be someone carrying a lantern, but as the light approached, Simon saw there was no one there."

Shortly thereafter, while all were seated at the dinner table, according to Mrs. Glover, there was a "furious yelping of the hounds," followed by three soft knocks on the door. "Uncle Simon called for the person to enter, but nothing happened. He only heard more rapping. He got up and went to the door, but there was no one there."

The incident was repeated over the ensuing months to the extent that the local newspaper began reporting on it. On several occasions the "spirit" caused such a commotion that local police and firemen were called out to disperse crowds that had gathered to try to get a glimpse of it.

"My mother and all the grownups talked about the spirit. My mother and grandmother, Matilda Perkins, said they had heard that spirits couldn't cross water, so my mother took Sister across a creek to our house in town, about ten miles from Uncle Simon's place," Mrs. Glover said.

"But the spirit came there, too. One night while we listened to the knocking a piece of pasteboard covering a broken window fell to the floor, frightening us. Mother said the spirit had come in through the window, and she asked aloud what the spirit wanted. There was a strange whispering noise. The spirit was talking through the girl—Sister—who was asleep in bed. She started squirming, as if someone was trying to get into bed with her.

"Mother recognized the voice, called the spirit by name, and asked what she wanted. The voice replied that she was angry and said, 'I don't want my little girl spanked. Simon, that bald-headed son-of-a-bitch, promised on my deathbed he wouldn't lay a hand on the girl. If he ever does it again, I will go to his house and tear it down.'

"My mother told the spirit there would be no more spanking."

Mrs. Glover and her brother listened wide-eyed and frightened as the strange voice gave instructions to their grandmother, Mrs. Perkins, that she wanted her daughter to live with a certain family in New York City. The voice then explained how the family could be located.

"My grandmother wrote to the address the dead mother had given, and the people came and got the girl. After that, the harassment of Uncle Simon stopped," according to Mrs. Glover. "I was a witness to this, and so was my brother. There is a supernatural power."

And what about Teresita Basa? Did she really enter the body of Remebios Chua in order to bring her killer to justice? Bill Swano, had this to say:

"There are four possibilities as to how Mrs. Chua got her information. One, she knew something about the murder. Two, Showery might have told her. Three, she was just guessing. And four, she had a true psychic experience."

There you have it. Allan Showery's own defense lawyer allows that the chances are one in four that Teresita did, indeed, come back from the grave and project her presence through another woman's body.

Chicago police, after thoroughly investigating the Chuas, discount the first two possibilities. As to whether Mrs. Chua was making an educated guess, Detective Joe Stachula reasoned: "Mrs. Chua is no dummy. But, if she had put two and two together, why didn't she just call the police? Why did she put her husband in that predicament of having to testify under oath that she had this psychic experience?"

Again, that leaves only possibility number four—a true psychic experience.

Both Stachula and Prosecutor Tom Organ are convinced of the Chuas' sincerity. They describe them as having been almost embarrassed over the incident, and the Chuas' refusal to discuss the case with the media certainly precludes the suggestion that they might have been publicity seekers.

Joseph DeLeonardi, citywide homicide commander at the time of the slaying, and later superintendent of police, said, "Mrs. Chua gave us the evidence we needed. It doesn't matter whether she had a psychic dream or not."

Two well-known psychics, who have worked with police on a variety of criminal cases throughout the country, are convinced that the experience, as described by the Chuas, happened that way indeed. They are Irene Hughes and Joseph DeLouise.

Mrs. Hughes said she believes a "psychic bond" existed between Teresita Basa and Remebios Chua. She said she feels Teresita picked Mrs. Chua as her messenger because this was the person who would have the greatest impact. "Teresita picked Mrs. Chua to make justice happen."

DeLouise, who worked with police on both the Sharon Tate Hollywood murder and ex-Teamster boss Jimmy Hoffa's disappearance, suggested that Teresita was angry after her death and wanted to right an injustice. "She was saying, 'Get this guy!' She was shocked, and murdered, at the best time of her life, and she didn't like it at all."

He believes Teresita chose Mrs. Chua because they may have been compatible "chemistry-wise and psychic-wise," even though they had not been close to one another in life. Both were from the Philippines, and had much in common. Mrs. Chua might have subconsciously reached out to Teresita by wondering what really happened to her on the night of February 21.

And what of Allan Showery? What did he think of the phenomenon that put him behind prison bars?

"Mrs. Chua faked this. Without a doubt, she faked it," he told reporter John O'Brien in a jailhouse interview before being packed off to Stateville. "She was definitely upset about something. She was very nervous after the murder. I don't know why she named me. I think it was designed for somebody else, but I was caught by my Achilles heel, so to speak. I had been critical of her job performance with patients. That is a motive."

Showery added, "I was reading and doing research on witchcraft and voodoo and things like that. I used to bring a few books to the job and read them. We were working together on the evening shift, and she didn't like these interests of mine.

"I was always curious about strange things. There were some groups I knew on the North Side that were into the occult. I was both amused and fascinated, because I am the sort of person who wants to learn a little bit of everything. There was something that happened in my family back in New York City, but I don't want to involve them. I, myself, have had strange experiences a few times."

In other words, Showery might be a believer in some cases, but he didn't believe Mrs. Chua.

He then turned the conversation to the Good Book, and stated, "My conscience and feelings are governed by the words in the Bible."

"Don't you feel your interest in the occult might have conflicted with the words in the Bible?" he was asked.

"There is no conflict. In order to understand good you have to understand evil."

No matter who, or what, put him behind bars, Showery was philosophical.

"I look at the whole thing as an experience," he said. "Some day, when I am released, I want to be known—not as Allan Showery, the ex-convict or the 'voice from the grave' killer—but as Allan Showery, the man."

Showery, alias Allam Sowry—as he was also known—served four and a half years before being released on parole in July of 1983. He did not go back to Yanka and his love child, but instead took up with "Naomi," the mysterious red-coated woman who had appeared in court daily as a spectator during his trial.

The Basa mansion on Colon Street in Dumaguete City, back in the Philippines where it all began, and across the street from Santa Catalina Cemetery where Teresita now lies buried, remains in the family. It is presently occupied by Socorro Basa's sister, Lourdes Calumpang, Teresita's aunt, and her family.

"I tell you the past is a bucket of ashes."

—Carl Sandburg

APPENDIX

████████████████████████████████

ALLAN SHOWERY'S SIGNED CONFESSION

RE: PEOPLE VS. ALLAN SHOWERY (DEATH OF
TERESITA BASA)

STATEMENT
OF
ALLAN SHOWERY

taken in an Interview Room, Criminal Investigation Division,
Area 6 Homicide, 2452 West Belmont, Chicago, Cook County,
Illinois, on Friday, August 12, 1977, at 2:53 o'clock a.m.

PRESENT: MR. PAUL LINTON,
Assistant State's Attorney.
INV. LEE EPPLEN #14244
Area 6 Homicide-Sex Unit
Reported by Blanca Lara
Book No. 7708-27

MR. LINTON: Let the record reflect that it is now 2:53
a.m. on August 12, 1977. We are in an Interview Room at the
Area 6 Criminal Investigation Division.

Present are myself, Assistant State's Attorney Paul
Linton; Investigator Lee Epplen from Area 6 Homicide and
Mr. Allan Showery.

Mr. Showery, you recall that you had a conversation with myself and the investigator a little while ago. Do you remember that conversation?

MR. SHOWERY: A Yes, I do.

Q Do you also remember earlier tonight before you talked to myself you had a conversation with other investigators?

A Yes, I did.

Q All right. At the conclusion of your oral statement, which was approximately ten to 2:00 this morning, you indicated you would give a written statement going over the matters that we covered at that time. Do you recall that?

A Yes, I do.

Q Do you wish to do that?

A Yes, I do.

Q Before we go into that I wish to re-advise you of your rights and go over some other preliminary matters. Okay?

A All right.

Q First of all, do you understand you have the right to remain silent?

A Yes, I do.

Q If you do not remain silent anything you say, do or write can and will be used against you in a court of law. Do you understand that?

A I do.

Q Do you also understand you have a right to have an attorney present before any questioning takes place and during any questioning that may take place?

A I understand.

Q You also have the right to have an attorney present that will be appointed for you by the court if you cannot afford your own attorney, to be with you before any questioning takes place and during any questioning. Do you understand that?

A Yes, I do.

Q All right. Should you decide to answer any questions, whether with or without an attorney, you may decide to stop answering the questions at any time and the questioning will cease. Do you understand that?

A Yes.

Q Did I also explain these matters to you before we had a conversation earlier this morning?

A Yes, you did.

Q Did you understand them at that time?

A Yes.

Ω And did you never-the-less give a statement at that time?

A Yes, I did.

Q And were you also advised of your rights earlier by the investigators?

A Yes.

Q Did you understand them at that time?

A Yes.

Q You also talked to them at that time?

A That's correct.

Q Do you understand what all your rights are at this time?

A Yes, I do.

Q Do you wish to give a statement relating what happened in February of this year?

A Yes.

Q Would you please state and spell your name?

A My name is Allan Showery. A-l-l-a-n S-h-o-w-e-r-y, Showery.

Q Where do you live?

A 630 West Schubert.

Q Since June of 1976, where have you been employed?

A Edgewater Hospital.

Q And what did you do there?

A Respiratory Technician.

Q How long have you lived in Chicago?

A Since '69.

Q Now, in the course of your employment at Edgewater Hospital, did you have occasion to know a Teresita Basa?

A Yes, I knew Teresita Basa.

Q And when did you first meet her?

A When I was hired at Edgewater Hospital in June of '76.

Q And what did she do for Edgewater Hospital?

A Respiratory Therapist.

Q Did you have occasion to work with her?

A Yes, I did, many times.

Q Did you work in the same department?

A Yes, we did.

Q How many times on the average week did you see her?

A Five days a week.

Q Did you have occasion to learn what her address and phone number was?

A Yes, I did.

Q And this was in connection with what?

A Helping her with immigration, becoming a citizen.

Q She was not a citizen?

A No, she wasn't.

Q You were attempting to help her become a citizen. Is that correct?

A Yes, that's correct.

Q Did you ever take her to the immigration office?

A Yes, I did.

Q Do you remember how many times?

A Twice.

Q Now, once you got to know her, did you have occasion to go over to her apartment?

A Yes, I did.

Q And this was at 2740 North Pine Grove. Is that correct?

A That's correct.

Q Apartment 15-B?

A Right.

Q How many times on the average did you go over to her apartment from July '76 to February of this year?

A Well, about three times a month.

Q When you were over there, what did you discuss?

A Her background, a lot about her background. A lot of her problems with her T.V.

Q And television?

A Yeah.

Q What was the matter with the television?

A There was a problem with the circuit breaker on the T.V. that was broken.

Q When did this come to your attention?

A Either the early part of October or the first week of November.

Q Of '76?

A '76.

Q All right. On these visitations when you used to go over there, did she ever cook food for you?

A No, she never cooked for me.

Q Did she ever serve any beverages?

A Yes, beer or coffee.

Q All right. In January of this year did you have a conversation with her regarding a circuit breaker for her television?

A Yes, I did.

Q What did you tell her at that time?

A Well, when I had talked with her I told her—she wanted me to go—come over to look at it because she had an electrician look at the T.V. and apparently he didn't fix it right. So she wanted me to come over to see if I could repair it.

Q In February of '77, did you go over to look at the television set?

A Yes, I did.

Q Do you remember what part of February it was?

A Off hand, no.

Q Approximately what time did you arrive over there in February, the day that you went there?

A 5:00.

Q 5:00 p.m.?

A 5:00 p.m. in the evening.

Q Are you familiar with electronics?

A Yes, I am.

Q When you got there at 5:00 did you examine the television?

A Yes, I did.

Q What did you discover?

A The electrician put the circuit breaker in wrong, and I told her that I was going to go home, that I had some wiring diagrams of similar patterns for her T.V., and see if I could repair them.

Q While you were there did you have anything to drink?

A A can and a half of beer.

Q How long were you there before you left?

A First time was ten, about fifteen minutes.

Q And did you later come back that evening?

A Yes, I did.

Q Approximately what time did you get back?

A Close to 7:30.

Q All right. Now, before you got back, had you been considering your financial condition at that time?

A Yes.

Q What was that at that time?

A My financial situation was very low.

Q Meaning what?

A I was in arrears on my rent and electricity. The rent was in arrears three months.

Q And, are you married?

A Common law marriage, yes. Legally, no.

Q On occasions, because of the favors that you did for her with the immigration authorities and transporting her places, did she ever give you any money?

A Yes, she gave me sometimes five dollars, sometimes ten dollars. It depended on how much time I spent with her in taking her to the Immigration Bureau and doing different odds and favors.

Q What did that mean to you, that she was able to give you ten dollars from time to time?

A That she had money.

Q When you returned at 7:30, did you have anything in mind?

A Yes, I did. I had—and as I left out of my house, which at the time I was living at 445 West Surf, only a three-minute walk. I decided what I was going to do. I was going to go there and kill her and rob her.

Q When you got there at 7:30, was she there?

A Yes, she was there.

Q Did anybody else live with her there?

A No, she lived alone.

Q Did she let you in?

A Yes.

Q Do you recall what she was wearing at the time?

A She was wearing pants, or slacks, and a sweater top.

Q And what happened immediately after she let you in?

A Immediately after she let me in she was proceeding to lock the door. I choked her into subconsciousness and later on left her on the living room floor.

Q How did you choke her into subconsciousness?

A She was locking the door and I came in back of her and I did what you call a Japanese Full Nelson, and I choked her using that technique.

Q Are you familiar with the Martial Arts?

A Yes, I am quite familiar.

Q What background do you have in that?

A I have a Black Belt in Karate.

Q What degree?

A Third Degree Black Belt and two other degrees in Brown Belt and Judo Akido.

Q Would you spell that?

A A-k-i-k-o. A-k-i-d-o, I'm sorry.

Q After you dropped her on the floor was she unconscious?

A Yes, she was completely unconscious.

Q What did you do immediately after that?

A I went to her purse to see if she had any money.

Q Did she have any money?

A Yes, she did. She had about thirty dollars.

Q What did you do immediately after that?

A After that I went into the bedroom, searched through her things, and didn't find anything. So, as I was searching through her things, I went to check the bedroom. I proceeded to carry her, picked her up from where she was lying on the living room floor, and carried her in the bedroom. In the bedroom I disrobed her, proceeded in the kitchen and got a kitchen knife and stabbed her in the mediastinum of her body. I then ransacked the living room and the rest of the house. I returned back into the bedroom, got a piece of paper of some kind, lit a fire to it, threw it on the mattress, and picked up the mattress and overturned it.

Q What did you do after that?

A I left immediately after that. After that I caught the elevator downstairs and came home.

Q When you left, what property did you have from the apartment?

A A jade piece, a ring that I can remember very accurately, and a lot of miscellaneous jewelry.

Q Did you have the thirty dollars at that time?

A Yes, I did.

Q What did you do with the jewelry?

A The majority of the jewelry, except for the jade piece and a ring, I threw in Diversey Park. I walked over and threw it in the park.

Q What did you do with the other two pieces of jewelry?

A I saved those and larger one I gave it to my wife.

Q Do you recall when you gave it to your wife?

A It had to be sometime about the end of February, going into March.

Q Why did you ransack the house and take her clothes off of her and set the fire?

A To make it look like a burglary and robbery, and rape and murder.

Q Did she ever regain consciousness from the time you initially rendered her unconscious until you stabbed her?

A No, she didn't.

Q Did you have intercourse with her?

A No, I did not.

Q All right. In the course of your conversation earlier did you identify these items of jewelry which you took from her apartment?

A Yes, I did identify it.

Q Were they taken from her bedroom, living room, or from where?

A Bedroom.

Q Are you—would you describe—in layman's language would you describe that sternum or mediastinum of the chest?

A Sternum of the chest.

Q Would you indicate on yourself where that is?

A (Indicating.)

Q Indicating, for the record, the center of the chest.

A The center.

Q How long were you there from the beginning to the end of this incident?

A Fifteen minutes.

Q When you were in the kitchen, did you notice whether or not there was anything on the stove?

A I noticed there were some pots on the stove, but it wasn't cooked, or if it had it might've been earlier, or maybe another day, I don't exactly remember, but she wasn't cooking anything.

Q From what door did you leave?

A The front door.

Q How did that door lock when you left?

A It has a tumbler action that when you turn it from the inside it locks automatically as you leave the apartment.

Q Did you leave the knife in her after you stabbed her?

A Yes, I did.

Q What kind of knife was it?

A About ten to twelve inch kitchen knife.

Q What—where did you obtain the knife?

A From her kitchen.

Q All right. While you've been here tonight have you been given coffee and food?

A Yes, I have.

Q You feel alert at the present time?

A Yes, I am.

Q Have the police officers and myself treated you satisfactory?

A Yes, they have.

Q Have you given this statement freely, of your own free will?

A Freely, and of my own free will.

Q At the conclusion of this, when the court reporter types up the statement, would you examine the statement, make corrections on it, and sign the statement?

A Yes, I will.

MR. LINTON: That's all I have, thank you.

(Signed) <u>Allan Showery</u>

WITNESSES TO SIGNATURE

<u>Lee R. Epplen</u>

<u>Paul Benjamin Linton</u>

INDEX

ABOUT THE AUTHORS

Between them, Edward Baumann and John O'Brien have covered every major Chicago and Midwestern crime in the last half of this century. They have worked together as a team since 1974.

O'Brien is an ex-Marine whose assignments as a reporter for the *Chicago Tribune* have taken him to police stations and county morgues from coast to coast. He has done in-depth stories on criminal justice in Michigan and California, exposés on child abuse in Texas and political dirty tricks in North Dakota, covered mob chief Tony Accardo in Florida, and joined investigators in tracking down suspects in a fortune of stolen cash all the way to the British West Indies. He shared the *Tribune's* coveted Edward Scott Beck Award for investigative reporting in 1989. A native Chicagoan, he now lives in south suburban Calumet City.

Baumann, a native of Kenosha, Wisconsin, served with the Army Air Corps in New Guinea and the Philippines during World War II. He worked as a reporter or editor on the *Waukegan News-Sun*, *Chicago Daily News*, *Chicago's American*, *Chicago Today* and the *Chicago Tribune* before turning to free-lancing full time in 1988. He is a past president of the Chicago Press Club, former chairman of the Chicago Press

Veterans Association, a director of the Chicago Newspaper Reporters Association, and winner of two Chicago Newspaper Guild Stick-O-Type Awards for investigative reporting. In 1988 he was honored by his peers as Chicago Press Veteran of the Year. He is the author of *Step Into My Parlor*, the chilling story of serial killer Jeffrey Dahmer.

Baumann and O'Brien are also the authors of *Chicago Heist*, *Getting Away with Murder*, and *Murder Next Door*, and more than 300 internationally published detective magazine articles. Baumann is also the co-author, with Kenan Heise, of *Chicago Originals: A Cast of the City's Colorful Characters*.